P9-DCR-981

HITLER, MUSSOLINI, AND THE VATICAN

HITLER, MUSSOLINI, AND THE VATICAN

Pope Pius XI and the Speech that was Never Made

EMMA FATTORINI

Translated by Carl Ipsen

polity

First published in Italian as *Pio XI, Hitler e Mussolini* © Giulio Einaudi Editore S.p.A, 2007

This English edition © Polity Press, 2011

Polity Press
65 Bridge Street
Cambridge CB2 1UR, UK

Polity Press
350 Main Street
Malden, MA 02148, USA

All rights reserved. Except for the quotation of short passages for the purpose of criticism and review, no part of this publication may be reproduced, stored in a retrieval system, or transmitted, in any form or by any means, electronic, mechanical, photocopying, recording or otherwise, without the prior permission of the publisher.

ISBN-13: 978-0-7456-4488-2

A catalogue record for this book is available from the British Library.

Typeset in 10.5 on 12 pt Sabon by Toppan Best-set Premedia Limited
Printed and bound in Great Britain by MPG Books Group Limited, Bodmin, Cornwall

The publisher has used its best endeavours to ensure that the URLs for external websites referred to in this book are correct and active at the time of going to press. However, the publisher has no responsibility for the websites and can make no guarantee that a site will remain live or that the content is or will remain appropriate.

Every effort has been made to trace all copyright holders, but if any have been inadvertently overlooked the publisher will be pleased to include any necessary credits in any subsequent reprint or edition.

For further information on Polity, visit our website: www.politybooks.com

The translation of this work has been funded by SEPS
SEGRETARIATO EUROPEO PER LE PUBBLICAZIONI SCIENTIFICHE

CONTENTS

LIST OF ABBREVIATIONS

ACDF	Archivio della Congregazione per la Dottrina della Fede
ACS	Archivio Centrale dello Stato
ADSS	Actes et documents du Saint Siège relatifs à la seconde guerre mondiale
AES	Affari Ecclesiastici Straordinari
ASDMEI	Archivio Storico del Ministero degli Affari Esteri Italiano
ASV	Archivio Segreto Vaticano
DBFP	*Documents on British Foreign Policy, 1919–39*, London
DDF	*Documenti diplomatici francesi*
FRUS	*Papers relating to the Foreign Relations of the United States*, Department of State, Washington
RSCI	*Rivista di Storia della Chiesa in Italia*
VKZG	Veröffentlichungen der Kommission für Zeitgeschichte

ACKNOWLEDGMENTS

I would like to extend heartfelt thanks to the many friends and colleagues who have helped me with this research, for their support, generosity, and suggestions.

Special thanks go to Cardinal Achille Silvestrini for his valuable suggestions on how to disentangle the complexities of Vatican diplomacy and also to Professor Giuseppe Bonfrate, who offered no less valuable guidance in the area of theology.

I would also like to express profound gratitude to the prefect of the Vatican Secret Archive, Barnabite Father Sergio Pagano, for his availability and the equilibrium he has displayed in managing the difficult opening of these sources. And finally, thanks to all the personnel of the Secret Archive, a rare island of competence and courtesy, and a special thanks to Carl Ipsen for the excellent translation.

This book is dedicated to my father, who in those years was a young physician and a lover of freedom and of the gospel.

PREFACE

On 23 September 1924, Mussolini declared: "A people will not become great and powerful if it does not embrace religion and consider it an essential element of public and private life." And fully consistent with many currents of nineteenth-century reactionary thought, from nationalism to the ideology of Maurras, *il Duce* held throughout his twenty years in power that religion was a necessary *instrumentum regni*. The relationship between the Church and Italian fascism, ranging as it did from enthusiasm to disillusionment, is one of the key elements that make it an "imperfect totalitarianism." The presence of the Vatican in Italy, together with the monarchy and a weak bourgeoisie, made fascism fundamentally different from German National Socialism.

Likewise, the Church sought in Mussolini a "man of providence." It was as though Mussolini would serve not only to settle the Roman Question and the conflict with liberal Italy, but would indeed resolve the situation created by the French Revolution, which saw the Church relegated to a corner, internally divided and lacking its former compactness. The Church had become just one social element and no longer encompassed society in its entirety. The Church expected not just material compensation, but that moral and spiritual comfort it needed to feel less isolated and alone in the modern world. And so there developed an intimate understanding with the new totalitarian order, one in which the Church would once again play the leading role. It was these expectations that explain the sense of elation that welcomed the "man whom providence has sent us." The Church wanted more than an alliance of convenience with fascism or a simple exchange of favors. Mussolini's arrival on the scene responded to deep needs and moral and social expectations that went well beyond a preference for the lesser of several evils. That elation becomes even more comprehensible if we consider the comforting agreement on certain fundamental principles: authority and hierarchy, family and property, order and discipline.

Reciprocal expectations led, however, to reciprocal manipulations, as Mussolini sought to fascistize the Church while Pius XI sought to Catholicize fascism. It was an alliance cemented by important material interests but founded, as we have suggested, on that intimate understanding and sharing of fundamental values that served to distinguish fascism from Nazism. Ironically, Pius XI preferred the modernist Mussolini while distrusting Hitler, the defender of tradition. Hitler's, though, was a tradition that usurped that of the Church, as his totalitarianism was so complete as to be subjectively and objectively not just in competition with the Church but incompatible with it. This distinction, paradoxical only in appearance, explains the different sorts of relationship Pius XI had with fascism and Nazism.

Messianic expectations for a man of providence found their origin in the firm conviction that the liberal political world, with its array of parties and unrealistic democratic aims, could no longer cope with a situation of increasing disorder. From his first encyclicals (*Ubi arcano* of 1922 and *Quas primas* of 1925), Pius XI seemed to go beyond the condemnation of all forms of secularism to arrive at a true program of re-Christianization. His papacy, indeed, was always demonstrative and regal, entirely in keeping with the authoritarian spirit of the age. With Pius XI, Catholicism shared that regenerative myth of collective participation that had been frustrated by the cathartic expectations issuing from the Great War, expectations that transformed millenarian prophecies into the dangerous myths of nationalism and communism.

So, while the convergence of Church and fascism relied upon fascism's character as a civil religion and the disillusionment of the post-war period, that convergence began to break down as the regime gradually assumed the nature of a true political religion. And it was at that very moment when fascism reached its apogee of sacredness, the very sacredness that had proved so reassuring, that the Church recognized its terrible miscalculation, the trap into which it had trustingly fallen. And so the conflict with the Catholic Church became inevitable when the regime moved from a religion of superficial liturgies to the attempt to penetrate consciousness and control individual subjectivity in permanent and structural ways – that is, to a true political religion. It was no accident that the Church came into conflict with the regime in 1931 over Catholic Action and the education of youth or in 1938 over the racial laws only insofar as they "violated" Catholic authority relative to mixed marriages.

And so, while the Church had happily supported the "sacralization of politics," it also constituted the best antidote. For, as Pius XI pointedly summed up his relationships with the totalitarian regimes, the Church was "the only truly totalitarian institution." The pope, however, made this unshakeable indictment of fascism only after 1937; by then the pact with Hitler seemed inevitable, and, in a threatening crescendo, the more totalitarian characteristics of fascism came to the fore as, according to Pius XI, it ever more dangerously resembled Nazism. The advance of this absolute unitary totalitarianism was incompatible with the only institution that could legitimately define itself as "totalitarian," namely the Roman Catholic Church. In September of 1938, Pius XI went so far as to state: ". . . if there is a totalitarian regime – totalitarian in fact and by rights – it is the regime of the Church, as man belongs wholly to the Church, must belong to it as man is the creation of the good Lord . . ."

Much has been written about the ambiguous and variable nature of totalitarianism, so that even communism has been included under the rubric; a constant, however, in these discussions is the sacralization and absolutization of politics. We do not encounter a clear theorization of totalitarianism in the thought of Pius XI; his view evolves instead from terms that include statolatry, neo-paganism, authoritarianism, exaggerated nationalism, statist absolutism – often used as neologisms or synonyms.

The pope only spoke of totalitarianism and its many attributes starting in spring 1938; his condemnation derived not from illumination but was, rather, the fruit of a long process in which the interplay of external events and interior reflection led to a highly significant conclusion. Just as the totalitarianisms had initially offered reassuring models, after a decade they appeared instead to threaten a dangerous revolt at the heart of the Church and of faith.

Pius XI's rejection of totalitarianism was born of the idea that the Church itself was the most true and genuine totalitarian organism – the *societas perfecta* – and of the total identification between man's belonging to God and, *therefore*, man's belonging to the Church. He went further still, asserting that the Church legitimately represented the *totality* of humankind and the *totality* of the individual, because only the Church finds the foundation of its authority and so of its power in transcendence. We will not explore this theme here, but only underline the fact that *Transcendence* and *Power*, so intimately connected, are the cornerstones of that perfect *complexio oppositorum* that is the Catholic Church in the theology of Carl Schmitt.

The pope, then, felt the need to return to universal principles and their roots which lie in *natural rights*, the only true principle of absolute equality. His interpretation of natural rights seemed to suggest a sort of political theology of the Church, a theology that derived from that very encounter and struggle with the totalitarianisms of the twentieth century. Documents from the Vatican Secret Archive reveal that the Vatican's grappling with totalitarian regimes, consisting as it did of moments of convergence and others of conflict, ultimately modified in a profound way the theological and pastoral apparatus of the Church; it would never be the same again.

Pius XI then defended the unity of humankind against the separatisms of racism and nationalism, placing the Jewish question in the theological and pastoral context we have described. His defense of the Jews derived from natural rights and developed into the rejection of anti-Jewishness: "spiritually we are all Semites." Our concern here is not to measure the different gradations of influence that anti-Jewishness had on the more practical anti-Semitism, but rather to understand that the pope's reference to a common descent from Abraham gave greater weight to his condemnation of the persecution of the Jews. For, in the thought of Pius XI, Christian and Jew shared a human identity. The point is not so much to celebrate that the pope overcame anti-Jewishness, but to underline that the root of that condemnation is theological. The common descent from Abraham is invoked because anti-Semitism attacks the heart of Christianity and so the Church. If concern about the fate of the Jews always begins and ends with Christianity, then the religious and even the theological basis of that concern reinforces its value greatly, as nothing could be more radical.

The new sources available from the Vatican Secret Archive draw an extraordinary picture of the evolution, growth, and maturity first of great expectations and then of equally great disillusionment with the concordats. Pius XI was at first surprised, then disappointed, and finally angry. His anxious concern grew as he saw, sooner and more clearly than others, the precipice down which the world was about to plummet; that growth can be reconstructed with great clarity from the documentation available from the second half of the 1930s, and that is the subject of the present work now offered to an English-speaking audience. At the risk even of falling into apology, my book emphasizes this need for "religious totality" and seeks its roots in areas typically ignored, including, for example, the pope's relation-ships with women. These roots are crucial for my purpose, as a pope does not cease to be a man, nor, and fortunately for the Church, does he cease to be a man of faith once he becomes pope. Pius XI regarded the impending situation with a sensibility that was spiritual rather than political, but one that paradoxically allowed him to intuit and decipher the imminent catastrophe more ably than other diplo-matic analysts who continued to reason within the logic of the concordats.

Pius XI died at 5:31 a.m. on 10 February 1939, on the eve of the anniversary of the Lateran Pact. Gravely ill and in bed, he had until just a few hours before been at work revising in a shaky hand the text of an address that would have been his strongest condemnation of fascism – a text that was then made immediately to disappear.

The publication of this book in Italy has inspired heated contro-versy. Many have maintained that Pacelli, who on the death of the pope was no longer secretary of state but instead camerlengo – the individual responsible for administering the vacancy of the Holy See – had no option but to destroy the text of the pope's last address, one that presaged a complete break with the fascist regime, and so also with the Nazi one.

Certainly, as camerlengo, Pacelli could destroy the last address, but he was not obliged to do so, and he certainly was not prevented from making it public at a later date. He *was within his rights* to follow that course of action, but he certainly was not *forced to*. No one had been closer than he to Pius XI; and no one knew better than he how important that address was to the pope. Our task, though, is not to judge a single act, however significant, but rather to reconstruct the climate of those days, the air of expectation, the pastoral and emo-tional choices of Pius XI. And while the present work of reconstruc-tion is not intended as yet another occasion to point a finger of accusation at Pacelli, it provides nonetheless a further sign, among many, that the secretary of state, along with the majority of the Curia, did not share the intransigent positions of the dying pope. The cam-erlengo, soon to be pope himself, had solid reasons to fear should the conclave be conducted with the Church openly defying Mussolini. Indeed, it would have been far more surprising if Pacelli, rather than suppressing the address, had made sure that it was circulated. And yet one cannot help but wonder at the diligence and speed with which he decided to deny the last wishes of the pope. It all seemed to come as a sigh of relief.

We need not downplay the differences between Eugenio Pacelli (Pius XII) and Achille Ratti (Pius XI), two tragic individuals so different in character and so indissolubly linked together. The make-up of their personalities, their family backgrounds, and their spiritual dimensions were almost diametrically opposed. And yet they were irresistibly attracted one to the other, perhaps because of those very differences and in keeping with the rule that opposites attract in search of a complementarity – complementarity for which both men felt a strong need. The sanguine Ratti would likely never have allowed himself to make such strong attacks had he not known that the diligent and faithful Pacelli was there to smooth things out and heal the diplomatic wounds. The two men held each other in high esteem, but it was above all mutual dependence that tied them together. Pacelli was the perfect secretary of state, so perfect that we might even say that once he himself became pope he nonetheless remained his own secretary of state.

Examination of the relationship between the prudent and diplomatic Pacelli and his impetuous pope can easily get tied up in the interminable debate over the silences of Pius XII, but that would be a distraction. The question of Pius XII's silences has unfortunately become a field of venomous debate, coming even to incorporate inappropriate anachronisms that project post-Vatican II expectations onto the question of the Vatican and the Jews. Only calm and balanced historical research can hope to transcend the temptation to fall either into the apologetic trap of those who would see Pius XII as the greatest saint of the twentieth century or into the opposite one depicting him as Hitler's pope. It is a conflict that the campaign to canonize Pius XII inevitably inspires. The imminent opening of Pius XII's archive may help to shed light on these questions. The last years of Ratti's papacy also add new elements to the debate and confirm Pacelli's prudent approach.

We should not, however, draw quick or simple conclusions. Who can deny, without the benefit of hindsight, that Pacelli's prudence did have its "justifications"? To my mind, we are on more solid ground when we lament that the spirit of Pius XI at the end of his life did not live on in his successor; indeed, Pius XII seems to have done just that in a tortured correspondence with Cardinal Clemens August von Galen, whose resoluteness Pacelli admired. It is right and legitimate to regret that Ratti's papacy was interrupted too suddenly by his death, just at that moment when, rather than coming to an end, it seemed about to begin anew. It was an end filled with hopes and expectations that, rather than being taken up, were instead and definitively canceled out.

INTRODUCTION

If Pius XI, energetic and impulsive man that he was, had lived a bit longer, there would in all likelihood have been a break in the relationship between the Reich and the Vatican.

From the memoir of Ernst von Weizsäcker,[1]
German ambassador to the Holy See

In the last years of his life, Pius XI developed a sharp and growing rejection of totalitarianism. From the end of 1936 till his death on 10 February 1939, his condemnation of the "anti-Christian" and "inhuman" aspects of Nazism, and also fascism, became ever more radical. The aging, ill pope came to reject racial discrimination, exaggerated nationalism, and the persecution of Jews as entirely unacceptable. Yet he experienced his intolerance largely in solitude. Now, thanks to documentation newly made available by the Vatican Secret Archive, the rumors of a Pius XI who during his final years found himself isolated in the Vatican and nearly alone in his opposition to Nazism lose their air of legend. Together with the reported sense of relief that came with his death, those rumors now take their place as a confirmed chapter in the contemporary history of the Church.[2]

My research examines this new material and focuses in particular on the final years of Pius XI's papacy, the years when he broke openly with Nazism and in many ways also with fascism. By that time, the ideal to which he had aspired in the 1920s of a Catholic front of conservative regimes had been dashed, and there grew in him instead ever greater disillusionment even with Mussolini, the man "whom providence has sent us."

This line of research has already been identified, if not fully pursued, in the work of Giovanni Miccoli,[3] and in some aspects also by

1

Giacomo Martina;[4] it now finds significant support in the new documentary sources made available for the entire papacy of Pius XI. Those sources confirm in no uncertain terms the pope's increasing dissatisfaction with diplomacy and the attempt to contain the growing conflict with Hitler within the framework of the Concordat. It was a dissatisfaction that went well beyond that of many other members of his entourage and in particular of his secretary of state, Eugenio Pacelli (the future Pius XII). This line has been little pursued in part because the Vatican archives have been closed until now, but also because of the fear that emphasizing the intransigence of Pius XI in his final years would fuel once again the suspicions surrounding the presumed shortcomings of his successor, Pius XII, around whom doubts and questions continue to swirl. The richness of these documents allows us to emerge finally from the drawn-out discussion of the silences and guilt of Pius XII. This latter historiography is too often built upon our present-day anxieties and the sensibilities constructed following the Second World War and the Second Vatican Council. Those anxieties are understandable, but end up reducing history to a series of condemnations and absolutions that distract us from the effort to understand better what actually happened and to maintain the delicate balance between judgment and historical research. The new documentation allows us to follow closely the maturation of Pius XI's thought and so to avoid certain simplistic dichotomies, such as that according to which Vatican diplomacy can maintain fidelity to Christian principles only by avoiding the need to make real-world choices.

To start with, we have to do away with many of the stereotypes that surround the figure of Achille Ratti (Pius XI), the last years of whose life have been progressively reduced to mere anecdote. The intransigence of his final years – a commonplace of the history of the Church in the twentieth century – has often been attributed to his authoritarian character, to his forceful will, to his age, and to his illness. Yet a revisiting of his life and the final years of his papacy reveals a man who was lucid and aware, determined and fully in contact with himself and the world around him.

The most interesting discovery, however, that emerges from a first look at the new documents has to do with the nature and modality of his intransigence. It was anything but sudden and improvised, and grew instead out of a profound "interior conversion." Although that conversion did not find expression in a coherent and explicit political theology,[5] we can instead define it as a "theology of history" based on a spiritual approach to wisdom that derives the values and respon-

2

sibilities of the faithful in daily life from divine grace. In the context of the irreducibility of faith (or the institutions of the Church) to any sort of political manipulation – so strongly defended by Pius XI – it is as if the pope wanted nonetheless to test the limits of the institution in order to inform institutional, diplomatic, and political positions as far as possible with the light of his interior faith. Put another way, the very person who occupied the highest position in the ecclesiastical institution, a pope who never abandoned the conservative tradition based upon the proud character of his native Lombardy, attempted a spiritual expansion of that institution.

The impulse to condemn and assign blame finds its opposite and reaction in defensive positions that reduce the internal divisions of the Church to a uniformity that does not exist. The world that we shall explore is complex, varied, and fungible, starting with the pope himself. He was impulsive, strong-willed, and passionate and so very different from his careful and solemn secretary of state. With Pacelli, in fact, he established a particular relationship, a sort of complementarity that allowed his own excesses to be tempered by Pacelli's diplomacy and the latter's indecision to find a more resolute position in the pope himself. Between 1937 and 1939 the differences between the pope and his secretary of state became explicit: Pacelli was always determined to pursue diplomatic mediation with the Nazi regime – the position that he anxiously sought to recover as soon as he assumed the papal mantle himself – while Ratti seemed to be moving toward an open break. Ratti, however, never lost confidence in his invaluable secretary of state, the faithful executor who moderated and tempered the pope's impulsive desires in a continual work of mediation. And Pacelli always remained Pius XI's chosen successor for the dark years that evidently lay ahead – an intention that does not, however, lessen their profound differences.

Between 10 August 1930 and 3 December 1938, Eugenio Pacelli took down notes on small unbound sheets of paper following his daily audience with the pope. Gathered together, these "Pacelli notebooks" tell us a great deal about these two very different but mutually attracted personalities. Other individuals from the office of the Secretariat have also left important records, among them the sustituto Domenico Tardini, who shared many of Pius XI's views and noted them down in diaries – for example, that for the month of October 1938, when he served as Pacelli's substitute, and that of January 1941, when he gathered together in a detailed and concise dossier all the documentation relating to the pope's last weeks. We also have the observations of the young Giovanni Battista Montini (later Paul VI).

Reports sent to Rome from the various nunciatures offer a privileged view of the national churches and the challenges they faced: in Germany the bishops encountered a dramatic conflict between loyalty to their homeland and to their faith, while in Spain during the first months of the Civil War they were trapped between the "violence of the reds," who massacred the clergy, and Franco, who slaughtered the Basque priests. But those reports also provide insight into periods of national crisis: the explosion of the Civil War in Spain, the beginning of the persecutions in Germany, the Popular Front coalition in France, the pro-Nazism of Austrian Catholicism, and the dangerous rapprochement between Italian fascism and Hitler. And there were of course problematic figures within the Roman Curia itself: pro-fascist councilors such as the noted Father Pietro Tacchi-Venturi, official and unfailing conduit to the fascist hierarchs; pro-Nazi monsignors such as Hudal, rector of the congregation of Santa Maria dell'Anima; or indefatigable fascist professors such as Guido Manacorda, who bombarded the Secretariat with appeals for a policy of pacification between the pope and Hitler. Others occupied more subtle positions, such as Agostino Gemelli, who had an important relationship with the pope, and also left-leaning Catholics such as the French democrat Francisque Gay, who, together with many other exponents of European Catholic anti-fascism and also modernist elements, in particular Tommaso Gallarati Scotti, saw in the pope's late positions a ray of hope. Over this whole range weighed heavily the figure of the Polish Count Ledóchowski, superior general of the Jesuits and a fierce anti-Semite and anti-communist. Ledóchowski was the force behind the anti-communist encyclical *Divini Redemptoris* and played an important role in opposing that condemning anti-Semitism desired by Pius XI in summer 1938 but which never saw the light of day.

We are faced then not simply with a monolithic and pyramidal Church, and yet these differences were resolved by the taking of positions that find their explanation and articulation in the newly available documentation.

Pius XI was certainly not a liberal pope, and his opposition to totalitarianism did not derive from an alliance with democratic ideals. His own doctrine was in fact profoundly traditional. And we should not be deceived by the favorable view that certain modernist, democratic, and progressive Catholic elements took of his papacy in the final years. Pius XI did not become a democrat; nor did he choose a new political path but rather underwent a true "spiritual conversion." Assuming the papal mantle following the death of Benedict XV, Pius XI inherited his predecessor's concern for the spiritual dimension of the institution but did not share Benedict's faith in the intervention of the Church in international organizations or the engagement of Catholics in political activity, least of all in political parties. Pius XI – strong-willed, active, headstrong, and authoritarian – devoted his considerable energies instead to building a new Christianity on the model of Christ the King, including a political revival of cults such as the Sacred Heart and the Kingdom of Christ as promoted in his *Quas primas* encyclical of late 1925.[6] He championed these devotions as the basis of a metaphysics of both interior and public action aimed at combating modernity and the evils born of secularization. They were cults intended to reconquer ground the Church had lost but which, as carefully noted by Giorgio Rumi,[7] in the anthropological conception of Pius XI, contained a strong spiritual and interior tension. Freed of their strictest trappings and mortifications, these devotions were intended to foster a virtuous dialectic between divine grace and freedom with an eye to authentic personal conversion and its consequent social and public impact.

Even the more political cults needed to be consolidated according to a more interior formation, "a true piety, pure habits, so that grace may speak." The clerical elite needed to act with purity and sanctity and so maintain coherence between their personal lives and their preaching. Pius XI explained as much to the cardinals on the occasion of the 13 December 1937 consistory, when he stated that to "do good," in biblical terms, was achieved above all through interiority and to the degree that one maintained coherence between intention and action, and so the need to "begin with oneself and one's own experience before speaking, before preaching the gospel." He seemed to want to recapture the practice of self-knowledge that had been so dear to the fathers of the Church who reinterpreted Greek philosophy in light of the gospel. His was not a generic appeal for coherence or for ethically correct exterior behavior; it was precisely the opposite: the unacceptability (if only because useless and ineffective) of Christian proselytizing in the absence of a true interior conversion.

Ratti's sensibility was informed by his fundamental encounter with Thérèse de Lisieux, mediator of small things in a world of despoilment and abandonment. She was his spiritual opposite, the "star of his papacy" who tempered his impulsive imperiousness, his frenetic tendency to organize, construct, and advance an ecclesiastic politics. Canonizing her on 17 May 1925, Pius XI transformed Thérèse from an icon of searing and romantic nineteenth-century devotion into the modern model of a serious and sober spirituality as well as patron of the Catholic missions (so proclaimed in 1927 along with Francis Xavier); she was a figure who facilitated interpretation of the acute anxieties afflicting French Catholicism in the period of the popular fronts.

The biography of this Lombard priest further reveals the importance in his life of strong women, beginning with his mother, of the sort who might be drawn from the works of that greatest of Lombard novelists, Alessandro Manzoni. From them he learned always to strive for something higher without losing sight of concrete reality, moving forward step by step while looking neither too far into the future nor into the past but remaining firmly in the present. His spiritual path resembled that of the mountain climber, a passion that Ratti never viewed as a heroic challenge.

His strength derived from an awareness of his own weakness as he measured himself against both the great events of history and small everyday things; this was not an easy task given his strong-willed character and inclination to command. Indeed, he spoke with horror of the ordinary day-to-day routine of life, of its senseless repetition, boredom, and lack of concrete results. And yet Ratti's spiritual path would be ever more marked by a confidence in self-abandonment derived from feminine influences, not only from his mother and Thérèse de Lisieux, but also as a result of his spiritual cohabitation with the Sisters of the Cenacle in Milan, for whom he was spiritual assistant during the years of his Milanese priesthood.

This attitude guided him in his first political and diplomatic experiences when he was sent as papal nuncio to Poland and found himself involved in – overwhelmed by, really – the conflicts between Poles and Germans over the border of Upper Silesia. It was a bitter experience that left Ratti drained and tested spiritually, as Benedict XV well observed: "His letter was shrouded in sadness, though not for personal reasons, and I admired his ability to understand the most secular of issues in spiritual terms."[8]

That interior evolution was tested by the illness that struck him in the winter of 1936–7. His body, which till then had never shown signs of weakness, was forced to cope with a dangerous bout of heart disease, and the recovery constituted both an experience of "impermanence" and training for the acceptance of passivity and the taking up again of new initiatives. It is often suggested that his intolerance for totalitarianism derived from his illness, thereby minimizing the significance of that intolerance and depriving it of meaning. Precisely the opposite was the case: it was from an awareness of his own fragility that Pius achieved detachment from earthly things and a firm conviction to allow himself to be led by the supernatural. Pius XI fell ill at the end of 1936; from March 1937 almost till his death on 10 February 1939 he was clear headed and watched the development of world affairs with increasing alarm while always in touch with his own interiority. It is as though the external and the internal, politics and faith, were in a dialogue, as though history were no longer simply observed, judged, and governed, but instead passed through a spiritual sphere transforming its sensibility and vice versa. This was a rare co-penetration and created no small difficulty for the man who was the incarnation of the institution of the Church. It represented a vital modulation of the religious experience that translated into a theology of history focused on the living presence of divine grace.

Fascist memoirs, starting with the diaries of Galeazzo Ciano and Giuseppe Bottai,[9] contain broad and intriguing testimony to Pius XI's passionate character or to his impatience, symptoms of an authoritarian temperament so accustomed to command, also revealed more than once by Domenico Tardini. We would do well not to leave these more personal and private details to the hagiographies, as typically happens with the historical study of twentieth-century popes. Even though we have witnessed greater attention paid to the full unity of character of more recent popes, such as John Paul II, the tendency of historical work is still to treat the ecclesiastical-diplomatic side as though distinct from personal biography, from private and emotional life. What we get then is a disembodied pope, one for whom the important choices of papal administration are somehow independent from his interior dimension. And yet it is just that interior dimension, that spiritual and psychological life – which is to say, as for *his* Thérèse, the *history of the soul* – that is indissolubly tied up with spiritual inclination and faith.

The evolution that characterized the final years of the life of Pius XI, then, was not a chance illumination, but rather the endpoint of a spiritual path that developed during his illness as he came face to face with the bitter disillusionment he felt for that fascist conservatism in which he had placed so much hope, presumed ally of his theocratic design.

Signs of this break had already appeared, the most notable being his well-studied condemnation of the Italo-Ethiopian War (1935–6), a war he "characterized as an unjust war of conquest. He condemned those who would provoke the war . . . and made it clear that (according to him) Italy's war against Ethiopia was unjust."[10] This according to Domenico Tardini, who spent an entire night trying to manipulate, temper, and soften the text of Pius XI's address to Catholic nurses of 27 August 1937. "It was a document made intentionally obscure," according to Gaetano Salvemini,[11] to the point that its sense was overturned and it appeared that the Church was, if not enthusiastic, certainly supportive of the fascist war in Ethiopia. It is a case already well studied and reconstructed using documentation from the Ministry of Foreign Affairs; and now that reconstruction finds full confirmation in the papers newly available from the Vatican archive.[12]

Between 1937 and 1938 the hope for an international Catholic front bringing together Italy, Austria, Spain, and Portugal also faded. The *Anschluß* and the racial laws threatened the accord with fascism and initiated a period of uncertainty.

The crisis of the 1930s seemed a true "conflict of civilizations" and could only be resolved by means of a "Catholic solution," by a return to the Christian roots of Western civilization.[13] It is as if two totalitarian conceptions, one Christian and the other anti-Christian, faced one another in what was truly viewed as a "battle between civilizations." As one can read in the *Rivista Liturgica*, "It was not a difference of opinions or of competing programs or of contingent institutions, but rather the perfect antithesis of two totalitarian concepts: Christian and anti-Christian."[14]

The pope too was convinced of the battle between Christianity and anti-Christianity, a challenge for which the tools of the Concordat were unfortunately impotent. So it was that he of the "mania for concordats" – he used to comment "I would make a concordat with the devil if it benefited the Church" – was forced to go to the root of this conflict that was spiritual before it was political – except that this time Italy and Germany would not be on the "side of Christianity" and the anti-Bolshevik front would not suffice. More aware than even his own entourage of the gravity of the situation, Pius XI no longer believed that diplomatic solutions of the type used up to that time in the conflict between states and the Holy See would be up to the challenge; indeed, he was never a champion of Munich and saw the Munich Accords instead as the final bluff.

Hitler and Mussolini repeatedly accused Pius of "practicing politics and not religion," a charge he rejected while at the same time not attempting to minimize the importance of his positions, given that the practice of religion need not be any less powerful, incisive, and resolute than that of politics. Indeed, he claimed to speak from a purely religious standpoint in order to sharpen, not alleviate, the conflict. Pacelli would often use similar argumentation but completely reversed, convinced that he could better placate the two dictators by sticking to a purely religious plane and guaranteeing that the Church would continue to operate within the confines of the existing concordats and standard diplomatic practices. The secretary of state in fact replied to the furious reaction of the German ambassador, Diego von Bergen, following the issuance of *Mit brennender Sorge* with the explanation that the encyclical derived "simply" from religious concerns, when in fact it represented a complete break with Nazi Germany.

The destiny of the Church was inseparable from that of humankind, and so its enemies no longer included just communism but also Hitler's Nazism, which seemed in fact to be taking the place of the other. The assessment that D'Arcy Osborne, British ambassador to the Holy See, delivered to Lord Halifax is well known: "There is no doubt that Nazi Germany has taken the place of communism as the most dangerous enemy of the Church." Communism was condemned in the encyclical *Divini Redemptoris*, issued at the same time as that against Nazism, as "intrinsically perverse," and so as a movement with which any sort of collaboration was impossible. However, while the text condemning communism is stronger, given that there is no possibility of its redemption, it is more doctrinal, less ringing and biblical, than that against the twisted cross that had been erected in place of the cross of Christ. Communism was by this time an old foe. Its atheism was too materialist and rationalist to compete with Christianity, while Nazism was more pervasive and vitalistic, more falsely sacred, and so it was better able to galvanize the need for spiritualism felt by the masses in the 1930s.

It is in fact with regard to communism that the new documentation holds some interesting surprises, in particular regarding the coalition policy and a meeting proposed to the Catholics by the French communists in the period of the Popular Front in the late 1930s. In contrast to the hostility and complete rejection by the secretary of state and the Jesuits, the pope saw in this proposal an opportunity for the Church to demonstrate both compassion and the ability to listen. His was not a political choice; indeed, he never came to any sort of agreement with the communists. Instead it was a sign of openness: the Christian does not turn away the hand that is offered to him but instead puts forward his own as an act of good faith. On 16 November 1937, he confided to Pacelli: "We must think carefully about leaving unanswered this offer of cooperation. What gives us the right to refuse an act of good faith? If we take into due consideration their overture, no one will be able to launch accusations against us."[15] This was a position that alarmed everyone: Pacelli and the entire Secretariat of State to begin with, but also the French nuncio, who sought to calm the French cardinals regarding the pope's excesses by issuing an assurance that one need not be overly concerned, and Cardinal Verdier of Paris, who was much struck by the incident.

The distinction made by the pope was a profound one, entirely spiritual and so free; it would subsequently give way to "more reasonable" policies. Yet the exquisite passages we discuss below, as well as one of his nocturnal meditations, reveal his ability to read current events in a spiritual light. It is the same religious position that he took when confronted with the internationalization of the Spanish Civil War, a conflict that left him disturbed, contemplative, and deep in prayer, rather than quick to take sides. The years and months that preceded the Vatican's recognition of Francisco Franco, a figure whom in any case Pius openly disliked, were ones of great uncertainty.

Although the Holy See received many and early protests regarding the persecution of the Jews – for example, the letter Edith Stein sent to the pope in 1933 and many others sent to the Berlin nuncio – the Vatican and the German bishops were eager to interpret every possible sign of amelioration and restricted their condemnations of Nazism to its elements of neo-paganism, particularly the positions advanced in Alfred Rosenberg's *Myth of the Twentieth Century*. Such in any event was the case until the bishops' letter that came out of the Fulda Conference of 1 August 1938 abandoned the hope that mild acts of compromise could move the Nazis to more conciliatory positions. The break instead took place in the first half of 1937 and became complete after the first months of 1938, coming to threaten even the relationship with fascism, especially insofar as the denunciation touched on the issues of race and anti-Semitism.

The new archival material, coming on the heels of the opening of the German nunciature in 2003, confirms and deepens the more serious lines of research already undertaken regarding the growing rift between Pius XI, Hitler, and eventually also Mussolini.[16] Though now we can identify subtleties that throw light on differences among various currents within the Curia and the Vatican diplomatic corps and allow a much clearer understanding of alliances and contrasts.

The pope found himself isolated, and Hitler himself reminded Pius of this fact. Following their failure to meet during the Nazi leader's visit to Rome in May 1938, Hitler issued a sort of curse, claiming that Pius's brandishing of the cross as a weapon "left him desperately alone to pray, pray, and pray some more . . . in the company of free-masons and Bolsheviks." There were, however, figures close to the pope, such as Cardinal Mundelein of Chicago, and the more anti-Nazi of the German bishops, such as Konrad von Preysing and Clemens von Galen, individuals who spoke a different language from that of pro-Nazi elements such as Monsignor Hudal or virulent anti-communists such as the Jesuit Superior General Ledóchowski. Pacelli maintained close relationships with all of these individuals, performing a balancing act while maintaining complete loyalty to Pius XI, if not a loyalty based on empathy.

We have looked in detail at the case of Austria following the *Anschluß*, as the new documentation offers fascinating material. The pope was particularly critical of Cardinal Innitzer of Vienna, a weak and frightened man who praised the annexation and was immediately disciplined by the Vatican. And those comments were nearly contemporaneous with his enthusiastic praise for Mundelein, who described Hitler as "an Austrian paper hanger, and a poor one at that." Documents from the Austrian nunciature offer a vivid and distressing picture of the days of the German occupation and of the silence that surrounded the persecution of the Jews. And none other than Sigmund Freud offers additional insight into in those same months:

> We are living in a specially remarkable period . . . it is precisely the institution of the Catholic Church which puts up a powerful defence against the spread of this danger to civilization – the Church which has hitherto been the relentless foe to freedom of thought and to advances toward the discovery of the truth!
>
> We are living here in a Catholic country under the protection of that Church, uncertain how long that protection will hold out.

The above was written before March 1938 in the prefatory note to the third essay of *Moses and Monotheism*. In June, by which time he had escaped to London, Freud added a second warning: "At the earlier date I was living under the protection of the Catholic Church and was afraid that the publication of my work would result in the loss of that protection . . . Then, suddenly came the German invasion and Catholicism proved, to use the words of the Bible, 'a broken reed.'"[17] Freud's comments, and the context in which they were made, point to a sort of awareness that Hitlerite paganism would ultimately move Jewish consciousness toward a position sympathetic with the Catholic Church in their common defense of biblical monotheism.

Pius's repeated criticisms of racism, and in some passages also of anti-Semitism, from the summer of 1938 and in the never published encyclical, depend upon the shared spiritual inheritance from Abraham of both Jews and Catholics. His moving comments of 6 September 1938 are well known: "Listen well, Abraham is our Patriarch, our ancestor . . . Anti-Semitism is irreconcilable . . . It is a hateful movement with which we Christians must have no relationship . . . through Christ we are the descendants of Abraham . . . Spiritually we are all Semites."[18] The etymology of the word Hebrew, a migrant or one passing over, intersects with the destiny of Abraham, the wandering one, a title that remains engraved in the Jewish faith (Deuteronomy 26:5). This derivation comes from the exegetic contact between ancient hermeneutics of Jewish and Christian extraction, to the point that it takes on the value of a necessary historical paradigm: all of humanity, under the sign of Judeo-Christian inheritance, takes on the quality of the pilgrim. Pius XI retrieved it according to the acceptance of a *common destiny, to proceed together, and to come from*, as he wrote in a document that accompanied the request for help for Jewish scientists sent to American cardinals.[19]

Similarly, Edith Stein's declaration to the pope was not made in the name of a generic "violation of human rights," but grew instead out of these common theological roots: "Is this war of extermination against the Jews not an outrage against the sacred humanity of our Savior, the Virgin Mary, and the apostles?"[20] The future Carmelite nun, a converted Jew, saw in the persecution of the Jews an attempt also to eliminate the source from which they historically traced their origin, namely the Judeo-Christian faith. Nazism then was battling not only against Judaism but also against Catholic Christianity, considered dangerous because organized in a centralized structure, the Roman Catholic Church:[21] "You cannot imagine how important it is for me to repeat, every morning when I go to the chapel and raise my eyes to the crucifix and to the image of the Madonna, that we came of the same blood . . . what it means to me to be a daughter of the chosen people."[22]

We have no documentary evidence of how the pope reacted to these words. Stein herself reflected in December 1938: "Later on I often wondered if he ever recalled that letter. What I had then predicted for the German Catholics effectively took place point by point over the following years."[23] Even though we do not know if Stein's appeal influenced the pope, it is certainly the case that her reflections on the

12

indissoluble links between Christianity and its Jewish roots point to a substantial spiritual affinity between the aging pontiff and the Jewish philosopher.

At the height of the Sudetenland crisis, on 18 September 1938, Pius XI touched upon a particularly important "doctrinal point." The true and profound nature of the conflict between Nazism and the Church lay in the fact that they were "two totalitarianisms": "One hears it bandied about, that all must be within the state. And so we have the totalitarian state: nothing outside of the state, all belongs to the state . . . And this represents a great usurpation, since if there exists a totalitarian regime – totalitarian in fact and in law – it is the regime of the Church; man belongs wholly to the Church, as indeed he must, for man is the creation of the good Lord."[24]

Ratti's indignation did not of course derive from a liberal-democratic consideration of the rights of man, or even from a generic appeal to natural law, but rather from the objective competition between the totality of the Church and Nazi veneration of the state. Nazi totalitarianism became for the pope the most advanced phase of that process of secularization that started with the French Revolution and sought to affirm the autonomy of modern man. Yet the support that the Church had given to totalitarianism created a problem for the Church itself, one more theological than political. And if that problem does not really foreshadow the theology of the "impotence of God" and the responsibility of man that followed the *Shoah*, it does demonstrate that the pope lived his faith as *Kénosis* – emptying, prostration, abandonment – entrusting himself to prayer, not as a form of surrender, and to the grace and spirituality of Thérèse de Lisieux.

The nature of the condemnation of Nazism reflected on Italian fascism as well. Giuseppe Bottai, then minister of education, saw this clearly and in July 1938 noted as much in relation to Pacelli's oration to the French *Semaines Sociales*: "the Church is progressively taking up positions contrary to the 'totalitarian' state, whether fascist or otherwise." The new documentation offers interesting evidence of the various attitudes taken with regard to fascism in the late 1930s and makes one regret that more effort has not gone into publishing source material relative to the relationship between fascism and the Church.[25] By comparison, there has been a huge publishing project in Germany on Church–Nazi relations.[26] Consider the publications of the *Kommission für Zeitgeschichte* – nearly forty volumes of correspondence, private notes, police reports, official documents, sermons, and transcripts – or the six volumes of the *Akten deutscher Bischöfe über die Lage die Kirche*, which help to clarify the choices of the bishopric and the Holy See. Currently underway is the publication of the complete correspondence between Eugenio Pacelli and the German nunciatures of Munich and Berlin, a collection of over 5,000 documents that surely holds interesting surprises regarding then Nuncio Pacelli's role relative to the politics of the Catholics in the *Zentrum* during Weimar.[27]

Had the papers of Pius XI been available sooner, studies of the relationship between the Church and the totalitarian regimes would have been fundamentally different. Those papers enrich our understanding of how Catholicism confronted the crisis of the 1930s and in places substantially change it; and they certainly help us to understand better the variety of positions that coexisted at the highest levels of the Vatican hierarchy. The inaccessibility of these sources has also meant that historical research has been hampered and credit given to a simplified version, according to which the Church was simply subordinate to fascism, while it has been impossible to follow up on the work of Catholic historians such as Pietro Scoppola that has taken a more measured view of fascism. The "a-fascist" category (a politically neutral historiography relative to fascist or, more often, antifascist positions), while useful, has not been able to keep pace with the more interesting developments of the lay histories of totalitarianism and so make a significant contribution to those lines of research that have departed from the work of Renzo De Felice. I have in mind here studies of the sacralization of politics, a process that has much in common with the Roman Catholic Church.[28]

Pope Pius XI died on 10 February 1939, though his demise did not seem to mark the end of a pontificate. His death rather seemed a beginning, as though his legacy still lay ahead, a project to take up and build upon. All expected that his end was near, and many even hoped for it, so that the sentiment of the Roman Curia on the occasion of his death was one of relief. In the final years of his life he had become an ever more cumbersome presence, in some sense an embarrassment.

Luigi Salvatorelli describes this climate well in a work whose title translates as *Pius XI and his Legacy*, a book published by the young Giulio Einaudi in April 1939 and written when the papacy of Ratti's successor had not yet begun. Inspired by a sense of anticipation, these are pages that reflect the hopes raised by the aged Pius XI, ever more intransigent in his opposition to totalitarianism.[29]

14

Liberal forces in England and France looked to him with hope, an autocratic and conservative pope. In January of 1939, Edouard Herriot wrote: "In Rome an old man, to whom our spontaneous homage is due, armed by his spiritual gallantry, renews the grand tradition of the great Popes, as protectors of outraged weakness."[30] But these hopes quickly met with disappointment, as Giuseppe Dossetti well expresses in a sharp analysis of the papal succession: "In spite of the quick succession that had the appearance of insuring a direct and immediate continuity, the months that passed between the death of Pius XI and the outbreak of the war were essentially wasted."[31]

The aging pope had gained the sympathy of many of the exponents of modernism, including his great friend Tommaso Gallarati Scotti, to whom a few days before his death he confided a sort of spiritual testimony. This was an alliance that challenged the anti-fascist exiles tied to the positions of don Luigi Sturzo,[32] positions that Achille Ratti had never liked and that in fact soured him to the idea of Catholic parties and in general to democracy.

His legacy would be taken up by a startlingly diverse group of Church figures. Bishop Oscar Romero felt a true dedication to Pius XI and had internalized the latter's emphasis on spirituality already during his training as a priest in Rome; indeed that direction would serve as his moral compass during the trying experience of his martyrdom.[33] Pius XI created a pastoral model of considerable scope: it influenced bishops who felt a keen sensibility as civil witnesses, among them the Italian Cardinal Alfredo Schuster and the French Cardinal Léon-Etienne Duval, who were particularly attentive to combining their allegiance to Rome with responsibility toward their own parishioners.[34]

The final years of Ratti's papacy speak primarily, as we have already pointed out, to a "spiritual conversion," more even than they do to his foresight and political-pastoral intuition in opposing the totalitarian regimes of the 1930s. He returned in those years not so much to the theme of the decline of Christianity but rather to the centrality of Christ, leaving aside the various integralist forms of political Catholicism. He did not develop a new political theology but reverted instead to the origins of faith, a faith that not only demanded the harmonious coherence of soul and action, but also from which derived a complete understanding of the world. He was very clearly invoking the identity of universalism and Catholicism when he spoke of a return to Universals and the unity of humankind while rejecting the divisiveness of race and nation. His orations took as their starting point the rejection of any manipulation of the human person. The universal scope of his thought made him still more sensitive to relationships with other religions, "to those who still believe in God and adore Him," according to the expression that Paul VI liked to repeat and which he had taken directly from Pius XI (as the later pope confided to Monsignor Rossano, the committed champion of inter-religious dialog).[35]

On 12 January 1941, Domenico Tardini gathered together all the documents relative to the final weeks of the pope's life. Those were days during which the pope, ever more debilitated by disease, prayed to God and asked the physicians to help him live until the tenth anniversary of the Lateran Pact. That event had taken on great importance for him, almost as though it were an appointment for the completion of his interior transfiguration.

The celebration fell during a period of acute conflict with Mussolini. The alliance with Germany had been forged, and among its bitter fruits were the racial laws about which Mussolini was unwilling to make concessions, even for cases of mixed marriages between Christians and converted Jews. The conflict with Catholic Action intensified. In those final days, the dying pope fought a hard battle, spending his nights writing the oration he intended to deliver to the bishops convened for the celebration. It was to be a damning one, and its prospect worried Mussolini. An air of tension surrounded the pope, and all those around him were alarmed. Pacelli advised him no fewer than three times not to proceed with his plan. Yet the pope succeeded in completing the text and then died directly afterward. Pacelli immediately had it destroyed: "not even one line must survive." It was an act of great symbolism and announced a new and less combative relationship with fascism and, between then and the subsequent conclave, also with Nazism. A new pontificate began, one that did not take up the legacy of the last years of Achille Ratti.

— 1 —

A POPE'S ILLUSIONS AND THE REBIRTH OF CHRISTIAN SOCIETY

It is above all when abroad that one understands the extent to which the pope is truly Italy's greatest ornament ... and the prestige and advantages that our country can gain from his presence.

From Cardinal Ratti's first oration in Milan Cathedral

"Aim higher"

Achille Ratti was born in Brianza and would jealously guard the characteristics of his native region: tenacity, perseverance, self-help, traditional faith, moderation, hard work, together with an understanding of construction, results, trade, and money.[1] He was often pleased to recall the working, pragmatic religiosity of Brianza as its social foundation: "We speak of a solid piety, not an empty one":

> "Look – he said to me – it is God's inspiration that has made me spend; so that now I have the parish buildings, churches, seminaries, and other structures. Money instead has lost its value; interest dissipates; and capital vanishes." But was it wise – Tardini asked – to invest the wealth of the Holy See in certain titles, in foreign currency and the like? And is it prudent today to purchase real estate in various countries? Have we not entered a bit too much into the area of speculation?[2]

Ratti's family origins were firmly rooted in the productivity of his native Lombardy. His mother was the daughter of a hotelier, and his father was a silk merchant. He felt a full range of emotions toward his parents, as we would expect: "He happily recalled the erect figure of his father, who ran a business, and his mother, one of those women who seem born to manage something more than a home, who was good at everything, and whom it was difficult to disobey."[3]

Of the many hagiographies, Carlo Confalonieri, his faithful and devoted secretary, has left us a tender portrait of the pope, one that is moreover highly revealing. Ratti's mother was named Teresa, just like the saint whom he would most love throughout his life. She was a strong and sturdy mother, a female figure of the sort one finds in Manzoni and in the background of many a Lombard priest from the beginning of the twentieth century.[4] He held her in true veneration: "I dedicate these plants, the oldest that we know in this our great and beloved Lombard city, to you, a mother both traditional and rare . . . I dedicate them to you on your saint's day and am happy in the thought that someday, perhaps far in the future, a scholar will read your name and find here a testimony to the affection and veneration your children have for you."[5] Achille Ratti recalled his mother often and with great affection. He jokingly repeated the words she said to him as a child: "to think well we rely on doctrine; but to think poorly we can rely on guesswork." It was then thanks to Ratti's mother that this epigram found its way into the Italian political vocabulary, by way of Giulio Andreotti.

Ratti always had a special respect for women, more internalized than declared, and better understood by indirect methods than from his official statements (which rarely speak to this issue). This aspect is worth noting not so much for its direct relevance, but because it tells us something about his personality, domineering but easily moved; he was a champion of ambitious projects but also attentive to detail. It was as though a feminine element tempered his more combative side. We can find that element in his interior journey, one always reflecting the spirituality of Thérèse de Lisieux, who, "if in her seductive humility, she wanted to be called 'little Thérèse' . . . was however a great saint, and indeed a 'great man, this Saint Thérèse.' "[6]

The pope in fact assigned many of his "omnipotent" expectations to women: to aim higher, to ask much of oneself and not give up. These were expectations that lived in the spirit of the mountains, and more than once he assigned to women unusual characterizations for the masculine world of that time. To aim higher and ask much of oneself, but in the spirit of the Alpinist, gradually overcoming difficulties one step at a time, steady and dogged progress without excess or heroism – this was his spiritual path, consistent in fact with any true spiritual path. On 19 May 1938 he appealed to female Catholic youth:

Aiming a bit higher than even seems possible is the only way to reach the right point. The Holy Father found confirmation of this in the words of his mother, a mother in the fine old tradition and whose memory is especially dear to us . . . She busied herself not only with what her children needed to do and the chores they needed to complete, but also often repeated: "you must always do a little more than seems possible." Strong, energetic words, and words of great pedagogical value, that tell us we must always aim not just short of but beyond the possible.[7]

He was especially concerned with issues relating to youth and the formation of female religious. Many times, he turned to the female orders with a sense of their intellectual dignity still greater than that of their moral dignity, even though, as women, the latter better suited them. In response to the request to declare his beloved Thérèse a doctor of the Church, he replied: "Oh! She is indeed mistress of a high and honest spirituality," but then, smiling, added the recommendation of Saint Paul – *mulieres in Ecclesia taceant* (I Corinthians 14:34) – and wondered what her older sister, Saint Teresa d'Ávila, would have thought of such a proposal.[8]

Not betraying the conservative tradition of which he was a product, Pius XI nonetheless in the last period of his life expressed an interest that the female orders take on the same responsibilities as the male orders in certain areas. In an audience with Pacelli on 2 July 1938, the pope spoke of the Sisters of the Cenacle, describing the ways in which the nuns should devote themselves to education and the formation of youth and what should be the relationship between their religiosity and their intellectual formation:

They should not succumb to intellectualism, but at the same time encourage greater cultural development . . . It will be up to the mothers superior to identify and choose those best suited to higher levels of learning and to whom the greater intellectual tasks will be assigned. In Milan, for example, we have always sponsored a society of female municipal teachers, and indeed of female teachers generally. It is of course important that these teachers come into contact with religious who have themselves attained a certain degree of education; it would be awkward otherwise. Naturally these women must be concerned above all with piety and the sanctification of the soul, but culture can serve as a tool in the service of piety, sanctification, and a more perfect illumination. The Church has always taken this approach with the clergy; the first priority is piety, but study also has a role to play. Even the Jesuits are not all specialists; most of them are working priests, assigned to an ordinary ministry.[9]

This statement, recorded by Pacelli near the end of the pope's life, recalls Ratti's experience as a young priest when he worked in poor relief and served as spiritual assistant to the Sisters of the Cenacle.[10] These were years that Ratti would describe as "the most beautiful of my life, given that I had only been ordained three years before":

> I attribute great importance to those years, as the Cenacle had a much greater influence than one might imagine on both my interior and priestly life . . . I knew all the souls who attended the Cenacle, individuals of every sort of importance, character, age, status, or condition . . . and so I gained a greater understanding of the soul there than I would have elsewhere and also, I would add, of society and the world.[11]

"The women of the Cenacle" were in fact mostly involved with young girls from the highest social circles in Milan. They held spiritual retreats of special intensity, inspired by Saint Ignatius Loyola. It was thanks to these occasions that Ratti would say he had "found the spirit of perpetual prayer . . . and the spirit of meditation." The sisters retained fond memories of this fervent young priest so intense in his devotion that when he brought the Host to his heart it was "as if he wanted to clasp his divine Friend in his arms."[12]

In 1888 Ratti was accepted into the college of doctors at the prestigious Ambrosian Library founded by Cardinal Federico Borromeo. At the age of just over thirty, Don Ratti immersed himself in intensive study, associated with foreign scholars, undertook research abroad, and naturally intensified his contacts with the political and intellectual elite. He was the frequent confidant for tortured interior struggles. At the Ambrosiana, Don Ratti established an intense relationship with the prefect, Monsignor Ceriani.[13] Antonio Ceriani was his teacher and introduced him to the world of archives, manuscripts, and learning, a world that Ceriani sent him off to explore in foreign libraries as well. It was in the natural course of things that, following Ceriani's death in 1907, Ratti took his place as prefect of the Ambrosian Library.

He also followed Ceriani in teaching a course of Hebrew at the major seminary in Milan. It was on this latter occasion that he intensified his relationship with Alessandro da Fano, the chief rabbi of Milan; and Ratti in fact took his seminary students with him to hear da Fano in the synagogue. This is a little-known or researched relationship, though one finds some mention of it in the special issue of *Israel* dedicated to Rabbi da Fano on the occasion of his death.[14] It was a relationship that continued into the years of Ratti's papacy, when he received da Fano for a number of audiences. As we shall learn from the accounts of Monsignor Tardini's audiences, those meetings would be recalled by Ratti as an example of the good relationships he enjoyed with the Jews.[15]

In spite of his defense of Cardinal Andrea Ferrari of Milan, accused of making too many concessions to modernism, Monsignor Ratti was named prefect of the Vatican Library by Pius X in October 1910. During his years at the Vatican Library, Ratti was always diligent but solitary and reserved, almost misanthropic. His only friendship was with the Jesuit Father Hagen, astronomer of the Vatican observatory and also noted for his extreme reserve.[16]

Ratti maintained a passion for books throughout his life. As Domenico Tardini recalled, "he maintained all the inclinations and preferences of a librarian":

> He was always happy when he got a book, and he received many. As undersecretary of state, it was my job to write the thank you notes. The pope, though, wouldn't let me take the books. I had to copy out their frontispieces exactly on separate pieces of paper. Pius XI meanwhile described to me the contents of the book, its importance, and the merits of its author. He knew many important authors and would recall when and why he had met them the first time (at the Ambrosiana or the Vatican) . . . it was a true cultural and bibliographical lesson.[17]

The reserve and solitude of his Roman period, when he served as prefect of the Vatican Library, provide a contrast to the intense sociability of his time in Milan. Through contact with the female elite who attended the Cenacle in Milan he came to know the most important Milanese families, and he further deepened those relationships while prefect at the Ambrosiana. Those families included the Gonzaga, the Castiglione, the Borromeo, the Belgioioso, the Greppi, the Thaon de Revel, and the Gallarati Scotti, families whose attitudes relative to liberalism and the monarchy ranged from conciliatory to intransigent. Nor is it easy to say on which side Ratti stood. According to Filippo Meda, himself an exponent of liberal Milanese Catholicism, "He did not avoid this debate but remained above it. Neither the liberals nor the intransigents could count him on their side. He was not motivated by opportunism, but rather enjoyed a tranquil and unostentatious superiority that allowed him to stay at his post and command general respect."[18]

Rather than align himself with a particular faction, Ratti seemed more concerned about the influence that secular liberalism might have on the Milanese upper classes, fearing that the bourgeoisie and nobility might lose their solid ties to Christian anthropology. The dukes of Gallarati Scotti were surely among the most important families with which Ratti associated. The family head, a fierce intransigent, entrusted his youngest child, Tommaso (born 1878), to the religious care of Don Ratti. That moment marked the beginning of an important relationship in the lives of both men. Great friends and intense correspondents, they experienced serious conflict when the disciple became an important exponent of Milanese modernism. Perhaps the most difficult moment started in 1907, when Tommaso and several of his friends founded the modernist periodical *Il Rinnovamento* – a journal that the prefect of the Congregation of the Index asked Cardinal Ferrari of Milan to condemn.[19] Following the publication of Pius X's encyclical *Pascendi*, condemning modernism, Ratti repeatedly asked his friend to terminate the magazine. When Gallarati Scotti decided to resign from the magazine on 24 December, a decree excommunicated all three directors. Ratti meanwhile supported the Milanese archbishop's decision to refuse them communion at the Christmas celebration.

It was a sad moment and a painful falling out that did not, however, lessen the intellectual and moral esteem in which Ratti held his modernist friend throughout his life. And it was indeed at the end of that life that he made a sort of spiritual testimony to his old friend, a summing up of the religious and political changes that marked the final years of his papacy. Gallarati Scotti's report of his final encounter with Pius XI – discussed below in the final chapter – reflects the full historical and spiritual awareness of the vanity of nations, of their madness for power. At the same time it reveals not only disillusionment with a Church policy that had sought to negotiate with the dictators, but also the possibility of a different and opposite strategy, namely that of a head-on conflict and challenge. That final colloquium betrays the spiritual intensity of his battle with the totalitarian regimes, a battle that he kept up till his last breath.

The intrepid mountaineer

Ratti was well known as an Alpinist, an activity that he continued without interruption throughout years of intense activity at the Ambrosiana and that ceased only when he was appointed nuncio in Poland. His career as a serious mountaineer ran from 1885 to 1913:

Of all possible recreations, none more than this – once fear has been overcome – feeds both the soul and the body. The hard effort required to climb up to where the air is clear invigorates and renews one's energy, while confronting difficulties of all sorts and overcoming them hardens one for the challenges of life. And, finally, the immense beauty and spectacle that opens before one's contemplation from the high peaks of the Alps lifts the soul easily to God, creator and lord of that nature.[20]

The conclusion of this pastoral letter in honor of Bernard of Menthon, patron saint of mountain climbers, delivered on 20 August 1923, encapsulates the special meaning that the mountains had for the Catholicism of the late nineteenth and early twentieth centuries: effort; determination to achieve a goal, shorn however of heroics and competitiveness; the marriage of mind and body in contact with nature; contemplation of the sublime as a reflection of God. It was a true cult of the mountain that became a social and pedagogic dimension of twentieth-century Italian Catholicism. As Pius XI himself put it, Alpinism was not "just a scramble up the mountain, but, on the contrary, a question of caution (with some courage), of strength and determination, a sense of nature and its hidden beauties."[21]

One might imagine that the first of those papal audiences transcribed by Pacelli in 1930 would be filled with weighty matters; instead it includes the thanks the pope wanted to send to the bishop of Chicago for the gift of a fine book on mountaineering that he had much appreciated.[22] The *Bulletin* of the Italian Alpine Club – Ratti was a member – recounts some of his adventures, moments he would recall with pleasure as pope, in particular a descent from Mont Blanc following a till then untried path and in fact subsequently known as Ratti's route.

Comparing the first Italian Alpine Club, founded in Turin in 1863 by Quintino Sella, with that of the early twentieth century, one can see how the initial dominance of the Savoy and Italian aristocracy was later joined by an important professional and bourgeois element, well-to-do but varied in its political and cultural tendencies.[23] A publication celebrating the foundation of the Milanese section of the club insisted that its "Alpine spirit" overcame ideological differences and cited as an example "of the perfect harmony of the section the fact that those two philosophical opposites, the atheist Gaetano Negri and the future Pope Doctor Ratti, were both named directors in December 1890."[24] It was a sign of Ratti's openness to secular elements and involvement with Milanese bourgeois society in the period before mountaineering became associated with fascist mythology.

The 1910s and 1920s, however, saw an explosion of patriotic and military enthusiasm for the mountains, so that a political and nationalist emphasis overcame the more Alpinist and sporting approach. Following the First World War, memories of the link between civil and military life during the conflict found expression in the affinity between the experience of the Alpine troops and the practice of Alpinism; nor was Catholic Alpinism immune from this tendency.[25]

The progressive slide of Alpinism toward politics and propaganda led to the international isolation of the organization: in the late 1930s, German and Austrian members were in fact excluded from the London Alpine Club. Among those proposed as honorary members was instead Pius XI, who had previously, on 22 May 1922, declined the invitation, offering thanks for "the kind thought" that had taken him back to "happy days gone by."

In meetings of the Italian Alpine Club between 1939 and 1940, Pius XI's virtues as a mountaineer were invoked on a fascist note, as if to erase the memory of his great opposition to *il Duce* at the end of his life. His climbing ability was linked to the achievement of the Lateran Pact with Mussolini and to the courage he displayed in confronting the Bolsheviks while nuncio to Poland.[26] It was an awkward attempt to fascistize the Alpine pope.

A first disappointment: the Polish case

Achille Ratti did not follow the usual career path of a prefect, one that normally leads to appointment as a cardinal. Instead he first spent a period in political-diplomatic service. That encounter with real politics began when Benedict XV had the fortunate idea to appoint him nuncio to Poland and Lithuania on 25 April 1918, and then, in March 1920, papal commissary to Upper Silesia.

It was through that experience that he came to know first hand the risks of nationalism, as distinguished from a legitimate and laudable patriotism. While that enthusiasm may at first have seemed to him providential, strengthening the Catholic soul of the country, after his first few months in Poland he realized that exactly the opposite was the case. The tension between Poles, Germans, Lithuanians, Ukrainians, and Russians left a permanent mark on the future pope. It was not so much that he realized the degree to which exasperated nationalism could cloud reason, but rather that he witnessed the scuttling of a possible happy encounter between national identity and that Polish Catholicism he found so passionate and seductive. It was

24

a first taste of the disappointment he would experience in later years, namely the failed hope to see that Christian society that touched him so deeply supported by those conservative regimes – and first of all the fascists – that described themselves as Catholic.

In his excellent reconstruction of Achille Ratti's Polish nunciature, from 1918 to 1921, Roberto Morozzo della Rocca describes with great clarity the evolution of Ratti's disillusionment, all the greater for the expectations he brought with him. Received in triumphant fashion on his arrival, the nuncio met with enthusiasm wherever he went, both in the city and the countryside: "Wherever he goes he is met with great fanfare. Ratti himself is much impressed by the devotion of the Poles, who accompany him through the country with groups of flag-waving cavalry; thousands patiently await his arrival and then fall all together to their knees, 'as one,' and raise triumphal banners with the Vatican colors."[27] Poland was enchanted with the pope's visitor, and he in turn was captivated by their courageous and expansive Catholicism, far – as he himself wrote – from the reserve and "human dignity" that restrained religious practice in Italy.

All of Eastern Europe was plunged into chaos following the First World War. In the vacuum left by the defeat of the Central Powers, and with the threat of the Bolshevik Revolution at its doorstep, Poland sought territorial definition. When Ratti arrived, there were two competing plans for foreign policy. Piłsudski favored the creation of friendly countries to the east, including Ukraine, White Russia, and the Baltic States. Dmowski on the other hand wanted to absorb all the Polish nuclei in the region and leave Ukraine to the Russians, with whom he hoped to maintain friendly relations. These two positions shared hatred for the Germans, and both sides asked for unconditional approval from the Holy See to achieve their different but equally nationalist goals. The nuncio then came to be seen more as Poland's representative to the Holy See rather than vice versa, a point he made ironically to his faithful secretary Pelegrinetti.

Extreme Polish nationalism, partially justified in Ratti's eyes because of its resistance to Russian oppression, included, however, an impulse to subjugate religion to national identity and so ran the risk of producing a national faith indifferent to the universal values of Catholicism. With their background of resistance to centuries of oppression, Polish nationalists felt the need to control all of the surrounding peoples and were hostile even to Orthodox Christians in Galicia and Ukraine. The nuncio was distressed by the obstinate refusal to consider any compromise. Commenting on the many examples of Polish intransigence regarding any sort of mediation, he wrote:

"the morbid sensibility one encounters is incredible, even among the well meaning, among priests and bishops."[28]

But it was not so much the nationalism that bothered Ratti – for him good healthy patriotism, even when extreme, was a "providential value" – or even the blind exuberance with which the Catholic masses embraced it. The future Pius XI instead criticized the superficiality of faith, excessively devout and too easily bent to the political plans of the nation. In this, his first fundamental political experience, Ratti saw and feared an external faith operating as a tool of politics, a Catholicism that was too generic, too emotional, irrational. In a letter from September 1920, as the elections approached, he hoped for the formation of a Catholic centrist party: "I will try as far as possible to be persuasive in that regard (taking the necessary precautions), particularly in view of the upcoming elections. But it is a difficult task; here everyone claims to be Catholic, but it is a generic and inefficient Catholicism that blocks a more specific and active faith."[29]

Ratti hoped that Polish Catholics would found a party and a Catholic press, and above all a Catholic Action as in Italy and France, but it was a model that enjoyed only partial realization in Posen; he made his case to the Polish bishops, who replied that all of Poland was Catholic so why bother to create a separate Catholic movement? Ratti's call for a Catholic party is significant and unusual. He was highly skeptical of using political parties to advance Catholic interests and would view with relief their disappearance a few years later in Italy and Germany. It is interesting to note that in Poland he favored a political party not to insure the expansion of Catholicism, but rather to intensify it and render it less generic and superficial. His idea in any case was for a party modeled on Catholic Action. It was not that he did not appreciate the homogeneity and compactness of Polish Catholicism. What he tried, though, to explain to local bishops was that it was not enough to be Polish to be Catholic, an observation that alienated many of those within the Church who had initially so welcomed him.

Yet Ratti too shared the commonplaces of Catholic circles in the 1920s, conservative and not, as evidenced by his own harsh statements against the Jews and regarding what he saw as their undermining of that very Polish unity: "For Ratti, the many Jews in the cities of Poland were the most 'untrustworthy' element in Polish life, a dangerous anti-national force, a mass that 'infested' public life."[30] Ratti's statements are one more sign of the fluid way in which Catholic hostility toward Judaism could translate into the fierce anti-Semitism of the interwar years, even in a figure like Ratti, who would devote the last years of his life to combating just that. In the 1920s similar sentiments were widespread among Catholics, and could be found in other important nuncios, such as Eugenio Pacelli.[31]

Ratti's courage and constancy showed themselves above all during the dangerous Russian invasion of summer 1920, when he asked Rome to let him stay in Warsaw and defend the interests of the Church. Fearing for the life of his nuncio, Benedict XV instructed that he follow both the Polish government and the diplomatic corps in retreat. A convoy left carrying with it the archive of the nunciature but not the nuncio himself, who joined it only later and so was the last diplomatic presence to leave Warsaw; it was a gesture much appreciated by the Polish authorities. Yet already in the following weeks, on the occasion of the Battle of the Vistula River, he fell from favor once again, as he encouraged moderation on the Poles following their victory against the Bolsheviks.

It is difficult to resist comparing Ratti's behavior with the much less courageous conduct of Pacelli, nuncio to Munich since 1917. As he reported to Rome, a frightened Pacelli witnessed attacks on the nunciature by "Russo-Judeo-revolutionary tyranny" during the November Revolution; after intense correspondence with the Holy See, and following the advice of Bishop Michael von Faulhaber, he fled to Switzerland[32] and sent the following justification via Pietro Gasparri: "Regarding any threat to my own person, I had no fear then nor do I now. But let me ask if it is expedient for the papal nuncio to attend a communist government."[33]

The two nuncios crossed paths regarding a diplomatic issue that would profoundly mark the future pope, namely the plebiscite conducted in the territories of Upper Silesia, where Ratti was sent as papal commissary. On one side, Pacelli sought to mediate for the Germans[34] and, on the other, Ratti for the Poles.[35] The nationality of these territories was to be determined by a plebiscite, and both the German and Polish clergy employed violent and bitter rhetoric in hopes of achieving victory.[36] Ratti's attempt at moderation was foiled in part because of the behavior of the German Cardinal Bertram from Breslau, who boasted of a papal decree dated 25 November regarding the election of diocesan priests, one that heavily penalized the Poles.

The Poles, however, felt betrayed by Ratti, who found himself caught between the two factions and bitter about the maneuver of Bertram, who acted without informing him. The nuncio, however, maintained his calm, "more spiritual than reactive." Ratti had, in fact, already expressed his concern about the German nationalism of Bertram, but did not find a receptive ear with Benedict XV, who thought his nuncio a bit too Polish. And so, injured, ignored, and battered by the winds of nationalism, Ratti was recalled to Rome.

Ratti's pragmatism and ability to transcend ideological partisanship – qualities seemingly well adapted to a situation riven by strong emotions and recriminations – did not serve him well on this occasion. It was his first major test, a sort of laboratory for the wounds of interwar Europe, wounds that would not soon heal but would indeed fester in the years to come.

It was an apprenticeship that saw Ratti accused of partisanship from both sides; the Poles criticized his support of Bertram against the more chauvinist priests, while the Germans thought him too friendly with the Poles and so under their sway. And even those who recognized his impartiality nonetheless found his actions confusing and improvident.[37] Under this double attack, Ratti left Poland, and Gasparri sent in his place Giovanni Ogno Serra, who remained till the completion of the plebiscite. Ogno Serra in turn faced a series of incredible difficulties that highlight the dramatic situations in which the papal delegates operated during those tumultuous years.[38]

Ratti learned two important lessons from his bitter experience in Poland. He began to understand the risk that Catholicism be yoked to nationalism; and he took spiritual measure of historical processes, that same attention to human nature that would so occupy the final years of his life. Benedict XV perceived clearly the balance in Ratti between faith and history:

> Your letter is shrouded in sadness, not for personal reasons – indeed, I admire your ability to understand the spiritual dimension of secular matters – but rather for what I would describe as reasons of office. The situation has in truth become delicate and difficult, and I would never have imagined that the Poles could be still more superficial than the French. Perhaps it is because they are no longer accustomed to govern. They are overly suspicious, and especially of the Holy See that has done so much for them. I understand in any case the difficulties you have faced . . . and even if there are some who fail to appreciate your efforts, know that you enjoy my esteem and good will. May God bless us all.[39]

The pope's perceptive reading and admiration of Ratti's "ability to understand the spiritual dimension of secular matters" is notable. It was a quality that would mature fully only during Ratti's own papacy.

Monsignor Ratti left Poland on 4 June 1921. At the secret consistory of 13 June, Benedict XV named him cardinal, and after only a few weeks in Rome, Ratti returned to Milan as its archbishop. During his first homily, delivered in the cathedral and before the memory of his Warsaw experience had faded, he made important statements relative to Italy:

> It is above all when abroad that one understands the extent to which the pope is truly Italy's greatest ornament, an asset to his second homeland; thanks to him Rome is truly the capital of the world. And one has to close one's eyes not to see in the overtures that all countries are making to the pope in the present situation the prestige and advantages that our country can gain from his presence. Catholics throughout the world recognize the international and supernational sovereignty he exerts over this divine institution.[40]

The response of then prime minister Giovanni Giolitti and his circle to these comments was highly critical; they considered Vatican pretensions overreaching. Meanwhile, Ratti's comments struck a chord with Mussolini, who on 16 July stated his belief that "the Latin and Roman traditions are embodied in Catholicism." This may have been the moment when Ratti first came to an understanding with "the man whom providence has sent us." According to Luc Valit, a journalist for *L'Illustration*, Ratti said as much of Mussolini at the time. Valit met Ratti in Milan in January 1922 but transcribed his comments only much later, on 9 January 1937: "Mussolini is a formidable man . . . recently converted, originally an exponent of the extreme left, he has all the zeal of the novitiate and acts with resolution . . . the future is his." Though later he also added:

> It remains to be seen how all this will end and what use he will make of all his energy. What direction will he take, when the day comes that he is forced to choose one? Will he resist the temptation that all leaders face to establish himself as an absolute dictator? . . . It is never a good thing when one man becomes omnipotent.[41]

A "totalitarian Church" for a theocratic society

Benedict XV died on 22 January 1922. Ratti's candidacy emerged from the conclave as a compromise between the intransigent wing, recalling Pius X and represented by Rafael Merry del Val and Pietro La Fontaine, and Gasparri's more conciliatory position, inspired by Benedict XV's papacy. It was not, however, a compromise reached *in extremis*. Ratti was a recently elevated cardinal who had ties to neither tendency and had not risen through the Vatican ranks; as was evident in his first discourse from Milan Cathedral, Ratti harbored an interest in Italy that did not diminish his desire to defend the Holy See. His first symbolic innovation was to issue a blessing from the external colonnade of Saint Peter's, a practice his predecessors had abandoned as a sign of protest against their "imprisonment" in the Vatican. His election, then, occurred just a few months before the coming to power of fascism, a movement with which the new pope would establish a relationship of trusting collaboration.

Continuing the international policies of Benedict XV, Pius XI appointed Gasparri as secretary of state. It was a novel choice – neither Mariano Rampolla nor Merry del Val had straddled papacies – as the usual practice was for the newly elected pope to rearrange his group of collaborators. His first encyclical, *Ubi arcano* of December 1922, in fact bears many resemblances to the spirit of Benedict XV: international peace as the internalization of a choice that was not only "political" but also religious, and the condemnation of nationalisms. He continued to emphasize the need to apply religious criteria to the diplomacy of the Church in the twentieth century. The fundamental idea behind *Ubi arcano* is the centrality of the individual and humanity as a unitary whole; neither nationalism nor class struggle contained this sense of humanity in its wholeness. It was a wholeness that the pope deceived himself was to be found in the organicism of conservative Catholic-leaning regimes like those in Austria, Spain, Portugal, and also Italy, regimes that would take on ever more dangerous totalitarian forms in the course of the 1930s. The idea that a "spirit of separation" that divided humanity by means of racism and nationalism was contrary to Christianity, and so to mankind itself, would fuel his disillusionment with those regimes. It was again to this sense of the unity of mankind that he would return repeatedly in the summer of 1938, when, as we shall see, he identified the "spirit of separation" as the root of that totalitarianism to which he dedicated his mature reflections on the insidious nature of nationalism: "There is alas something still worse than this or that racism or nationalism, namely the spirit that lies behind them: this spirit of separation, of exaggerated nationalism, ultimately lacks humanity because neither Christian nor religious."[42]

An organic conception of society could be achieved by means of the unity of the individual with the family and other intermediate organs that brought humanity together into a movement of distinction and aggregation. "Love of homeland and the nation" should be encouraged only insofar as it favors "the dignity and sanctity of life, the need for obedience, the divine organization of society, the sanctity of the family."

Public power must not block the return of society to God, because only the re-Christianization of society can bring peace and prosperity. Within this theocratic view, there was not much space for other human institutions except insofar as they could support and integrate themselves into that larger context. A major discontinuity relative to Benedict XV, noted at the time by Luigi Salvatorelli, was that, for Pius XI, no secular institution was capable of providing the nation with "an international code that can respond to the modern conditions," like that which had existed in the Middle Ages:

> That true League of Nations that was Christianity . . . the Church of Christ was instead the divine institution best suited to guard the sanctity of human law. So not only the League of Nations but the international politics of all nations have in some sense been left to their own whims . . . In these ideas and formulas it was as though a theocratic society was to be laid over the organization of secular nations.[43]

But Ratti's profound lack of faith in secular institutions made a number of important exceptions: support for the Locarno Treaties; a persistent policy of pacification in relation to Germany (blocked, however, by the French right wing, including Catholics in the Action Française); and support of the Genoa Conference of April–May 1922 for global economic recovery.

And yet, even on those occasions, Pius XI's radical skepticism relative to secular institutions showed through, as in his comments during the Genoa Conference made to the XXVI Eucharistic Congress of 1922, which "highlighted the differences between the failed diplomacies of the participating countries meeting in Genoa and the success of the only true king and his Vicariate."[44] *Civiltà Cattolica* described the event in the following triumphal terms: "Both victor and vanquished looked to him with fervid hope. They bowed their heads before him to receive his paternal blessing; they applauded him with faith and enthusiasm; they joined together in impassioned praise for Jesus."[45]

The Holy See stuck to its previous policy of greater justice for the losers and revision of the peace treaties with an eye to reducing German reparations. The pope, however, aimed not so much to create new spaces for the Church within the existing post-war framework, but rather proposed to the states a strong and self-sufficient model of Christian society.

The French were unhappy with Vatican opposition to occupation of the Ruhr, and it is also within that context that one should understand the hopes for good relations with Russia; the famous menu change at the lunch for Čičerin has entered into the annals of Vatican diplomatic history.[46] Between 1924 and 1929 hope for peace grew, and 1925 was both a Holy Year and the year of Locarno, namely the attempt on the part of liberal forces to resolve the post-war problems. That attempt was further aided by the passing of the French *bleu horizon* parliament that had so radicalized post-war debates. The pope seemed to want to repair the damage done by Versailles, urging world leaders to commit themselves to solid Christian principles rather than diplomatic balancing acts. The Christmas Eve encyclical of 1929 reflected this season of greater hope; the Church could strike a positive note in light of lessening nationalism and class conflict and champion the positions of German Catholics in the spirit of Locarno. Those hopes were, however, soon dashed with the crisis of 1929, an event that coincided on 16 December of that year with Gasparri's being replaced as secretary of state by Pacelli, who, among other things, adopted a much more combative position relative to communism. The culture of peace, ever more difficult to attain, became an imperative for Catholics who sought to wed it with conservatism.

Immediately after the war, the positions of the pope and Italian Catholics who supported him were broadly applauded. It was liberalism instead that faded, a fact appreciated neither by Catholics nor by the pope himself. The seduction of nationalism, though toned down relative to the war years, continued to exercise its evil influence in various ways: in France through national-imperial currents with dreams of hegemony; in Germany and Hungary through dreams of victory and revenge; and in Italy in the form of the clerico-fascism of Catholic conservatives.[47]

Nationalism/imperialism was also the prime target of *Ubi arcano*, though the distance between the pope and the Popular Party regarding how best to combat it was enormous:

> Many Catholics fail to see the danger as long as nationalism claims to support religion. But, in nationalism, religion has value only insofar as it serves the nation: for nationalists the conflict between Church and state has been resolved, as the nation hovers over both of them as a dialectic process and the highest spiritual value. In this same way, the moral conflict caused by illicit actions is also resolved.[48]

The "social nature" and individualism of liberal thought, combined with the need that the religious dimension not be relegated simply to the realm of conscience, leads to a model for the re-Christianization of society that sits uneasily in a democratic context, but rather favors an authoritarian one, though the Church must never for any reason find itself subordinate to those authoritarian forces.

An anti-democratic pope condemns Action Française

Pius XI was not a democrat, either by nature or by conviction. His liberalism, if we can even speak of liberalism in his case, was moderate and subordinate to his theocratic vision. He viewed political parties skeptically and as instruments of personal power and negotiation rather than of social progress. His religious approach tended to minimize the secular political world; and he certainly had no confidence in the democratic system that inspired both Catholic parties, like that of Sturzo, and the French right under Charles Maurras, a force that poisoned youth with its integral nationalism. Although fundamentally atheist and naturalist, Action Française had achieved ever greater consensus among French Catholic conservatives, who were convinced that it provided a front against republican and anti-clerical tendencies. Even Pius X, who sympathized with some of the movement's positions, sought in a timid way to rein it in, describing Maurras as "condemnable but not condemned" after six of his works were put on the Index in 1914. But with Pius XI, the definitive condemnation arrived.

The situation changed in 1925, not so much because of the pressure applied by the French government, tired of the constant attacks of Action Française, but for basically religious reasons and concern about the negative influence Maurras and Daudet were having on French and Belgian youth.[49]

The pope was very close to the Action catholique de la jeunesse belge. It was a movement possessing great spiritual and liturgical energy and, like many of the francophone Catholic lay youth movements of its day, conveyed the political and social significance of the liturgical and eucharistic movement. At the moment of greatest conflict with the totalitarian movements, in 1938, the general assistant of the Belgian movement, Louis Picard, emphasized the special relationship between the spiritual and worldly realms in Catholicism. Picard concluded that, when compared to Judaism or the lay religions – namely liberalism, with its insistence on the separation between the two spheres and its view of faith as a "private affair," and extreme "pagan" nationalism – only Christianity did not conflate the two spheres but managed to maintain the distinction between spiritual and temporal without separating them.[50] He sought to make this point following the condemnation of the Action Française movement for which Catholic youth felt a strong affinity.[51]

On 29 December 1926, the Sacred Office published its decree condemning Maurras's publications and his newspaper, *Action Française*, which had been in existence since 1914. The motivations offered were religious ones: the French *ligue* was a dangerous organization, as it was imbued with naturalism and paganism. It was already clear at that time, as we shall also see again at the end of Pius XI's life, that the Catholic religion must never and for any reason become a political "tool."

This insistence may be the most obvious discontinuity with Benedict XV and at the same time the uninterrupted thread that ties together the early years of Pius XI's papacy with its final ones in the 1930s, namely a distancing of the Church from that Catholic politics that had been trying so hard to establish itself in a democratic context. It was a rejection of any *politique d'abord*; his entire papacy was characterized by the rejection of autonomy for the political sphere and a clear demarcation of its limits.

It is difficult to distinguish the religious motives of the condemnation from the political ones. Indeed much of the historiography on the Action Française[52] revolves around this question, as the pope himself considered the distinction a difficult one to make, and in this case the two were intertwined. As we know, Pius XI would frequently return to the relationship between religion and politics and in terms that would become for him habitual:

> It is important to guard against the confusion that can arise when we or the Episcopal Councils or the clergy or Catholic lay organizations seem to be engaging in politics but are instead simply practicing religion. For we are simply practicing religion when we fight for the freedom of the Church and for the sanctity of the family, of the schools, and of the days dedicated to God. In all of these cases and other analogous ones, we are not engaging in politics; but politics has sullied the altar and so it is our duty to defend God and His religion.[53]

The pope did not want political arguments to be ascribed to the religious motivations that lay behind the condemnation of Action

Française, as Jacques Maritain implied with his *Primauté du spirituel*.[54] Pius XI rejected any interpretation that read a partisan political move in the condemnation. For this reason he censored Monsignor Julien, bishop of Arras – a supporter of the League of Nations and of attempts to achieve a rapprochement between Germany and France[55] – because Julien interpreted the condemnation as directed also against French nationalism; nor did the pope want it to appear that his move presaged an endorsement by Catholics of the republic. The condemnation was not born out of "political preconceptions or preferences, or out of personal considerations or influences ... it was solely out of the awareness of our responsibility, our obligation to honor our divine Lord, and for the salvation of souls that we were moved to speak."[56]

The excommunication, then, was politically significant only in a general sense, for example as a warning to Mussolini. That interpretation finds support in the consistorial allocution of 20 December 1926: "Our words may find utility and application outside of the borders of France."[57]

The complicated story of Action Française and its interpretations serve as a metaphor for the relationship between politics and religion throughout Ratti's papacy. It throws light on his so-called theocratic politics, on that "political Augustinianism" that has led some to describe Pius XI as practicing a true political theology.[58]

Pius XI initiated a number of beatifications that would be exceeded only by John Paul II, though, ironically, he is the only twentieth-century pope for whom no beatification process has been started. As is well known, a pope's beatification strategy provides a significant insight into the general orientation of his papacy. One significant example that is often left out of the histories of Pius XI is the beatification of the martyrs of the French Revolution, that event which the pope in 1922 described as having led to "universal perturbations during which the rights of man were affirmed with exceeding arrogance." On 17 October 1926, he declared the beatification of 191 martyrs, the culmination of a long process begun in 1916 by Benedict XV.

The coincidence of the beatification of these priests with the condemnation of Action Française is profoundly significant. It was in part owing to the rhythms of the hagiographic process; but, as Philippe Boutry has pointed out, by privileging the sacrifice of these victims at the same time that he rejected the beatification of Louis XVI, Ratti affirmed once again the centuries-long tradition of the Church's religious intransigence and political independence.[59]

As Pietro Scoppola has observed, the papal allocution condemning Action Française of 14 December 1926 has too often been interpreted as a simple tactical concession to the French government, intended to aid the revival of diplomatic relations following the tempestuous break at the beginning of the century; it formed instead an essential part of Pius XI's worldview.[60]

Toward the end of his papacy, there was moreover the beginning of a rapprochement: Maurras wrote a letter to the pope from prison, a gesture that comforted the latter in his illness, but led to no reconciliation or retraction. It was only following Ratti's death, in July 1939, that the Sacred Office lifted the interdiction against Action Française. But that was under the papacy of Pius XII and constitutes a separate history.

Mussolini, "the man whom providence has sent us"

Both Ratti's relief over the demise of the Partito Poplare and his firm condemnation of Action Française should be understood in this light. On 2 October 1922, just weeks before the fascist "March on Rome," the pope issued a circular instructing bishops and priests not to join political parties, including Catholic ones. The correspondence between Pius XI and Don Sturzo regarding the resignation of the latter can now be consulted and includes a number of Ratti's annotations, though it does little to change the generally accepted interpretation. The file begins with a letter from Gasparri to Tacchi-Venturi in which, "in the name of the Holy Father, Don Sturzo is invited to offer his resignation from the Italian Popular Party." Sturzo replied to the pope that his resignation would be understood to signify that the Church supported "fascism and the fascist government, whose methods both in politics and in the ethical realm offer much to condemn." The letter continues, expressing fear over the effect that his resignation will have, given that it comes in response to "an action by the Holy See on the eve of the Chamber of Deputies' vote on reforming electoral politics":

> How can one deny that? With what means? Perhaps by lying? [At this point a papal notation states: "Certainly not; but with due reflection: the good of the PPI and the Catholic Church."] I would not be able to . . . I believe that my repentant withdrawal at this point will do damage to the one party that is truly inspired by a Christian vision of civil society . . . in the letter . . . it is suggested that behind the opposi-

36

tion I have led against the government lurks the hand of freemasonry. [And here the pope comments: "In Pisa in fact the masons decided to support Sturzo against the government."] I must add that freemasonry has never had any ties with the Popular Party, either directly or indirectly.[61]

While Sturzo considered democracy a value inseparable from Christianity, the pope preferred instead to bypass political parties, even Catholic ones, and speak directly to the state. It is this position that helps to explain his so-called mania for concordats and so his willingness to sign one with any state that showed the least inclination. Pius XI's preference for conservative and authoritarian states correlated directly with his hostility toward democracy, as in the latter he perceived an unacceptable breakdown of authority. His initial close affinity for fascism derived above all from the belief that he and Mussolini shared a common goal – namely a revival of those values dear to nineteenth-century intransigents: authority, family, order, moderation. The question of whether that illusion characterized his entire papacy or primarily the 1920s has split historians. On the one hand, some find that his strict ecclesiastic conception, authoritarian though it was, bred substantial hostility to the fascist state already in the 1920s. Others find instead that Pius XI broke with fascism only in the second half of the 1930s,[62] the Lateran Treaties representing the turning point.

The Lateran Treaties granted the Church the sovereign autonomy it had lacked in unified Italy, and just at that moment when the state was itself exercising an unprecedented degree of sovereignty. This innate contradiction, in spite of the considerable advantages gained by the Church, soon led to conflict. Less than a month after the regime's victory in the plebiscite of 24 March 1929, welcomed by *Civiltà Cattolica* as the beginning of a "Christian restoration of society," Mussolini delivered two of his best-known speeches (13 and 25 May), in which he sought to minimize the importance of the Concordat:

We find ourselves before an equivocation that must be cleared up immediately . . . "*A free and sovereign Church; a free and sovereign state*" . . . this formulation may lead one to believe that there are two coexistent authorities: on the one hand the Vatican, on the other the Kingdom of Italy – that is, the Italian state. We need to emphasize that the distance between the state and the Vatican can be measured in thousands of kilometers, even though by chance it happens to take five minutes to go to this state and ten minutes more to cross the border.

[Applause] There are then two entirely distinct and different sovereignties that perfectly and reciprocally recognize one another. But, within the state, the Church is neither sovereign nor free . . . because its institutions and operatives are subject to the laws of the state, just as it is also subject to the specific clauses of the Concordat.[63]

The pope responded immediately the next day. In a famous letter to Cardinal Gasparri, he took issue with *il Duce*'s interpretation of 25 May and re-emphasized the indivisibility of the Treaty and the Concordat. The Treaty recognized the existence of a city-state, more symbolic than real and able to guarantee the sovereignty of the pope, while the Concordat guaranteed the influence of the Catholic Church in the Kingdom of Italy: "The Treaty and the Concordat . . . are each the necessary complement of the other and are inseparable and indissoluble. And from this it derives that *simul stabunt vel simul cadent*." The pope's firm resolution in this regard was based on his unshakeable faith:

The state has nothing to fear from the education offered by the Church and under its direction; this is the education that has prepared the best of modern civilization, all that is good and lofty . . . One says and repeats "Catholic state", but also "fascist state." Of this we are aware; it presents no special difficulties for us; indeed, we welcome it insofar as it obviously means that the fascist state – in its ideas, doctrine, and actions – does not allow anything that is not in accordance with Catholic practice and doctrine. Without this there would not be, nor could there be, a Catholic state.[64]

Sturzo's comments on the accords focus rather on the inherent conflict and so the irreconcilable nature of the competing objectives – namely between the fascist intention to use the Church as a tool in its "ethical-social conception" of the state, a conception that Sturzo defines as pantheistic, and the Church's goal to craft a confessional state and so garner greater guarantees. Ultimately, fascism sought to employ Catholic universalism to strengthen its nationalism, while the Church hoped to use the authoritarianism of the regime to erect a Catholic state:

Initially Italian fascism did not aspire to universalism in the way that Moscow did, or to racial domination like Berlin. Italian fascism instead assumed a national and political character; its goal was to make Italy into an imperial power. To that end it needed a myth . . . to which all other ideals and activities would be subordinate. And as for Catholicism and the papacy? In the grand ideal of the fascist state, they too were subordinate to this goal . . . Having modeled its state after a totalizing ethical conception (we would call it pantheistic), fascism sought in any way possible to insert the Church too into this concept, while at the same time not losing its secular character . . . The Vatican sought rather to put a Catholic seal on the Italian state in order to insure that Catholicism was truly, and not just in name, the state religion. However, while the terms of the Concordat spoke in confessional tones, the spirit of the fascist state remained unaltered.[65]

The regime's position on youth was another source of conflict; the pope would oppose it just six months after the Concordat, in *Divinis illius magisteri*, but to no avail, and their differences culminated in the conflict over Azione Cattolica in April–May 1931, coincident with the encyclical on the social question, *Quadrigesimo anno*. The pope's response to this conflict took the form of another encyclical that he drafted himself, *Non abbiamo bisogno* of 29 June, and in which he invoked the natural rights of man and the defense of the individual against the totalitarian pretensions of the state. The resultant compromise was destined to endure, with its ups and downs, until Mussolini forged his alliance with Hitler.

— 2 —

THE SPIRITUAL TURN

It would be a grave error, on the other hand, to say that Christ has no
authority whatever in civil affairs . . . He is the author of happiness
and true prosperity for every man and for every nation.

Quas primas

Political religion and religious politics:
the heart of the King

Published on 11 December 1925, at the close of the Holy Year, the
encyclical *Quas primas* deals with the universal Kingdom of Jesus
Christ. The pope introduced the solemn holiday of Christ the King
on 31 December and then subsequently on the last Sunday of October.
The Kingdom of Christ the savior applied to all men, not only
Christians and Catholics, not only members of the community.
Because of the universal relevance of Jesus to the entire human race,
both believers and non-believers, all governments owed Him
obedience and reverence in response to "the plague of our times:
anti-clericalism." To deny His Kingdom was to deny the Church
responsibility for managing the human race, for conditioning the laws
of human governments. It meant putting Christianity on the same
level as other religions and so subjecting it to that civil power which,
because of its secularism, the Church could not recognize.

The papacy invoked the Kingdom of Christ as juridical basis for
the government of the Church in this world and also in other ways
recalled the *Unam Sanctam* of Boniface VIII. Azione Cattolica pre-
dictably figured among the primary instruments that would serve to
erect this Kingdom, and so the design of the theocracy was entrusted

40

no longer to the hands of the clergy but to the laity, with the understanding, however, that lay participation would differ from the energetic network established under Leo XIII, with its strong political and economic overtones. The laity were called upon to engage in a new militancy in the world in order to re-Christianize it, but were to take as their starting point an internal conversion. To those attending the Congress of Catholic Youth on 10 September 1922, the pope intoned: "neither politics nor social economics, nor even culture, but first of all the Christian formation of the individual."[1]

The idea of the Kingdom of Christ grew out of the venerable cult of the Sacred Heart, that pillar of nineteenth-century devotion which originated in the sixteenth century at Paray-le-Monial following the visions of the nun Marguerite Marie Alacoque (beatified in 1864). It was a complex cult characterized by a variety of different branches and developments. Its spread at the end of the nineteenth century, especially thanks to the efforts of the Jesuit Henri Ramière, depended on the bleeding heart of Christ as a symbol of remorse for the de-Christianization of the modern world. It was then a suffering and sensitive cult quick to condemn modern secular man for his misapplication of free will since the French Revolution, but at the same time neither militant nor combative. While opposed to secularization and quick to point out its errors, the Sacred Heart relied more on penitence and contrition than on excommunication. For these and other reasons, it could not always be mobilized for political ends.[2]

The proclamation of the social Kingdom of Christ could not be separated from the cult of the Sacred Heart, as maintained in the spiritual writing of Henri Ramière at the end of the nineteenth century.[3] Together they became the pillars of the papacy of Pius XI.

The strong spirit of voluntarism and opposition to determinism of Father Gemelli, derived from Saint Francis, had a significant impact in this regard. Pius XI adopted, though in a moderate way, the categories of *medievalism*, Gemelli's weapon against relativism, an influence that led to the reaffirmation of certain absolutes – certain truth, universal law, supreme authority – in order to "lead Italy back to Christ."[4] A militant political and temporal call to arms of this sort was essential to Pius XI's plan for revival. In *Quas primas*, he wrote:

> It would be a grave error, on the other hand, to say that Christ has no authority whatever in civil affairs ... He is the author of happiness and true prosperity for every man and for every nation ... If, therefore, the rulers of nations wish to preserve their authority, to promote and

41

increase the prosperity of their countries, they will not neglect the public duty of reverence and obedience to the rule of Christ . . . When once men recognize, both in private and in public life, that Christ is King, society will at last receive the great blessings of real liberty, well-ordered discipline, peace and harmony.[5]

Here is the teleological root of the doctrinal difference between Pius XI and Benedict XV. For Benedict the cult of the Sacred Heart was more spiritual and internal, while for Pius the Kingdom of Christ was at once both political and public and nonetheless inspired by the inward vision of the Sacred Heart. That vision itself had undergone a significant transformation. During the First World War, and with the tireless support of Armida Barelli, Gemelli had used the Sacred Heart for his own ends: linking it with a strong sense of *religious nationalism*, he entrusted the Italian army to its care, a maneuver that linked the doctrine of the Sacred Heart to the social Kingdom of Christ. The approach was decidedly *public* and *collective*, but held that *individual* commitment was a necessary element to achieve the *re-Christianization* of Italy. A visible public Catholic presence needed to take its place among the cultural and political leadership. Clearly, the foundation of the Catholic University (by Gemelli) responded to the need to form that ruling class, while allegiance to the Sacred Heart tempered its intellectualism. Cultural formation could not proceed divorced from spirituality, which in turn was of a profoundly personal nature. Pius XI's doctrinal commitment to the social Kingdom of Christ constituted a greater collective and obligatory force. Benedict XV insisted, even on the occasion of the consecration of Alfonso XIII as king of Spain, that "social importance not be measured in terms of the external act, but rather by the depth of the internal renovation that derives from it." The reign of the Sacred Heart may or may not be an "empire of love," and there is no banner or power that represents an alternative. Pius XI received the same Alfonso XIII in a different spirit in November 1923, when, following Primo de Rivera's coup d'état, he celebrated restoration of the monarchy that, thirty years after the disaster of 1898, would evoke a revival of the crusades. On that occasion, the pope announced that he shared the idea that consecration of the Sacred Heart represented the relaunching of an idea of *hispanidad* that assigned the Spanish nation the task of affirming the superiority of Catholic civilization. At the inauguration of the Catholic University, Benedict XV recognized the contrast with lay culture, but his point of reference remained the Sacred Heart, "which holds all the treasures of science and wisdom." In the same situation, while still archbishop of Milan, Ratti used the same citation but, as Giorgio Rumi has carefully noted, "his prospective was clearly different"; he started from the premise of a "catastrophic failure of science and human wisdom that we have witnessed in recent years," in order to proclaim "the need that all Catholic actions and organizations be directed toward the erection everywhere of the rights of Christ the savior and his Kingdom." Once again Ratti insisted that Jesus Christ command over the social, civil, and secular realms and so challenged official atheism. And, as the historian concludes:

> The encyclical *Quas primas* highlights the distinction between the two papacies. The Kingdom is now assigned directly to Christ without reference to the mediation of the Sacred Heart. The name of Ratti's predecessor disappeared from the scene; the holiday shifted from June to the last Sunday in October; even Marguerite Marie Alacoque disappeared . . . The main interest of the pope was the terrestrial crown.[6]

Quas primas in fact launched a true campaign against what it described as the "plague of anti-clericalism."

The spiritual roots of *Quas primas*, the practice of piety linked to the cult of the Sacred Heart, which is not immediate for Benedict XV – were re-emphasized in *Pacem Dei munus*, the first encyclical taking peace as its subject (and so prior to *Pacem in terris*). In it the cult was linked to evangelical charity toward one's enemies, and so that international brotherhood without which peace was impossible. In the reading of Benedict XV, the cult of the Sacred Heart meant leniency, gentleness, mercy, and forgiveness, equating family peace with international peace. Pius XI instead emphasized the "political" significance of the cult and made it, together with the cult of Christ the King, the foundation on which the reign of Christianity would rest, the only possible solution to the evils introduced by secularization.[7] The political implications then of the cult of the Kingdom of Christ were applied even more adamantly than in the interpretations of Ambrosians such as Armida Barelli and Agostino Gemelli, who themselves assigned it great political relevance.[8]

In 1926 Gemelli published a commentary on *Quas primas* in *Vita e Pensiero* that attempted to combine the cults of the Sacred Heart and the Kingdom of Christ and so salvage that combination of temporal and spiritual planes that had always characterized the Church in Milan. Previously, in July 1925, *L'Azione giovanile*, the journal of Catholic youth in Milan, had put forward the Sacred Heart as the means to achieve a reign of love. In the days following the delivery

43

of *Quas primas*, that same journal described the two devotions as overlapping and so linked interiority together with action. In May 1926, a congress was held at the Catholic University to better define the social Kingdom of Christ. Cardinal Mazzella placed spirituality first among the essential attributes of the Kingdom of Christ, without which one could not define the goals of the cult, while the means to achieve those goals must necessarily be temporal ones. The Kingdom of Christ must exercise the same concrete powers as any other kingdom.[9] On Pentecost Sunday, 23 May 1926, thousands of Catholics marched in Milan, bringing to a close Father Gemelli's conference. While the fascists asserted their control, masses of people expressed their Catholic identity, as if to demonstrate the incomplete nature of fascist cultural annexation.

The introduction of the holiday of Christ the King left open the question of what role the Sacred Heart would play in the restoration of theocratic power. Pius XI resolved this dilemma in 1928 with the encyclical *Miserantissimus redemptor*. The pope re-emphasized a point already made in *Quas primas* and following the formulation of Benedict XV, namely that "the great empire of Christ" must rule over not only the individual but also civil and domestic society.

In the face of these sins, contrition was added to consecration, as it was necessary to atone for the offense against God made by our sins and so re-establish, by way of penitence, the traditional order of society. It was then a social obligation that the errors of modernity be corrected in a public and collective forum, as it was the autonomy of modern man that had deprived the Church of leadership in the temporal realm. The encyclical *Caritate Christi* of 1932 underlined still more forcefully this need for atonement.

The Holy Year saw a transition from the King disguised to the King revealed and triumphant, as He assumed a universal character: a Christian society of all peoples under a single King. The Church's mission under fascism, then, was naturally to re-Christianize the Italian nation; there was, however, an underlying and universal tension, as that re-Christianization would take place under the sign of a Roman tradition to which Catholics and fascists alike claimed to be the natural heirs. Collaboration then was essential, but not subservience.

The various expressions of both the liturgical and Eucharistic movements also served this purpose, as they took on an ever more social and political function, both for the Christian community and as a pole of attraction for the de-Christianized world. The appeal that liturgical celebrations – for example the triumphant religious ceremonies of the Holy Year – could exercise on the mass of non-believers proved to be a great resource for the liturgical movement as it sought to compete with the popular demonstrations of the totalitarian regimes. The liturgical movement could employ expressive forms both fascinating and suggestive in confronting the lay population – yet another example of the way in which spirituality in politics takes its inspiration from the spirituality of the Church.

Church liturgy could become an effective weapon to combat modern propaganda of just the sort spread by the fascist regime. As noted in one of the many comments made in the *Rivista Liturgica*, it was exactly the liturgy, "with its universal diffusion, daily repetition, and deep influence, that could wage a solid and triumphant battle against the modern, insidious, implacable, serpentine, and dynamic propaganda of evil."[10]

The spirituality of Thérèse de Lisieux

It was through the "little way" of Thérèse de Lisieux, a guide to humility and abandonment, that Pius XI made the spiritual journey culminating in the particular interpretation of historical events that characterized his later years. On the occasion of her canonization on 17 May 1925, he described her as the "Word of God": her life was a Word that revealed God in His mercy and grace. She taught us that "we must be small in the presence of God" and expect all of God "as a child expects all from his father."

In her own words, the essential tenets of Thérèse de Lisieux's meditations were as follows: "If God chooses to be for me only mercy and grace, then there is only one way for me to recognize His will (that is, to see the face of God), namely to have nothing in me that could justify His love for me." She seems to be saying that it is only by means of this "non-being/having nothing" that one can abandon oneself completely to grace and so "actuate being/have everything." What then is strength for Thérèse? To have no strength at all. In a word, man himself is nothingness, and so, precisely for this reason, he is everything in God. God transforms the nothingness of being by means of mercy and grace and so establishes confidence. According to Thérèse, this is the only way for man to achieve unity with God: "it is confidence and nothing other than confidence that can lead us to Love."[11] Thérèse felt that it was her mission to teach the whole Church about this "small path," this return to what is essential. From this derived an interior space that had no place for that "network or

45

rosary of practices" that she disliked.[12] She anticipated that final encounter with God as being all the more "secure" if she approached it with nothing. "I have no good deeds, so He cannot render to me 'according to my deeds' . . . So be it. He will render to me 'according to His deeds.'"[13]

The stream of Thérèse's thought, a sort of spiritual oxymoron, fed the character of Pius XI, who nonetheless did not hesitate to act, organize, promote, and engage in politics according to his own theocratic understanding. Paradoxically, it was exactly to the spirituality of Thérèse de Lisieux that the pope assigned many of his practical programs; for example he made her protectress of the Catholic missions. Those programs were infused with a sense of abandonment to God derived from his most beloved saint.

The spirituality of Thérèse de Lisieux that "had no place for a rosary of practices" sat uncomfortably with Pius XI's determined political application of the devotions; these were the same devotions that she had experienced in their interiority, with maternal benevolence "dans la solitude de ce délicieux coeur à coeur." By comparing Thérèse de Lisieux with such looming figures of sanctity as Ignatius Loyola, Francis Xavier, Charles Borromeo, and Teresa of Ávila, the pope identified in her the sense of the small linked to those of abandonment and confidence:

> It is her simplicity and sincere heartfelt humility, interior devotion to the needs of her station . . . incessant prayer, openness to all forms of sacrifice, constant immolation, and the abandonment and confidence in God she inspires that constitute her sanctity . . . some may point out that she neither preached nor taught, nor underwent austere penitence. Yet many, while desiring these qualities, are unable to achieve her simplicity and patience, humility, prayer, and love.[14]

The pope was not a great lover of the quotidian. Indeed he would describe day-to-day tasks in exaggerated tones as "a cruel martyrdom," a true cross to bear: "the heaviness and agony, the at times crushing monotony deriving from the implacable, unavoidable weight of daily tasks."[15] And yet, inclined as he was to grand undertakings and to command, nonetheless he often spoke of the value of the ordinary: "But how much that is uncommon and unusual is there in what is common and quotidian! . . . It takes uncommon virtue to fulfill the tasks that fill up our daily lives with precision, concentration, piety, and an intimate fervor of the spirit."[16]

The canonization of Thérèse de Lisieux in 1925, coinciding symbolically with the condemnation of Action Française, marked the establishment of a new and important cult that would leave its mark on the history of contemporary spiritualism. Thérèse, the "little flower of Jesus," died in 1897 at the age of twenty-four in the Lisieux Carmel. Her internal voyage exerted great influence over French Catholicism, not, however, as an extension of nineteenth-century decadent religious romanticism, but rather as an icon of the most sober modern spirituality. She represented the authentic testimony of how the small can illuminate the great and indeed the world. It was a vision that greatly inspired the Petits Frères of Father Charles de Foucault, above all René Voillaume. The Petits Frères came into existence in September 1933 and commanded considerable attention among French Catholics. While they themselves would have preferred silence, Cardinal Verdier organized a solemn ceremony at Montmartre that deepened the influence of Thérèse de Lisieux on French Catholicism.

Ratti had been devoted to the saint since his days as a priest. He probably "discovered" her around 1900, as her spiritual autobiography, *The History of a Soul*, was published a year after her death and brought to Ratti's attention by Léopold Delisle, conservator at the National Library in Paris, who had close ties to the Lisieux Carmel and was a close friend of Ratti.[17] His attachment to the saint, to her genuine and simple spirituality, as he repeated countless times, grew over the years. He kept her relics both at the Vatican and at Castelgandolfo, and his most important decisions were filtered, read, and interpreted in the light of her spirituality. We learn from his audiences with Pacelli that, in response to the dramatic events of the Spanish Civil War or the ever more distressing news from Germany, the pope would often ask the sisters of the Lisieux Carmel to pray for him before he made a decision.

The spirituality of Thérèse, however, not only served as an anchor in difficult moments but also became a guide for reading historical events. And we must turn to her sensibility and abandonment if we are to understand the various elements that contributed to Ratti's interior conversion and break with the totalitarian regimes. She was his interpretive filter and his light, "the guiding star of his papacy," or, as he himself would say, "my advocate," "my counselor."

Pius XI re-elaborated and further internalized his relationship with Thérèse during his illness, the other crucial event to understanding the change he underwent, and indeed he attributed his recovery during the winter of 1936–7 to her. I do not believe, though, that his attribution referred exclusively to supernatural intervention; he found in Thérèse a sort of consonance, an intimate dialog on the experience of bodily suffering. We gain this insight from the way in which the pope dealt with the surprise caused by a body that had abandoned him, that no longer responded, and the introspection and awareness this produced in him, not only physically but also mentally. The way in which the pope bore his physical suffering recalls many passages on "coping with pain" in Thérèse de Lisieux's *History of a Soul*, passages in which the acceptance of suffering leads not to a sort of complacent pain but rather to a calm self-awareness.

That work's valuable suggestions for how to deal with suffering, and in particular devastating bodily pain, must have been illuminating and in tune with the pope's own ideas, as when she recommends that one "stay in the present moment" and confront suffering without heroism but one step at time, as when climbing a mountain, looking neither behind nor too far ahead. Thérèse is humility, dialog, tenderness without indulgence, resistance without heroism, steadfastness in reaching one's goal without pride, at once presence to oneself and abandonment. Pius XI, brusque, strong, authoritarian, with a strong ego, found in Thérèse his anchor, the guiding star of his papacy, his first beatification, his first saint.

Pius XI, who was sovereign pope and aspired to kingship, even in heaven, who called in his troops and recruited the laity to serve in the militia and undertake a crusade, found more and more in Thérèse "the importance of small things." We shall hear the echoes of this in his final discourse, the one that never saw the light of day because destroyed while his body was still warm. It was a text that would not be published till the 1950s, and then only partially, by John XXIII. It does call on priests and seminarians to oppose fascism, but also to pay attention to the importance of small domestic virtues, the order and harmony that, following Thérèse, constituted for him a true internal light, and not just that obsession with precision described in his biographies.

It was no accident that Pius XI declared Thérèse protectress of the missions, a particularly important choice in the context of his relaunching of the missionary movement. In the *Rerum Ecclesiae gestarum* of 28 February 1926, dedicated to the missions, he re-emphasized the importance of indigenous clergy, as opposed to that imported from the West, because the converted needed to see that the missions were truly at their service and not a Trojan horse of colonialism. Following the spirit of Benedict XV, he warned against the nationalist infiltration of the missionary movement. It was in this spirit, for example, that he made an opening to the Chinese nationalists and consecrated six Chinese bishops on 28 October 1928.

Looking ahead to his address to the Consistory College on 13 December 1937, he explained that to "do good" according to the Bible meant above all to leave oneself and one's usual role: more abandonment than command, more listening than injunction, as revealed in the call to extend a hand in the months of the politics of the proffered hand:

> To follow IIim then wherever and as long as He requires: in the tranquility of peace and in the difficulties of conflict . . . follow Him, the divine Lord, wherever . . . in the hopes of doing good for all those who appeal to the pope . . . offering a helping hand in all cases of suffering, of misery, in the hope of helping or at least comforting and consoling . . . providing that nothing at all be sacrificed in the way of sacred truth.[18]

In the late 1930s even the Kingdom of Christ underwent a transition that was more spiritual than political, a significant sign of the break between the 1920s and the 1930s. On 5 January 1938 Pius addressed the leaders of Azione Cattolica and offered an interpretation of the Kingdom of Christ that was more spiritual than political:

> The brothers of Azione Cattolica have both understood and put into practice the words of our Lord Jesus Christ and his sacred teaching. He did not come here to promote a political regime in the usual vulgar sense of the word, but rather to bring to all souls the benefits of the Kingdom of God . . . Such were the politics of the pope which are the politics of our Lord: the politics that give the polis to the citizens in the full awareness of their human and Christian dignity and of all their duties as well.[19]

An ailing pope and the virtue of limits

Between Christmas 1936 and Easter 1937, Pius XI was gravely ill and bed-ridden. On 16 December he asked Professor Aminta Milani pointedly how long it would take to recover: "Don't keep the truth from me."[20]

The pope's response to illness demonstrates how suffering can contribute to interior maturity and lead to great spiritual intuition. His path led to an awareness of limits that comes with an acceptance of finiteness, of impermanence, of the changeable nature of events and human fate. Giacomo Martina has understood how, during the last years of Pius's papacy, this illness "weakened the pope's very fiber and forced him into inactivity, causing him to think at length about the virtues of the Cross and its power for redemption."[21] Given Pius's extroverted and sanguine character, his growing aversion for Nazism and his profound disillusionment with fascism have often been attributed to his illness, almost as if his intransigence was a function of age and physical suffering. However, assigning his position primarily to these personal factors diminishes his condemnation of totalitarianism.

The fact that his firm denunciation was founded on intimate contact with suffering adds, rather, greater force and profundity to a vision that was more religious than political, to that rejection of the vanity of power that marked the spirituality of his papacy in its last years. Exactly on his eightieth birthday, the pope realized that he was not well. For the first time in his life he suffered from fatigue and pain in his legs. He had always enjoyed excellent health; it was said that only once in his life had he suffered from a sore throat. He was as hearty as the oak trees of his native Brianza and had employed that energy in scaling the Alps. "Perhaps the joy I got from climbing made me think that my feet were invincible; and yet how debilitated I am; what sort of man is he who is felled by pain! . . . One almost imagines a failure of science, unable as it is to fix two poor legs!"[22]

One month after the appearance of the most serious symptoms, L'Osservatore Romano published this medical report: "The primary cause of the illness lies in the artherosclerotic process and in particular in the myocardium, causing disruption of the normal heartbeat. Early in December, these symptoms precipitated a reduction in circulation and so the necessity of bed rest."[23] A team of physicians under the direction of Professor Milani monitored the pope's condition; one of these was Father Gemelli, who frequently traveled to Rome from Milan to check on the pope's progress. Ratti commented ironically that there were too many doctors, more than should be needed to kill off the patient. He insisted on being kept fully informed of his condition and of the latest treatments, as we read in the account of an audience with Pacelli at the beginning of January:

> Write to Mons. Hinsley: given that you are aware of the pope's illness, the Holy Father has learned (in the British Medical Journal of Saturday, 2 January 1937) that there is a center in London that deals specifically with varicose veins, exactly the Holy Father's affliction. Ask Monsignor

Hinsley to better inform us about this physician. Is he Catholic, or half-Catholic? Does he have a good professional reputation, as he seems to, and is he indeed a specialist in varicose veins and their treatment? And other similar information as soon as possible. All in secret. Greatest special blessings.[24]

The illness came suddenly and was surprising not only for its unexpected arrival but also for the rapidity with which it receded. It came and went like a heartbeat that speeds up and then slows down in a frightening fashion, that peaks and then suddenly drops. The pope's illness took him many times close to death, but then drew him back. This condition taught him to live in a constant state of impermanence, which is to say not simply to make the transition from health to illness, a process that "only" requires a linear passage through resignation and acceptance. He had instead to live with the continual possibility that he might die at any moment, with a rapidity that he had indeed hoped for since he was young, but may not have wanted to go through repeatedly.

This man, accustomed to dominating and managing his physical force, surprised himself with his own energy. Indeed he felt an affinity for the peasants of his native Brianza, not for the "heaviness of the work" but for the fact that only a true illness could make him rest. He was disoriented by the illness, as was his entourage, and amazed by his own fragility; nonetheless he faced up to pain in the same sanguine and forceful way that he had managed his exuberance. His secretary, Carlo Confalonieri, whose interest in science and physiology was not of the academic sort, has written moving pages describing these days, pages that go beyond the usual hagiography:

> He made observations that probably interest the doctors as well: on the relationship, for example, between pain and the cry that accompanies it; the existence of words, expressions, and tonalities that seem to lessen pain; and even the fact that pain can express itself in different visible colors and intensities. Pain always took him to a higher level, from purification to asceticism to sacrifice. He came in fact to meditate on the wealth of goodness that came with that pain that kissed his forehead; he climbed up with Christ on the cross; his life became sacrifice.[25]

It was a strange meeting of spirituality and scientific interest in the responses to bodily pain, the relation between the cry of one's voice and pain, the search for calming words, the colors that correspond with various parts of the body (as is well known in oriental medicine, though it is unlikely he was aware of this). The entire experience was understood in relation to God and His word, as abandonment to His will:

> It is in the midst of suffering that one understands the will of God. As long as things are good, following the precepts of God corresponds more or less to following our own desires, because ultimately it brings us pleasure. But when God strikes us, it is a different matter. We have to thank God for having given us the opportunity, before we die, to understand what it truly means to obey His will. . . . Write to Lisieux of the need to pray still more in order to rightly perform, as the pope would want, the will of God. Tell them to continue to pray so that he may know the will of the Lord, as the Lord will and as long as He will, in pain.[26]

He said "that the experience of life, as great as it is, misses something if it does not include the experience of pain, and so we have to thank God when he brings us suffering . . . I wish everyone to be happy, and this morning I said as much to Cardinal Pacelli; but I also hope that each one of us can find a corner of life for suffering."[27]

The pope involved Pacelli in the most private and intimate moments of his life, moments when he identified with the suffering on the cross and cried over the empathy of the experience. The tears were his own; the pope cried and revealed his emotions both in public and in private. On the radio, his emotional state might prove embarrassing, awkward, and disorienting, as in his message to the Munich Conference. Pacelli on a number of occasions exercised a sort of self-censorship and did not speak of these moments or record them. Tardini was more forthcoming, though with a degree of reserve, feeling at once fear over the exposure of such intimate sentiments and an intense sense of filial devotion. The pope himself did not immediately reveal his illness, and at first he and his entourage sought to hide it. He was, for example, forced to give the blessing from the balcony while seated, and a curtain was used to disguise the fact that he was unable to stand. And the sostituto complained when the correspondent for *La Stampa* wrote on 4 February 1937 that, "as one who has seen him . . . the Holy Father is not walking well."[28] In fact, he had been practically immobilized for over three months.

The way in which the pope's illness was managed and the reactions it inspired – at first reservation and then what for those times was something of a media blitz – seem to offer proof that in the twentieth century the body of the pope was once again "available" to all. As in the past, the people of Rome were informed of their pope's health, down to the minute details. And so this body was hailed from afar not only in its regality but in its misery. The frailty of the pope's body had been an important theme in the thirteenth century, when it had often been depicted in a powerful iconography.[29] Recall the intense Subiaco fresco that depicts Gregory the Great seated on his throne adorned in papal finery while Job sits naked and covered with sores on the ground:

> The contrast between the "nudity" represented by Job and the authority of the papal figure must certainly be placed in the long rhetorical series describing the decline of the pope's physical body, the roots of which reach back to the beginnings of the Gregorian reforms. It is a discourse that in underlining the physical decline of the pope in his human form emphasizes at the same time the superiority and universality of his institutional figure.[30]

The vulnerability of the body of the pope, that fed fantasies and imagination, was also perceived and represented in the course of the Middle Ages and the modern era through a series of objects and instruments, the liturgical accoutrements of his reign.

In this, Pius XI represented a bridge between the old and the new relationship with the body. During his illness he used a series of ingenious devices that he designed himself, including a sort of folding bed that was useful when he had to leave Rome. These were tools, like the modern Popemobile, that allowed him to maintain his relationship with the outside world: "A stretcher to get him to his audiences, the rolling chair inside the apartment, and a cane for short movements both indoors and in the garden. During solemn ceremonies in the Sistine Chapel and in the Basilica he got down from his throne as little as possible and, except for the essential liturgical movements, he remained seated."[31]

Following the four months during which he was bed-ridden, Pius began again to celebrate mass regularly in his private chapel on 19 March 1937. His recovery was vigorous, and that was in fact the month when he delivered three encyclicals against totalitarianism. It was the month that inaugurated the intense last two years of his life, years that witnessed a true change of course:

> A profound internal labor marked the spirit of the pope. He looked back over all the works and events of his papacy and in silence and calm must have effected a sort of review, something between a

53

historical judgment and personal examination of his conscience, with an emphasis on the latter as was natural for a believer, for a pope who in any case felt the nearness of eternity.[32]

A pope alone? Pius XI and his entourage

Who made up the pope's entourage in these last and crucial years of his life? Who were his collaborators and what was their relationship? Much has been made of the pope's solitude and of the relief that would be felt after his death, the removal from the scene of a nearly unmanageable personality. References to his brusqueness recur regularly in the descriptions of these months, as do depictions of the spy Pacelli, who was constantly trying to undermine the plans of the pope, or indeed of a pope subordinate to the will of his secretary of state. All of these depictions have about them an air of allusion and fantasy and rarely rely on documentary evidence of the sort that is now available to us.

The overall impression one gets from the relations in these years is more subtle and articulated. In many cases, the legends of course find confirmation, as we read in the recollections of a collaborator who knew him well. Federico Alessandrini, the mythical shadow correspondent of *L'Osservatore Romano*, who allegedly reported from the most important foreign capitals, regularly angered the chancelleries without in fact stepping outside of the Vatican, where he commanded a well-informed press office. He had close contacts with the office of the secretary of state, first Giuseppe Pizzardi and then Tardini, Montini (later Paul VI), and above all Pacelli. He wrote the following to his son Giorgio, himself a Roman priest:

> Pius XI was a centralizer. He possessed an authoritarian character and did not tolerate contradiction; but in fact sometimes "the offices" overruled even him and his "ornery character," insensitive to diplomatic paraphrasing and circumlocution . . . In his audiences with the young he was very affectionate . . . at times he would put his hand on the head of a youth and tousle his hair in a rough caress. When speaking he could easily be overcome by emotion, to the point of tears. Rather than discourses, he delivered meditations out loud. At times, he seemed to have finished, to be at the point of dismissal; but then he would continue and sometimes it was then that he spoke more or less directly about the current situation, without reserve or censure. Those were unforgettable encounters.[33]

"The offices": this was the term used not only in the Secretariat of State but generally by the Roman Curia to refer to the management of current affairs, entailing as it did all the more prosaic characteristics of a large bureaucracy. This was in fact the first aspect of the pope's "objective" solitude. He felt the need to express a new, if uncertain and vexed, vision of current events, one that in its uncertainty could not always be translated into the usual bureaucratic and diplomatic framework.

There is then that natural solitude that comes with illness and the creation of restrictions, dependence, and introspection. This new physical and mental condition affected the pope's relations with those who were closest to him, starting with his two secretaries, Monsignor Carlo Confalonieri and Monsignor Diego Venini.[34] It was with Confalonieri, the figure of greater stature, that he forged a true friendship.

Curious to note, even the most hagiographic and biographical treatments often overlook the presence in papal circles of women, who are nonetheless important and can in fact become problematic figures, as in the case of Sister Pascalina, to whom Pius XII would give such free rein. There was an important woman close to Pius XI – Linda, who had cared for him since his days at the Ambrosiana and who followed him to Rome. Aside from a few vulgar and predictable remarks from the fascist press, we know almost nothing about this discreet presence. Outside of the domestic sphere, his daily contacts were above all with Pacelli and the other collaborators of the secretary of state:

> Standing next to the pope was the master of the chamber, Monsignor Caccia Dominioni, tall and heavily built and with an incurable nervous tic so he constantly winces; the chamberlain, Monsignor Confalonieri, now a deacon of the Sacred College; or Monsignor Venini. And then Don Montini, not yet monsignor, who, wrapped in a *ferraiolo* of black silk, imposed the protocol and introduced us to the pope one by one. These were unforgettable meetings that offered strength and established the certainty that one was not alone in truth and justice. Were there any elements of political ambition in this group of young men? I couldn't say for sure, but I was never aware of it, and in any case such an ambition would have received no encouragement at all.[35]

Expanding the circle a bit, we have to include the director of *L'Osservatore Romano*, Count Dalla Torre, who had a direct line to the pope and could speak to him without the mediation of Pacelli,[36] as well as several cardinals and bishops especially close to the pope, such as Eugène Tisserant.

A few excerpts from unpublished documents reveal how the select group that made up the Secretariat of State was chosen. On 1 June 1936, Giovanni Battista Montini replied to Tardini, sustituto to the secretary of state, regarding Montini's nomination to the Sacred Congregation:

> The office exceeds my powers (my physical power, not to mention others); I am not adequately prepared; nor do I desire positions of greater responsibility. My nomination would not be well received by those in the offices who have attained higher rank; nor do I have any reason to change my current position, a position that requires more experience and study, not new activities.[37]

Through to the spring of 1937 Montini requested some moments of retreat and prayer, as in a letter of 3 March 1937 in which he asked for a period of spiritual exercises, of the sort he had not had since 1932, in his native Brescia. From there, in October 1937, he wrote Tardini asking "not to be assigned greater obligations or bureaucratic responsibilities, as for myself I am happy to leave both the greater burden and greater advantage to others."[38]

In December 1937, Tardini replaced Pizzardo as secretary for extraordinary ecclesiastical affairs in the Secretariat of State and Montini succeeded him as sustituto. The pope favored another candidate: "Monsignor Tardini recounted that Pius XI preferred Monsignor Confalonieri, but Cardinal Pacelli and Tardini himself insisted on Montini."[39]

On many occasions the pope confirmed his centralizing tendency, as for example in August 1937, following the death of the prefect of the Congregation of Seminaries and Universities, Cardinal Gaetano Bisleti. Failing to find an appropriate candidate he decided, in a burst of energy and sense of command, to assume the office himself: "Mussolini was not wrong to keep for himself various ministries. For that way, all runs smoothly without conflicts and interruptions. He added that he approved thoroughly of those cardinal prefects who held audiences in their own parishes during their office hours, rather than at home."[40]

Pius XI's special relationship with Pacelli

For more than eight years, from 10 August 1930 to 3 December 1938, Pacelli made notes every evening on his morning audience with the pope and his afternoon meeting with the diplomatic corps. We shall refer to these as the "Pacelli notebooks," though following the example of Pacelli himself they are now more correctly described as "audience notes."[41] They do not constitute a diary and contain neither analytical narcissism nor introspection. Nor are they a transcript. Some of the audiences in fact are missing, as are references to some of the most pressing questions. It is as if Pacelli practiced a sort of self-censorship, not wanting to leave behind any possibly compromising written documents. It was the same cautious approach that would lead him to burn many documents once he became pope. Sister Pascalina, as is well known, would describe in her memoir Pacelli's purging of his files; he often brought sheaves of papers into the kitchen to burn, especially during the German occupation of Rome. And in fact, when reading these notebooks, especially those for days following important events when one would expect immediate reactions, one finds instead only the occasional reference or no reference at all. Given that these "gaps" often coincide with controversial topics, we can imagine that the relevant pages were destroyed by Pacelli after he became pope.

For one reason or another, these Pacelli notebooks can be disappointing, rich as they are in minutiae while lacking in-depth discussion, from the very beginning: the first audience of 16 August 1930, for example, reports: "Cardinal of Chicago, thank for kind gift (books on Alpinism)."

And yet these notes do offer new insights on some important events, and on the figure of the pope and the special relationship that developed between him and Pacelli. Their laconic nature nonetheless possesses a tight communicative efficiency for at least two reasons. On the one hand, they reveal the daily rapport between two men who were at once so different and so united. On the other, at those moments of important events they offer, as we shall see, insight and lively commentary into those events, immediate and first hand and often escaping the self-censure of Pacelli himself.

The secretary of state never contradicted his pope directly; nor did he criticize him, even implicitly. But his differences, or better his hidden differences, are easy enough to discern, as we shall see in a number of the citations used below in this reconstruction. The reports are hurried, probably dashed down after long and wearying days. So, while they do not offer long explorations, they often capture the freshness of a chronicle.

Pius XI for his part had a unique relationship with his secretary of state. The two men differed in many ways: character, emotion, spirituality, political conviction, and analysis of a given situation. And yet they were linked by a sort of complementarity that rendered each indispensable to the other. It was as though the pope knew that he could publicly give vent to his impulses, as Pacelli would smooth things out afterward. By contrast, Pacelli's caution and timidity found in Ratti's resolution an anchor that allowed him his dithering, both because he could hesitate without great worry and because he knew he would never be scolded. It is surprising that a pope of this sort, often brusque and quick to correct his aides, had for Pacelli a sort of respect and delicacy, as though he feared injuring such an ethereal personality with his rough ways. A pope accustomed to lording it over others, of giving orders and having them obeyed, imbued with a spirit of command, approached his secretary with a respect that bordered on reverential. Achille Ratti saw in Eugenio Pacelli everything he was not or was in a different way: lofty, theocratic, noble, expert in languages, a fine preacher, exquisite, and courtly. Pacelli's first masterpiece of seduction and persuasion (even if it wasn't really that) he accomplished with his pope.

It is possible to analyze this complicated relationship by comparing the Pacelli notebooks with those kept by Tardini during the annual month of vacation the secretary of state spent in Switzerland; Pacelli did not alter this practice even during the Munich conference, though he was daily in touch with his Vatican contacts by telephone. During that month of October 1938, Tardini kept a detailed account of his audiences with the pope "in order to keep informed his eminence Cardinal Pacelli who was then on vacation in Switzerland."[42] The differences between the Pacelli notebooks and Tardini's diary jump out at anyone who compares the two, starting with the attention to detail, doubtless a product of the responsibility Tardini felt as substitute to give as full an account as possible. Tardini's style is looser and quicker to make on-the-spot judgments, more like the character of the pope himself, with whom he shared a taste for frequent and at times biting remarks.

Tardini had much more in common with the pope than did the reserved and prudent Pacelli. And yet the relationship between Tardini and the pope casts light upon that complicated and particular one between the pontiff and Pacelli. Tardini's presence allows us to make out some of the chiaroscuro of that mysterious relationship, one that defies the widespread stereotypes. From the first page (27 September 1938) one encounters Pius XI's heavy dependence on Pacelli: "The Holy Father immediately asked me at what time the secretary of state had left. To my reply and wish that he might find a degree of repose, his holiness replied: 'This had been a year of crushing work.'" And the next day, with regard to his radio message, Pius XI expressed his "pleasure that the message was well received and happiness that the secretary of state heard it in Switzerland and found it magnificent" [underlined].

We have already noted how the pope repressed his usual sense of command with Pacelli; he never felt the need to issue orders, largely because the secretary tended to anticipate the pope's wishes before they were expressed.[43] His relationship with Tardini was very different, as is clear from Tardini's book *Pio XII*, itself derived from Tardini's oration in honor of Pius XII in the Vatican Hall of Blessings on 11 October 1958. The text is one of solid praise on all levels, expressing unlimited admiration and devotion. And yet the extensive notes describing his relationship with Ratti reveal that his regard for Pius XII was not as fervid or emotional as had been that for his predecessor: "He once gave me – I don't recall why – a solemn upbraiding. He quickly calmed down, saying, 'I am much better now.' I dared to reply: 'It is I, Holy Father, who does not feel much better.' The pope, continuing the conversation, found a reason to give me a watch that I keep to this day."[44]

Traces of this rough affection appear frequently in Tardini's published diary. Among the most amusing are those regarding Pius XI's concern about good financial investments. As during the audience of 3 February 1934:

19:34, audience with the Holy Father. I found him more alert and livelier than usual, in excellent humor. He listened unperturbed to my financial requests, agreeing to many of them, and executing a few, but I feared the worst. He lamented our lack of money ... "I entreat you then! Find lots of money ..." I replied, "Your holiness, it is impossible. We cannot find money, but must ask for it." – "Alright" – he replied – "well, at least pray for it." ... Tardini added, "The pope was happy to speak with me about the issue that most troubled him, the world economic crisis ... he spoke almost more fervidly about the decline of the dollar than about moral decline and lamented with greater bitterness the loss of money than the destruction of souls."[45]

— 3 —

FRANCE AND COMMUNISM
AS CHRISTIAN HERESY

We take that hand and offer ours in return with the prayer that it be accepted. For we do not want the one nor offer the other except insofar as we make our own, as we have both the right and the duty, the words of our Lord Jesus Christ: "Come unto us all who are weary and burdened, I shall give you rest."

From a nocturnal meditation of Pius XI (6 November 1937)

The "proffered hand" and the fear of contagion

On 17 April 1936, one month before elections, Maurice Thorez, secretary of the French Communist Party, famously addressed Catholic voters over Radio Paris: "We who are secular offer our hand to you: Catholic, laborer, office worker, artisan, or peasant. Because you are our brother and so weighed down with the same worries . . . We offer you our hand, national volunteer, veteran who has joined the Croix de Feu, because you are a son of the people."

The seductive power of this appeal for votes was limited. François Mauriac's ironic commentary on the communist nightingale's song expressed widespread Catholic skepticism, and he reasserted his wary attitude following the Spanish massacres. From the start, the electoral campaign was a tense one. On 4 March 1936 Cardinal Luigi Maglione had warned the French bishops not to underestimate the appeal that a more flexible communist approach might have among Catholics. The secretary of the French Episcopal Assembly, Chollet, was urged to prevent the *noyautage*, communist infiltration "among the ranks of the Catholics and especially among the young on the pretense of pursuing humanitarian ends." The pope himself asked to be kept informed about the threat of this "communist infection."[1]

Following a heated electoral campaign, on 3 May the French elected 375 Popular Front deputies to the Chamber as compared to 220 for the right. It was not a massive shift as compared to the election four years previously, but a limited electoral advantage translated into a substantial difference in the fortunes of the two sides. On this occasion the *discipline républicaine* held for the first time since the end of the war, as radicals, socialists, and communists combined to back well-placed left-wing candidates in the second round of voting. The more appealing and democratic politics of the communists (the very politics championed by the Popular Front) in particular were rewarded, as that party saw a dramatic increase from eleven deputies to seventy-two. All the nightmares of the European right in the 1930s seemed to be realized when the Popular Front chose as prime minister Léon Blum, the man most hated by the opposition: socialist, intellectual, atheist, and Jew. As if that were not enough, a few days after the elections a factory occupation began that in a few weeks was joined by millions of workers around the country. Social revolution seemed to follow on the heels of political revolution.[2]

During these feverish weeks of spring 1936, a variety of positions found expression among Catholics as well. They ranged from those who applauded the victory of the left – on 1 June 1936, Mounier wrote in *Esprit* with typically Popular Front rhetoric: "We shall continue to help and encourage in any way we can ... I am thinking in particular about the battle of the unions against the war and against poverty, to disarm capitalism from within"[3] – to the more cautious *L'aube* and the hostile opposition of reactionary Catholics. The last seemed more in tune with Pius XI, who in those torrid weeks of May exhorted a group of Hungarian pilgrims visiting Rome not to follow the example of the many who had allowed themselves to be deceived by the communists: "everywhere they seek to infiltrate and may even seem to have the best intentions." The day before, 12 May, he had described communist propaganda to the international press as "still more dangerous when, as we have seen lately, it becomes less violent and apparently less impious in an effort to penetrate more deeply and achieve, as it has of late, incredible acceptance or at least silence and tolerance, a situation that constitutes a great victory for the forces of evil and brings with it sad consequences for the forces of good."[4]

Pius's position was adamant and forcefully repeated, as when he corrected the position of Francisque Gay, the director of *L'aube*, who sought to tone down the sense of direct confrontation and emphasized instead a principled distance from anti-clericalism and Marxist atheism: "The misgivings of the Church in this regard are not so much with specific political programs but rather with the persistent anti-clericalism of certain far-left elements and the congenital atheism of their doctrines."[5]

The pope was unhappy with this formulation and instructed Dalla Torre, editor of *L'Osservatore Romano*, to draft a "serious response" to the French communists, correcting the "imprecise interpretation" of his statements that had appeared in the French Catholic paper. Moreover, Gay himself published the headline "Catholique d'abord," a paraphase of Maurras' "Politique d'abord," and recalled the condemnation of communist atheism: "If *L'aube* has misinterpreted the pope's intentions, either directly or indirectly, we humbly submit without recourse to false pretext or diversionary tactics."[6] Gay had in any case established a good relationship with Pius XI, who received him at least ten times and praised his "crusade" against l'Action Française. On 16 June *L'Osservatore Romano* in the end limited itself to reprinting Gay's article. For his part, Gay kept his interaction with the left, including even the communists, discreet, meeting repeatedly with Thorez.[7] It would be up to Cardinal Verdier, following instructions from the pope, to define clearly the responsibilities of French Catholics in the context of the social and political agitation of spring 1936. He launched an appeal for social peace and invoked once again the justice of Catholic social doctrine, receiving praise from the pope for his handling of a delicate situation.

Italian Catholics also continued to be divided over how to approach the French communists, as is evident from the comments of Professor Guido Manacorda that appeared in *Corriere della Sera* and were sent together with a request for a papal audience. We will have occasion to return to Manacorda, a Catholic fascist and professor of German language and literature, as he would later seek to mediate for the Holy See in hopes of improving the relationship with Hitler. Manacorda wrote for *Critica fascista* and was a great friend of Bottai, who refers to him in several places in his diary. Bottai offers a precise sketch of this Florentine fascist of the first hour and describes an exchange of 17 August 1940 in which Manacorda, among other things, expresses a negative judgment of the "fundamentally democratic" pope:[8]

> He recalled with pride the role he had played in establishing links between fascism and Nazism. In September '35 he went on his own

initiative to Berlin, where he asked and managed to see Hitler, in order to present him with his Italian *Faust*. We were on the verge of the sanctions, and Hitler suddenly abandoned the literary discussion in order to attack Italian foreign policy. What sort of policy was Mussolini pursuing? Not European, not Italian, it was instead "Triestine." . . . In response to Manacorda's question, he protested that Germany would never support the sanctions, and concluded with words of praise for Mussolini . . . Mussolini in turn received the news with the comment: "So this way Germany will rebuild its gold reserve behind our back."[9]

We will explore later on Manacorda's failed attempts to mediate between the pope and Hitler. For now we shall look at his advice on the French situation included in a letter to the secretary of state, written from Florence on 24 September and including the articles referred to above. Manacorda offered a synthesis of his treatment of "communism and communist propaganda among Catholics, the political-religious situation in France, Germany, and Holland":

He will see the head of state and does not know if he will be assigned any new tasks. Before the meeting with *il Duce* he would like to meet with Pizzardo. He claims the deliberations of the League of Nations will only serve to speed things along. He thinks it urgent that an understanding be reached with the forces of order. He will arrive in Rome on 30 September for the meeting with *il Duce* that will occur in the first days of October; he would also like to meet with the pope on that occasion. He will write in the coming days to D'Annunzio.[10]

His article "Cattolici al bivio" [Catholics at the Crossroads], published in *Corriere della Sera* on 3 September 1936, included a harsh attack on the Dominican journal *Vie Intellectuelle*; the latter on 10 July had described the sincere desire of many men on the left for honest collaboration with the Catholics, "respecting freedom of conscience," and interpreted many points of the recent communist platform as close to the social doctrine of the Church. The Florentine professor explicitly attacked Congar and Maritain, as they judged fascism worse than communism, whose doctrines "can only lead to totalitarian oppression by means of self-negation." His stentorian condemnation of these strange Catholics allowed for no appeal and was pronounced in the name of imperial Rome:

On the one hand they burn incense at the idol in Geneva, egalitarian and masonic, while on the other they proffer a hand to communism in the economic sphere, as if communist economics were not inexorably tied to principles that are radically atheist and anti-Christian! It is the raising up of that so-called spiritual man outside and beyond the laws of civil society, as if the *homo spiritualis* of Augustine was seriously a vulgar anarchist and not instead a saint overflowing with grace. They harbor, finally, a deaf and poorly hidden aversion for higher and central authority, for any hierarchy, for any sort of organization; against Rome, finally, its spirit, history, and combined divine and human mission.

In another article on French politics, in *La Nazione* of 22 November, Manacorda offered a stereotypical sketch of all the vices of the French spirit: bureaucratic, individualist, secular, and denatalist heir of Malthusian egoism. The *fille aînée de l'Église* responded wearily to these vices as they were taking hold "in the more sophisticated religious quarters, strangely infused with old-style enlightenment and tolerant of spirits and forms clearly averse to Christianity."

Manacorda for his part did not limit to France alone his concern about the direction Catholics were taking. On 29 July he sent a letter to the secretary of state noting the position taken by the Dutch deputy Muller in a meeting with the Tilburg section of the Dutch Catholic Party: "If the Catholic should ever have to choose, he would choose communism over National Socialism. The former would indeed bring an immediate, open and cruel persecution, but that would have no effect on the Church. The latter instead would oppress the Church with a velvet glove like Julian the Apostate." According to this view, only Nazism, not communism, is totalitarian: "The fundamental principle of Nazism is the totalitarian state – the propaganda according to which the state comes first and the individual second, that even the Church is subordinate to the state. Man exists for the state, but this is pure heresy and atheism. The state exists for man. Such is Catholic teaching: man always comes first."

For Manacorda, the words of the Dutch deputy well represented the dangerous ideas that were spreading among too many European Catholics. The Church of Rome needed to intervene energetically: "Spain is in flames, with the likely victory of anarcho-communists. France is in the state that we all recognize. In Belgium and Holland the ember threatens to catch fire. Millions of Catholics wait for a guiding and comforting light from Rome. I rejoiced to see *Terre Nouvelle* placed on the Index; it was about time!"

This Catholic fascist was of course not the only voice worried about the need to build barricades against the left. In France itself, Jacques Chevalier, chair of the faculty of letters at Grenoble, after reviewing the positions of those Catholic intellectuals open to dialog with the communists and of their journals, called for a clear and decisive intervention from the Holy See:

> It is extremely urgent that the Holy See make it perfectly clear through the office of the papal nuncio to the spiritual and intellectual leaders of French Catholicism and to the archbishop of Paris (who vacillates and is overly conciliatory) . . . that the Holy See does not approve of these trends, indeed views them as dangerous, and forbids Catholics from any sort of consorting with communist doctrines or organizations. What is needed is not a public act but rather a stern and energetic warning: Catholics who are working with the communists need to know that Rome opposes them.
> It is absolutely necessary to banish the sad equivocation in which French Catholics are living and which has meant that even clear-eyed bishops dare not do anything for fear of disapproval from Rome. If the Holy See does not intervene soon, the damage will be irreparable and we can foresee serious problems.[11]

We have lingered over these minor figures in order to make clearer the pressure under which the secretary of state, and so also the pope, operated; letters and solicitations of all sorts urged them not to take a conciliatory position with the Popular Front. The closing of the Dominican journal *Sept* in August 1937 at the request of the Sacred Congregation – ostensibly for economic reasons, contradicted by its wide circulation and for which much documentation exists in the papers of the nunciature[12] – should be read in this light, as a reply to these sorts of worries. The pope himself sought to soften this condemnation, and indeed it seems that he was not himself fully informed about the *Sept* affair, indeed in some sense was left out of it.

Ledóchowski and the *Divini Redemptoris*

On 11 April 1936, the Jesuit superior general and great friend of Pacelli, Włodzimierz Ledóchowski, sent a hand-written and confidential letter to the pope, one not lacking in subservience:

> In our last audience, your Holiness told me that communism had made inroads even into the seminaries. Keeping in mind the words of the vicar of Christ, it occurred to me today, following the afternoon mass, that perhaps your Holiness would like to make known to the world this terrible danger, one that becomes every day more threatening. And

though the atheist propaganda from Moscow becomes ever more intense, nonetheless the world press, in the hands of the Jews, hardly makes a reference, just as it ignores the crimes committed in Russia . . . and while that propaganda becomes ever more able and devious, many are fooled, many who would not fall into this error if they knew the whole truth. An encyclical on this topic would, I think, be opportune, and would encourage not only Catholics but others as well to put up a stronger resistance. Your Holiness will excuse my ardor, and if he deems such an encyclical to be opportune, I think that we could also contribute.[13]

A penciled-in remark on the margin of this letter, perhaps written by Tardini, suggests that this may have been the "first idea for the encyclical against communism." Is that a credible remark? Did the initial inspiration for the anti-communist encyclical indeed come from the superior general of the Jesuits?

The reply can be only tentative, but it is more than likely as this letter is only one of many documents from the *Divini Redemptoris* file bearing Ledóchowski's name, and the Jesuits played an important role in drafting the encyclical. That contribution is in fact just the tip of the iceberg of the anti-communist activity carried out throughout the world in this period by the Jesuits and their energetic superior general.

Count Włodzimierz Ledóchowski was an Austrian aristocrat of Polish-Galician origins who identified closely with his Polish roots and was a rabid anti-communist; he ruled the Society of Jesus for twenty-seven years, from 1915 to 1942:

His generalship marked the high point of that theocratic conception that found expression in Jesuit obedience and a constant flow of instructions. Ledóchowski established close ties with Benedict XV and maintained them with Pius XI, a state of affairs that gave new meaning to the old Roman nickname for the superior general, namely the "black pope." And indeed it is not hard in the interwar period to identify a political-theological direction that emanates from the top and is carried out, at times interpreted, by the base.[14]

In the mid-1930s, Ledóchowski created his "Secretariat on Atheism," which between 1935 and 1939 published the *Lettres de Rome sur l'athéisme moderne* in five languages and under the direction of Joseph Ledit, professor at the Istituto Orientale. The journal was partly an informational bulletin and partly a collection of sources and analyses. It became an organ for the study of communism in all its aspects, employing news items as well as literary, historical, and philosophical sources. The superior general's ambition was to establish a Catholic International in Rome, just as there was a Communist International in Moscow and a center for international politics in Geneva. It was perhaps too great an ambition given the limited means available, or such in any case was the recollection of Friedrich Muckermann, another Jesuit activist who held strong anti-communist and anti-Nazi views and conducted a fierce campaign against Hitler.[15] It was in any case a huge undertaking of anti-communist propaganda and polemics that brought together an impressive amount of material, often first hand and important. These documents, gathered according to precise instructions from the Secretariat of State for the battle against communism, are now available for consultation.[16]

The Exposition of the Catholic Press held in Rome in spring 1936 included, among other things, much of the material gathered by the "Special Secretariat on Atheism." Father Ledóchowski summoned the Jesuit fathers to the Istituto Orientale and enlisted them in the battle against communism, made more urgent by the recent victories in France. The delegates, coming from various countries in Europe and America, listened to their superior general denounce the excessive indulgence shown by the capitalist forces in the face of the Bolshevik threat. Many sources noted the correlation between the Jesuit general's comments and the oration delivered by the pope on that same occasion.[17]

By way of comparison, the archival material relative to Germany for *Mit brennender Sorge* includes the various versions of Cardinal Faulhaber and the revisions of Pacelli, but none of the discussion of precedents or of how the encyclical might be used, nor any papers where one would most expect them, namely the Secretariat of State. The sources for *Divini Redemptoris*, on the other hand, are fairly complete and include a number of drafts and multiple contributions. Among Jesuits from the *Lettres de Rome* involved in the work on *Divini Redemptoris* were Father Gundlach – who, as we shall see, also participated in drafting the encyclical Pius XI wanted against anti-Semitism that was in all likelihood blocked by Ledóchowski – as well as Father Desbuquois, who, according to his biographer, was able to balance the condemnation of communism with the inclusion of some positive comments regarding the social doctrine of the Church.[18]

A file dated 1936, and labeled in the pope's handwriting "Outlines for an encyclical against communism," contains notes from Monsignor Valentini (probably an aide to Tardini) as well as documents by

Monsignor Pizzardi and an outline in pencil that listed the steps of its elaboration:

> 1936, 11 April Easter, letter from Ledóchowski, offer of collaboration to Pius XI – Note: communism dangers and remedies.
> Monsignor Valentini's prospectus, outline I and II.
> Outline dictated by Pius XI and sent by Confalonieri to Ledóchowski on behalf of Pius XI.
> I. Ottaviani text? By whom?
> 1937, 6 January, encyclical text in 35 pages by Pius XI, Monsignor Ottaviani.
> After 6 January the encyclical was placed under the protection of Saint Joseph.
> II. Outlines I and II Mons. Valentini.
> III. General outline Pius XI.
> 1937, 24 February, text sent to Ledóchowski (fathers from various groups collaborated).
> IV. Ledóchowski text missing.
> 28 February communication to the archive, Pius XI writes 28–2–37 encyclical communism.
> Typed observations Ledóchowski drafted in Italian (with titles and subtitles).
> 24–25 March manuscript of the Latin translation by Monsignor Bacci (observations on the translation from F. Ledóchowski).
> 23 March Latin draft sent to Ledóchowski.
> 29 March date of the encyclical.[19]

Pages 69–76 of this file include all of Ledóchowski's corrections; they are interesting for his requests for greater clarity, but even more so because they soften the criticisms of the fascist totalitarian states and emphasize instead the weight of "occult masonic forces etc., true threats to the Christian order," a sign of the cultural milieu from which the Jesuit traced his roots. Page 35, for example, suggests a variation:

> The owning classes . . . induced by whom? By the state? And yet already the states are dispossessing them: agrarian laws, devaluations, price controls, land reforms and so on. I would soften this part: "we are convinced of the urgent need for the sake of the common good . . ." And all of the paragraph that follows may make a poor impression in some countries, insofar as it is the large atheist and possibly Jewish companies that are profiting from the situation (protocols of Zion). I would call instead for a sacred crusade to realize those goals for which the Holy Father has called.

Ledóchowski's letter of 24 February, in which he assures the pope that he has "faithfully followed the points fully outlined by Your Holiness," allows us to measure his distance from the pope on a number of important issues. The notes sent by the Jesuit, along with various proposed insertions, are marked with at least three comments. Next to the gospel citations of James and Matthew, the pope has written "good," but he does not make that same annotation next to the lines that make allusion "to the role played by the Jews in this whole affair":

> It seems necessary to us that in an encyclical of this sort some reference be made, if only in passing, to the Jewish influence. For not only were all the intellectual fathers of communism Jewish (Marx, Lasalle, etc.), but the communist movement in Russia was staged by Jews [at this point the pope writes: "Verify"], and even now, if one digs deeply one finds that the primary authors of communist propaganda, though perhaps not always openly, are Jews.

At the head of this umpteenth rehashing of the "Judeo-Masonic-Bolshevik plot," the pope wrote again in pencil: "Verify!"

On 31 January, after the text had been finalized, Ledóchowski wrote to the pope about the communication of the encyclical, which he insisted should be rapid, efficient, and clear, ends not easily achieved in Latin: "As we are dealing with delicate arguments and modern concepts expressed in technical language, it is to be feared that Latin will not achieve the desired precision and clarity. And so it would seem opportune to include along with the official text a modern-language version."

Once the encyclical had been published, the Holy See naturally took note of its international reception. On 22 March the papal nuncio in Paris, Monsignor Valeri, reported on a range of French publications. The right-wing journals were obviously enthusiastic, including *Action Française*, which joined in the chorus by publishing "on the front page a fine commentary by Maurras himself, who is currently in prison and so has written under the pseudonym of 'Pellison.'" The press of the left was unhappy, however, especially the socialists, "who have displayed even more passion and acrimony than the communists. And that is saying a lot! Perhaps the communists continue to find hope in the policy of the proffered hand insofar as it serves to hide to some extent their claws." A couple of months later, at a reception, the French prime minister and great *patron* of the socialist newspaper, Léon Blum, personally apologized to the nuncio for the tone of André Leroux's article; his unpardonable excesses can perhaps be explained by the fact that the French pseudonym masked the passions of an Italian exile "who in the time of the Popular Party had some relations with Don Sturzo." Léon Blum failed to mention to Monsignor Valeri – and the nuncio makes no mention of the fact, probably because unaware of it – that the Italian anti-fascist exile was none other than Angelo Tasca.[20]

On 24 March, Nuncio Cicognani reported from Vienna on the good reception by the Austrian press.[21] The archbishop of Salzburg, Sigismund Waitz, was nothing if not enthusiastic about the publication of the two encyclicals: "It seemed to us a true Easter gift . . . a special act of divine providence that the Holy Father was able to overcome his illness and perform this great act. These encyclicals have had a special effect in Austria and are an efficient tool to combat serious dangers."[22]

In North America the encyclical did not enjoy a particularly warm welcome, but it is interesting to note appreciation of the willpower of the pope who, although seriously ill, found the energy to write this text. The vitality of the pope seems to have excited more enthusiasm than the "political" significance of an encyclical that risked moderating the condemnation of Nazism in *Mit brennender Sorge*.

The files include a note that reads: "the pope did not like the article, should we reply to M. Bordeaux?" The reference may be to the so-called Oxford group, a religious movement that had developed in English protestant circles and spread to the continent as well. Following their lead, French Catholics proposed a sort of "social rearming" for France herself and convening a broad array of forces "starting with the workers, for the sake of a spiritual restoration of France and of humanity": "The formula of human salvation was more specific to Catholics. The pope's concerns focused on this issue, as recounted by the French writer Henri Bordeaux in *Écho de Paris* of February 1938 when describing his visit with Pius XI."[23]

Pacelli's trip to Paris and to Lisieux

"The welcome offered to his eminence Cardinal Pacelli in Paris was truly grand. More solemn even than that normally reserved for crowned rulers."[24] So wrote an enthusiastic Monsignor Tardini from Paris on 9 July 1937 to those who had stayed behind at the Secretariat of State in Rome. His was a chronicle of triumph: the warm reception of the authorities, the hospitality, the boat trip to the International

Exposition on the banks of the Seine, Paris at its most seductive and welcoming. Many Parisians acclaimed the papal delegation: "the crowd gathered around his eminence in order to kiss his hand. It is now 14:30 and we are leaving for Lisieux."[25]

In comparison with Tardini, who was a great lover of France and a friend of its nuncio, Pacelli did not know France well, though he did speak the language with surprising eloquence. He had made another trip to France, for the Easter triduum between 25 and 28 April 1935 at Lourdes; it was an important visit, as it followed upon the improved relations deriving from Laval's visit to the Vatican on 7 January of that same year.

That détente between France and Italy on the eve of the Ethiopian War and immediately after the Stresa Accords led the Vatican to continue to hope for a bloc of Catholic countries. France was key to those hopes, which depended on the lifting of sanctions against Italy – hopes which fell, however, along with the Laval government at the end of 1935. Much as he favored these developments, Pacelli did not on that occasion go so far as to promise Vatican support for the lifting of sanctions. As has already been written, this whole affair left the impression of a Pacelli less "Italian than the pope . . . and closer to the League of Nations in terms of his ideas about resolving the Ethiopian crisis."[26]

The July 1937 trip, both for the moment that it took place and for the discourses that were made, had special political and symbolic importance. It seemed as if the Church was about to choose sides irrevocably. From the pulpit in Notre Dame, Secretary of State Pacelli delivered a wide-ranging discourse, one that attacked racism and praised liberty, citing *Mit brennender Sorge* but not *Divini Redemptoris*, while at the same time warning Catholics to beware of the proffered hand and the danger of "mistaking darkness for light." Pacelli was engaging with a social Catholicism of special force in France, one endowed with a vitality all its own that had just celebrated, at the end of June, the fiftieth anniversary of its labor union. The following September, at the International Labor Congress, it would relaunch the ideological premises of Christian neo-humanism.

The great popular demonstrations that accompanied the inauguration of the new basilica in honor of Saint Thérèse marked a moment of close friendship between the Chautemps–Blum government and the Holy See. The monastery was to be directed by the saint's sister, who, among other things, had important correspondence with both Tardini and Confalonieri on behalf of the pope. And the Lisieux

Carmel was certainly an important place for French Catholicism: the ecumenical journey of Abbé Coutrier found its inspiration there; it was the site of the reconciliation between Maurras and Rome; and it was there that Emmanuel Suhard organized the Mission de France seminary. It was a crossroads of intense French Catholic religiosity and had been the site of important spiritual retreats. It was at Lisieux that the first superior of the Mission de France, Reverend Louis Augros, asked Madeleine Delbrel to open a community linked to her spiritual mission: "Nous autres, gens des rues." Delbrel was the woman who perhaps best expressed a special French Catholic approach to the social question. In the very months of the "proffered hand," she and her group went to live in the most communist city in France, Ivry, stronghold of Thorez. She worked together with the communists, inspired by a concern for the workers that she shared with another woman, Simone Weil. Delbrel, however, did not come to the same gnostic conclusions of Weil, who returned to her life as an intellectual, but instead tied her destiny to the common people, following a spirit of sharing like that of Charles de Foucault. It was a vocation that contained many echoes of Thérèse de Lisieux:

> There are people whom God takes and sets apart. But there are others whom He leaves among the multitude, whom He does not withdraw from the world. These are people who do ordinary work and lead ordinary lives ... people whom you might encounter in any street ... people like us, people of the street. And we believe that this world where God has put us is where we will find our sanctity.[27]

Madeleine Delbrel was a figure on the front line and collaborated with communists in social activities without ever joining the party. And she was supported by the archbishop of Paris, who asked for her help at the beginning of the 1940s, at the Mission de France in Lisieux, to find more creative forms of evangelization for the new urban peripheries.

Given his great devotion to Thérèse de Lisieux, the pope himself would have liked to preside over the ceremony, but because of his weakness he stayed in Rome and delivered an important address over the radio. In the letter appointing Pacelli as his special legate, the pope used warm and sincere language to express his admiration for Thérèse, "a singular example of genuine and exquisite simplicity."[28]

Pacelli delivered two orations. The first, for the inauguration of the basilica, was strictly religious and referred to the continuity between the Old and New Testaments; it was essentially an invitation to pray for deliverance from present dangers. Pacelli's tone, bordering on pompous, highlighted the detachment of religious reflection, as though separate from current events. The second discourse, by contrast, was a passionate declaration that spoke directly to France:

> Here we find the soul of France herself, the soul of that daughter of the Church speaking to another soul. A France that marches forward, that advances in spite of everything, a France that . . . dies . . . we know the aspirations and the worries of France today. The present generation dreams of being a generation of pioneers . . . be true to your traditional vocation! Never has it been more important to take on your responsibilities; never before has it been more beautiful to respond . . . Do not let the gifts that God has given you be profaned in the service of some other mistaken ideal, inconsistent or less noble and less worthy of you.[29]

It was a great oration, a hymn to liberty, a triumphal speech that enthralled the French people. The newspapers spoke of jubilation, "an epoch-making speech." It was also an enormous personal success. Pacelli seemed direct, strong, sure of himself.

Following the lead of Tardini,[30] who urged that one not be misled by Pius XII's convoluted and ornate style, Chenaux has the following to say about the French orations: "These speeches, drafted with characteristic care and attention to detail, are never soothing. Their emphatic form and studied effect should not hide the urgency Cardinal Pacelli felt to get across a clear political and religious message to the public he was addressing."[31]

The point, however, was not so much that the excessively rhetorical nature of the argument might confuse the clarity of Pacelli's position. It was more one of substance. It was as if the religious dimension of the argument had become rarefied, almost detached from the political event. And so that event was confronted on both diplomatic and political levels without achieving communication between the two. During the French trip, this particular characteristic – product of both his own personality and his diplomatic role – seemed largely to have disappeared because his style was more direct. And yet on this occasion too the two levels, of political communication and religious reflection, remained side by side rather than combined.

He said of the communists: "with their passionate spirit and their warm and sincere hearts . . . their impetuosity and their social concerns, they risk going beyond that limit where truth slides into error."[32] This certainly was not an opening on Pacelli's part to the communists, but a way to understand their reasoning. It was not an a priori condemnation, though it was certainly a condemnation of communist atheism. And indeed various parties accused him of having given in to the Popular Front and so contributing to the encirclement of Germany. He rejected that accusation on 2 August 1937 in a letter to Faulhaber, Bertram, and Schulte in which he insisted that "there was no sort of ideological preclusion as regards National Socialism."

The German press was furious. Describing the mission as "grotesque," the *Börsen Zeitung* of Berlin wrote ironically on 14 July that, "in spite of the purely religious purpose of the trip, Pacelli had clearly spoken with Delbos of much else than the little saint of Lisieux," and concluded that praise from *L'Humanité* must have seemed to his eminence like the "kiss of Judas." The harshest condemnation, as always, came from *Der Angriff*, the Berlin Nazi paper. On 6 July, Goebbels's mouthpiece spoke of a true encirclement of Germany engineered by the Vatican, recalling Pizzardo's recent trip to England and Pacelli's to Lourdes in 1935. The secretary of state at once paraphrased and replied to these accusations:

> It is suggested that the words of the pope, even those emanating from the warmth of his paternal heart as supreme shepherd, are little more than a veil hiding political ends; that his most sublime thoughts, tinged with the mystery of faith, are nothing more than a pretense for achieving temporal goals. And the cult of Saint Thérèse of the baby Jesus, toward which the pope's personal devotion is well known – he has called it the "star of our papacy" – is a simple pretext for coming to an agreement with the Popular Front government in order to encircle Germany. Saint Thérèse as the mediator between communism and the Holy See? And yet the pope himself has declared communism "intrinsically perverse, so that no collaboration between Catholics and communism is admissible; and yet the first collaborator is his holiness's cardinal secretary of state?"[33]

It was a firm response and typical of the Church's relations with all governments, including those (and here the allusion to Germany is clear) "that under the veil of diplomatic relations are profoundly hostile to it": "And under that disguise they carry out a heedless and open attack against the Church, violent and insidious. These are cases when even many of her own children are surprised and tempted to view patience and tolerance as weakness."[34]

And yet, the note continues, the Church maintains these relations, and not only out of Christian charity but also, as in Germany, "to protect the religious interests of those of her children who are persecuted."[35] The conflict remained tense, as *Der Angriff* on 14 July described the "medieval" celebrations in Lisieux as an aggressive anti-German campaign and asked sarcastically if "the Moscow–France alliance of the Popular Front–Vatican had been finalized." And in case there were still any doubts, the Nazi paper added yet another accusation against the Holy See, namely that of being too soft on the Spanish Republicans.

French diplomacy instead underlined the importance that France attributed to Pacelli's visit, and expressed satisfaction over its success:

> Cardinal Pacelli came to France as a delegate for the inauguration of the Lisieux Basilica. His mission then was an exclusively ecclesiastical one. The French government sought to facilitate the visit and show due respect to the secretary of state of the Holy See . . . The very day of his arrival, before going to Lisieux, the cardinal secretary of state personally called on me and expressed his satisfaction at being in France.
>
> In his discourses, at Lisieux, Notre Dame, and the Hotel de Ville in Paris, he publicly expressed his admiration for our country. He acknowledged not only the official honors but also the warm reception that he received from crowds in both Lisieux and Paris.
>
> This visit and the demonstrations it inspired . . . show that one of the greatest spiritual powers of the world has ignored the campaigns being waged against France. That power has reaffirmed instead its faith in the French government and recognized the value of our democratic regime as a force for spiritual liberty.[36]

The reaction of international Catholic public opinion seemed to signal a change in the attitude of the Vatican relative to the global contest between fascism and democracy. In one example, the Peruvian embassy in Paris referred to the surprise of the conservative Peruvian Church, which was convinced "of the perfect coincidence of views between fascism and the Vatican":

> Who could imagine that the Rome–Berlin axis, a shield against communism for Europe and Western civilization, was not well regarded by the Church? . . . While the encyclical against communism was well publicized, the one on Nazism was virtually ignored. It was difficult to achieve that same end with regard to the ceremonies in Paris and Lisieux, though at first the papers limited themselves to brief descriptions without commentary. Nothing better expresses the general opinion than a piece that appeared in a satirical paper called *Cascabel*: "Certainly we must praise this rapprochement. Given the broad view displayed by the Church, we will not be surprised if the Third

International opens an office in Rome tomorrow and the Church sends a legate to Moscow."[37]

It was up to the organ of the local archbishop to explain that Pacelli's spectacular visit to France was testimony to the fact that "the Church does not engage in politics":

> If it were true that the Church engages in politics, it would logically find itself in conflict with France and not Germany, as the Church loves order and authority and strongly opposes communism. Nonetheless, its interests do not extend to the secular authority of governments, and so today it is a friend of the France of Chautemps and Blum and protests instead against the totalitarian abuse of the Nazis, who have proclaimed that "there is no other God than Hitler."[38]

A nocturnal meditation

On 6 November 1937, the pope confided to Pacelli a thought that had come to him "during a night without sleep, but still calm and relaxing." In his own words:

> With regard to the *main tendue*: We take that hand and offer ours in return with the prayer that it be accepted. For we do not want the one nor offer the other except insofar as we make our own, as we have both the right and the duty, the words of our Lord Jesus Christ: *venite a me, omnes qui laboratis et onerati estis, et ego reficiam vos*. We take your hands and offer ours in order to do good for you. This act represents no ideological commingling or confusion, as some are wont to say; it is not a betrayal of those principles that all the world recognizes as belonging to the Catholic Church. It is to do good for you. As this situation emerged in France, it might be best for the French episcopy to make a gesture of this sort. If they should do so, it would not be one bishopric praising another, but the Holy Father himself would respond: good, you have well interpreted the thought of the Holy Father as you have done nothing other than interpret the thought of Jesus Christ Himself. Jesus Christ came to this world to offer salvation and benefit to all. *Venite a me, omnes . . .*[39]

For the pope, who was ill and suffering from insomnia, night was a special time for prayer and spiritual concentration. This confession was the distillation of thoughts that had matured over time; it was a calm and clear reflection reached in the dead of night following a year during which his attention to the other had grown, starting with that which was closest at hand – for example, the Jews, with whom he had recognized a common spiritual heritage. It would seem that during 1937 the pope came to recognize that the true threat, or at least the most pressing one, was no longer communism but Nazism, "which had taken its place."

And yet once again the pope's meditations seem not to have found immediate expression in the politics of the Holy See. On 7 November, the day after his nocturnal meditation, the pope could read in the Catholic newspaper *Avvenire d'Italia* an article desired by Pacelli and Pizzardo that was a complete repudiation of the communist politics of the proffered hand. In this regard it cited *l'Humanité* as a reminder that the French Communist Party "was in fact nowhere near abandoning its defense of secularism or contemplating the abolition of this or that secular law." And while *Avvenire d'Italia* did not request that Catholics abandon any particular conviction, neither did it express any confidence in the left, concluding: "Catholics who support the communists or the radicals must realize that in doing so they are reinforcing that 'secularism' that is nothing less than a discreet synonym for atheist materialism."[40]

In order to strengthen this position, the article went so far as to cite the Nazi paper *Der Angriff*, which had sardonically asked how Thorez could still dare pursue the proffered hand six months after publication of *Divini Redemptoris*. According to the Nazi paper, the only possible explanation was that the encyclical was nothing more than a pretext for then issuing *Mit brennender Sorge*, an encyclical that was not "the condemnation of pagan heresy, but rather a political act against Germany." According to the Catholic paper, in turn, accepting the proffered hand would be a startling confirmation of the Nazi argument.[41]

This position apparently did not interrupt the path taken by the pope, if Pacelli's commentary is to be believed, on his long reflections on the origins of communism and its relationship with Christianity. An audience with Pacelli entitled "Catholics and Communists" contains ample discussion by the pope of communist reasoning on social justice and accepts the fact that the Church had benefited from serfdom. That discussion concludes of course with praise for the Christian model, because it is more equitable.[42]

A month after the pope's nocturnal meditation, the French communist leader forcefully renewed the "proffered hand." This time it was the bishop of Paris, Cardinal Verdier, who responded in his Christmas address, adopting a tone very different from that of the previous year:

The good physician never refuses to take the hand of the sick patient. We do not share your doctrines . . . Collaboration? Our work is suffused with spirituality, yours with materialism. If your gesture of the proffered hand signifies on your part the desire to know better your Christian brothers, to respect them better . . . the Church will not refuse to undertake its job of illumination.[43]

In this new and apparent willingness to listen, the French bishopric knew that it was not alone. Already on 10 November 1937, following a trip to Rome during which he had an audience with the pope and other French bishops on the very day after the nocturnal meditation, François-Jean-Marie Serrand, bishop of Saint-Brieuc, had gone to the Nuncio Valeri:

The prelate related to me that the Holy Father referred, among other things, to the question of collaboration proposed several times now by the French Communist Party. Mons. Serrand added that he and some of his colleagues noted with interest and surprise that, with regard to the "*main tendue*," the august Pope let it be understood that it might be inopportune to ignore wholly this oft-repeated invitation. It might instead be better to take up that invitation, "not of course so that we might be drawn toward the communists, but rather so that we can draw the communist proffered hand toward us."

The Holy Father then added that he had in mind to assign one of the most excellent bishops the task of exploring the possibility of a public declaration on the part of the French bishopric in this regard.[44]

Valeri sought to calm the enthusiasm of his interlocutor, suggesting "that it was perhaps better not to take the ideas expressed by the Holy Father too literally, as He likely put them forward as a simple and distant hypothesis meriting study, in the light, moreover, of His marvelous encyclicals, especially the *Divini Redemptoris*." If the French bishopric were ever to make an open statement on the "*main tendue*," it would do so with cautious circumspection, given "the serious consequences that could follow from a declaration that is not sufficiently clear and precise."[45]

The reply of the secretary of state to his nuncio in France was vexed. After at least five drafts, each one filled with revisions and corrections, the final version allowed that "the event related to Your Excellency by Mons. Serrand, bishop of Saint-Brieuc, has some foundation in truth in that, during an audience granted to several French bishops, the Holy Father opened his soul on the question of whether or not any consideration should be given to the offer – one cannot know how sincere it may be – of the *'main tendue.'*" Pacelli, however, is clear that "it was not a case of a definite proposal – the Holy Father is very far from that – but rather a simple thought inspired by the desire to open the way to the wellbeing which the Church offers to souls who have been deceived by communist error." This cautious text is a perfect example of the constant need felt by Pacelli to soften the initiatives of Pius XI: "The Holy Father knows well that this is a delicate matter and must be studied with the greatest calm and without taking rash measures, thinking only of the glory of God, the honor of the Church, and the salvation of human souls."[46]

The pope, however, was not offering a generic formula suitable for any occasion, but was instead grappling with a spiritual distinction, as the secretary of state himself was forced to admit:

> As pastor to all the faithful He hopes that the day will not come when He can be reproached for not having seized a favorable opportunity by rejecting a hand offered to Him. Indeed the Holy Father maintains that one does not have the right to deny the possibility of good faith behind an offer of this sort, and so He is obliged to keep alive the possibility of one day taking advantage of such an offer for the good of souls.[47]

Certainly one could not conclude "that the Church was somehow revoking the condemnation of atheist communism." And while the pope proposed a comparison between the social doctrines of the Church and the less radical versions of socialism, which were the true novelty of this period and so the forces which the pope sought to understand, Pacelli's reading continued to be weighed down with caution and vagueness:

> The Holy Father thinks, for example, that, should favorable conditions prevail for an initiative of this sort, the French bishops might ask those who are proffering their hand to tell us clearly in what manner we might take that hand that they offer us and offer ours in return in order to do good for them and with them on behalf of society . . . An opportunity might present itself, for example, with regard to some work of charity . . . In such a circumstance, we must demonstrate even more clearly and forcefully than in the past that the Catholic Church has always been the first to address social ills, even when civil society has remained indifferent, and it has done so not out of vain ostentation but to carry out the teachings of its Divine Founder, to Whom the communists themselves often appeal. So if the communists offer the Church an opportunity to reduce a social ill without destroying among

the masses the principles of morality and faith, then Catholics will be happy to find a way to carry out the evangelical teachings of their Divine Master.[48]

With his usual pragmatic and Lombard approach, attentive to the economic ramifications, "regarding those works of charity and assistance that the bishops may propose, the Holy Father makes available to the French bishopric the sum of one million francs."

In this way, the adoption of a shared program would not involve any sort of renunciation of "the principles of order and social justice proclaimed by the Catholic Church, especially in recent times." Instead, "any good that can be derived from the so-called conquests of socialism" would redound to the Catholic doctrine. Relevant in this regard are the broad observations in the Pacelli notebooks on the Christian origins of socialism, viewed as a grand heresy, and the benefit to be derived from making the socialists understand the possible common rationale for social justice.[49] According to Pacelli, the pope's initiative also reflected the fear that the Church might be viewed as not taking seriously a proposed collaboration that could contribute to the common good.

The pope shared none of this caution over the possibility of meeting over a concrete plan; Pacelli himself mentioned that the pope had discussed this possibility with Cardinal Achille Liénart, authorizing him to speak with Cardinal Jean Verdier. And so the secretary of state was forced, *malgré lui*, to authorize his nuncio to pursue this possibility, while continuing to urge prudence: "make the necessary contacts with the most excellent cardinal archbishop in order to study what might be done in the sense described above and with the necessary caution."[50]

A disconcerting reflection

The various drafts prepared by the secretary of state for the nuncio and the French bishops recount other interesting observations made by the pope – for example, an analogy between the "proffered hand" and the dissident churches:

> The Church finds itself today in a situation that bears comparison with the proposals made by the dissident churches in hopes of obtaining collaboration and achieving reunification. Certainly that invitation was a sincere one on the part of many, and the Church itself hoped to see the words of Our Lord realized: a single fold, a single God.[51]

As in this latter case, so with the communists good faith and sincerity were not enough, as it was important that the Church should not be "unjustly lowered to the level of having a sociology that derives from communist doctrine adopted to the Credo":

> So the proffered hand cannot be understood as an act by which the communists draw the Catholics into their ambit, but rather as an expression of the need felt by the communists to seek aid from the Catholics of a sort they cannot derive from their own philosophical doctrine. Nonetheless, just as the Church did not refuse contact with the dissident Christians, while never varying from the fundamental principle that it alone possessed the truth, so it is not out of the question that the Catholics may make contact and attempt to dialog with the communists.[52]

This draft seems to reflect more closely the thought of Ratti, in that the Church must respond to both the material and the spiritual suffering of humanity. It continues: "the Church no longer has the freedom it once had in charitable works; it cannot reject other means, providing they are not intrinsically evil, as these are secondary questions relative to the ends to be achieved."

The other times to which the pope refers are clear from the notes on the audience in which he speaks of primitive Christianity, the first centuries of the Church, the common property of the early Christian communities, and the inspiration that communist utopianism has taken from that example. He may also refer, however, to more recent times and the strictures imposed on the Church by the growth of the modern state and its intervention in the social realm – the nostalgia then of a new social Christianity combined with an acute sense of the limits imposed upon the space in which the Church might operate by secularism, on the one hand, and totalitarianism, on the other. In these last years of his life, the pope seemed concerned more with the original message of the Church, with its spiritual mission, than with the triumphant design of Christ the King. To my mind, the distinction between the means and the ends of communism should be read in this regard: not simply as the concern that Catholics not be manipulated by the communists – a defensive attitude that clearly inspired Pacelli's comments to Nuncio Valeri and the other bishops – but rather as a worry that the Church might lose a great opportunity to demonstrate its adherence to the gospel:

> The Church cannot remain indifferent to social suffering, to the evils that afflict humanity. If you offer it the means more easily to

reduce that suffering, to combat injustice, then it is happy in that way to practice its own principles of charity and justice. Just as in ancient times it did not hesitate to adapt pagan buildings to the needs of its own cult and Roman law to the needs of its life, so today it is willing to practice its charitable work in the forms imposed by modern life. The proffered hand can be contemplated in this regard, and the episcopacy would do well to study it so that, when the opportune moment presents itself, one bishop or another can respond with authority to those who repeatedly put forward the proffered hand.[53]

The weeks between 1937 and 1938 signaled a true *Wendepunkt*. In the allocution for the consistory of 13 December, the pope issued condemnations at once of what had happened in Germany, of the impious atrocities committed in Russia, and for the sad fate of Catholic Spain. But in the traditional Christmas Eve allocution to the College of Cardinals, the strongest attack was against Germany, a sign that Nazism had replaced communism as his greatest concern.

It was in this climate that Verdier, the archbishop of Paris, delivered a discourse on 10 December that exalted the value of the individual and admitted a partial concordance between this Christian premise and the Declaration of the Rights of Man of 1789. A few days before Christmas, Verdier spoke to the faithful of his recent meeting with the pope, who had confided to him that following his illness, an entirely new experience for him, he felt greater compassion for human suffering of all sorts, including that of brothers separated from the Church – as, for example, Muslims who appealed to him for help. Moreover, the pope added, "Men very far from us, in our own country, proffer their hand to us." It is almost an echo of the evangelical call: "Come unto me, all ye that labor and are heavy laden, and I will give you rest" – the "misereor super turbam" of Christ as practiced by the pope.[54]

In his Christmas message, Cardinal Verdier, while softening the pope's more explicit and passionate affirmations relative to the proffered hand, nonetheless echoed this spirit:

The good doctor does not refuse the hand that reaches out to him in pain. The Good Shepherd of the Gospel worries more about the one lost sheep than about the other ninety-nine who have remained in the fold. To those who call to us from far away, we must respond: "We salute you in the name of Christ who loves you. But tell us what you want, what you expect from us."[55]

82

While remaining more cautious than Ratti, the discourse of Verdier reveals how much his talk with the pope influenced him and how much his attitude had changed from that of a couple of weeks earlier. As recently as early December he had expressed perplexity regarding overtures made by the communist secretary, who himself risked a degree of isolation among his comrades; the nuncio wrote to Pacelli: "I don't believe that Monsieur Thorez has as important a role in the party as is normally ascribed to him, and for that reason I think it would be better to drop the question of the proffered hand."[56]

The Popular Front press praised the cardinal's discourse – "taking him for one of our own" – while the communist *l'Humanité* did not fail to note an element of caution greater than that of the pope. On Christmas Eve 1937, *L'aube* celebrated the moving spiritual message of the pope, describing as reductive and misleading any attempt to read it as a political statement: "The pope is thinking only of those souls that have come from so far away . . . we are witnessing one of the greatest acts of concrete apology that history has ever known . . . Charity is the greatest tool for bringing men to the truth."[57]

A note of Tardini from 20 December attenuates and modifies the sense of Verdier's discourse regarding a methodological premise:

> 1. The argument is highly delicate, as the communists have already clearly explained the meaning of the *main tendue*, asserting that they intend to leave their principles and ideologies unchanged. 2. Given that, the words of the Holy Father could be understood by anti-communists (not only in France but especially in Germany and Italy) as something approaching collaboration with the communists. 3. In that regard we would suggest certain corrections.[58]

The first correction would be simply to ignore the words of the pope.

L'Osservatore Romano on 29 December claimed that there had been no change in the positions of the Holy See. Intransigence in the face of communism remained, and, recalling the anti-communist encyclical, the prohibition against any sort of collaboration with the communists, even of a practical nature, was reaffirmed. The pope then had simply appealed to those who had strayed that they should correct their ways.

The piece in the Vatican paper derived in part from a note sent on the 26th from Tardini to its director:

> I have asked Count Dalla Torre to prepare a clearly stated article to explain that the pope has not changed his position. The encyclical and many other declarations remain in force. And if today he opens his

arms to these errant children, he does not rescind his condemnation of their errors; nor does he admit that collaboration he has already declared inadmissible.[59]

The note included an outline of the article that restated the essence of *Divini Redemptoris*: "Communism is intrinsically perverse and nowhere can collaboration be permitted between it and those who want to save Christian civilization." It is not only in the cultural realm that collaboration with the communists is forbidden, but "even in the social realm, as attaching a materialist identity to social assistance would give it a totally different spirit." One can instead collaborate with the governing authority, even if communist: "If the established authority, with which collaboration is necessary, happens to be communist, then this calls for special caution and reserve. 'Interficite errores, sed diligetis errantes (Saint Augustine).' That collaboration then is allowable, indeed necessary, for a Christian . . . But charitable works should be directed at individuals (even if in practice they gather in the masses)." Never to be allowed, however, is "collaboration with a communist entity *qua talis*; even if the individuals involved act in good faith, it must be absolutely denied to the various communist organizations." It was an appeal for prudence, then, in using expressions that could be misunderstood; the language of *l'Humanité* is cited as an example of political distortion and manipulation of the pope's words.

Whatever we are to make of all this caution, Catholic anti-communism was strictly religious. The papers of the French nunciature include many examples of caution and calls for prudence by Pacelli, Tardini, Verdier, the nuncio, and other unidentified hands. To take one example of many:

> To accept the proffered hand confounds our principles. It is impossible that those who say "there is no soul" can think in the same way as those who say "there is a soul." The pope has not said this and never will; indeed he cannot say it. If he were to say it he would no longer be pope and head of the Church, because he would be an apostate and no longer a member of the Church.

The pope then, according to the "explanation" given for his scandalous statements, had made these "overtures" only because required to do so by his position and not out of true conviction.

In a 29 December report in which the nuncio describes in detail the internal divisions and political distress among Catholics caused by the pope's statements, there is also a hand-written note by Tardini dated 27 December: "Praise the nuncio. It is clear that the Holy Father neither contradicts himself nor changes his position . . . The nuncio puts it well . . . Today there will be an article in OR to straighten out the situation." Referring to the issues raised by the director of *L'Osservatore Romano*, he added in parentheses a remark typical of his style: "(providing that Count Dalla Torre does not increase . . . the confusion)."

But it was the secretary of state himself who replied to the nuncio on 21 December with a telegram emphasizing the importance and urgent need for a reply:

> In conformity with the agreement taken relative to your note, please communicate to his excellency the cardinal archbishop that, in accordance with the desires of his Holiness, it is important to emphasize the inevitable intransigence regarding principles and to say that what you have communicated "is the sense of the words of the Holy Father, as you were able to understand them in a confidential conversation."

Apprehension grew even in protestant quarters, as noted by the Swiss nuncio Filippo Bernardini:

> I would go so far as to say that the *main tendue* is regarded with anxiety in protestant circles . . . and the painful impression created by the declarations of Cardinal Verdier . . . [was] fear that an agreement between us and the communists was not only possible but perhaps even desirable . . . Happily the OR article of the 29th has eliminated all doubts.[60]

And so the openness to dialog that grew out of the pope's purely spiritual concerns and that served him as a guide to illuminate the terrible events gathering on the horizon was buried in a flurry of caution and fear.

— 4 —

SPAIN AND THE CRUSADE

His Holiness ardently desires that Generalissimo Franco and his government understand how profoundly saddened he is by the Spanish–German cultural accord that has just been signed. It is an exceptionally grave accord as it opens the door to Nazi ideological propaganda.

Maglione to Yanguas Messía, ambassador of the National
Government of Francisco Franco to the Holy See

The Spanish Civil War

"The Spanish Civil War is a great massacre. All of the errors of Europe are gathered and putrefying here, the mortal suffering that Europe attempts to regurgitate amid frightening convulsions."[1] So wrote George Bernanos in the harshest Catholic denunciation of the Spanish Civil War. That conflict took on immediately an enormous political and symbolic significance as a contest between fascism and anti-fascism, between "reds" and "blacks." A fierce religious conflict was at the heart of the bloody civil war, and it witnessed a true popular "anti-religious obsession" against the priests, thousands of whom died as victims of the violence directed against a Catholic Church considered an accomplice of longstanding oppression. According to the well-known expression of Jemolo, it was "easy to give it the aspect of a crusade: for the faith of the fathers, for the freedom of the Church, against the emissaries of Moscow. There is no reserve here among the clergy; all bless the legionaries."[2] And yet, more interested in condemning "communist violence" than supporting Francoism, the Vatican itself did not initially cast the conflict as a religious crusade. Only after 1938–9 would it become – much more

86

so than the Mexican case – "the martial myth of the Christian militia," in the double sense of Catholic martyrdom in a war fought for the victory of Christ the King and of the possible installation of a Catholic totalitarian regime, in which direction fascist Italy too should be urged in the context of a European bloc of confessional states.[3] Once again, however, the position of the Holy See during this radical crisis must be reconstructed with great care, taking the trouble to sort out the many subtleties that argue against oversimplification.[4]

In the first place, we have to recognize that the Church for a time faced an anomalous situation, as the Holy See continued to maintain relationships with the "official government," namely the Republicans, and not with the Nationalists led by Franco.

On 4 June, just a few weeks before the attempted *coup d'état* by the "four generals," and purely by coincidence, there was a turnover at the Madrid nunciature: Nuncio Federico Tedeschini was nominated cardinal and so called back to Rome. He left the Spanish capital on 11 June and was replaced by Filippo Cortesi; however, because of the military uprising of 18 July Cortesi was unable to take up his post and on 24 December went to an entirely different one, as apostolic nuncio in Poland. Following the departure of Tedeschini, Monsignor Silvio Sericano took over in Madrid and handled relations with the regular government, as chargé d'affaires, until 4 November.

From a diplomatic perspective, the situation was resolved only on 16 May 1938, when Gaetano Cicognani was nominated as apostolic nuncio to the Nationalist government in Salamanca. The pope had great respect for Cicognani, and, following diplomatic appointments in Bolivia, Peru, and Austria (whence he left following the *Anschluß*), Pius XI decided to entrust him with the task of representing the Vatican in Spain, one of the most difficult appointments at the time.

The other protagonists in this period, the most representative members of the Spanish episcopacy, had complex backgrounds riven by conflicts of jurisdiction and profound political and ecclesiastic differences. Cardinal Francesc Vidal i Barraquer, archbishop of Tarragona and president of the Conference of the Metropolitan Bishops from 1931 to 1933, was openly liberal. Cardinal Isidro Gomá y Tomás became archbishop of Toledo and primate of Spain starting in 1933 following the forced retirement of Cardinal Pedro Segura, who was known for his strongly reactionary and monarchist positions, positions in part passed on to his successor. That appointment came after a year and a half of hesitation on the part of the Vatican; it was a difficult situation that divided the Curia between the supporters of the two bishops. The Jesuit superior general, Ledóchowski, not surprisingly took Gomá's side against the cardinal of Tarragona. The differences between Gomá and Vidal i Barraquer were finally resolved on 16 December 1935, when Cardinal Pizzardo, prefect of the Congregation for Extraordinary Ecclesiastic Affairs, informed the nuncio that the Holy See supported Gomá's claims regarding the integral nature of his functions in Toledo.

Such was the unpromising background against which the Spanish Church faced the military uprising of 18 July 1936. The diplomatic situation, as we have already mentioned, was complicated and in a sense paradoxical. In spite of the fact that thousands of religious were massacred in the zones occupied by the Republicans, the Vatican could not end diplomatic relations with what was still the legitimate government. It was an anomalous situation in the diplomatic relations of the Holy See, which as a rule never withdraws its nuncio from any country unless forced to do so, as in the case of the Soviet Union. Clearly, though, relations were strained, and in August the secretary of state called for condemnation of anti-religious atrocities in the pages of *L'Osservatore Romano*.

The National-Catholic ideology of the crusade was not long in asserting itself, and already in November 1936 the Catholic-friendly government of Burgos was pressuring the Holy See to provide it with some sort of legitimization. Pressure came from within the episcopacy as well: Cardinal Gomá y Tomás did not wait more than twenty days following the failed military *coup d'état* before openly supporting the *Alzamiento nacional*, certain that he was expressing a fundamental choice on the part of the Vatican, namely that of promoting a grand anti-communist campaign among the European powers.

The pope viewed with dismay the developments in Spain and the urgent need of the Spanish episcopacy to side with Franco, as though stunned by the combined seriousness and anomaly of events. Pacelli's audiences reveal a pope in serious difficulty, waiting several weeks before issuing a statement on Spain and constrained it seems to protect his "people" from persecution and violence. Following an initial complaint from the secretary of state to the ambassador of the Spanish Republic on 31 July, the pope himself sent a note to the Madrid government protesting the violence. The month of August was filled with questions from the pope about a situation whose gravity he seems not to have fully grasped, leaving him shocked by the growing violence and atrocities, as if paralyzed by events. Any response seemed to him inadequate to the drama being played out. It was in fact Pacelli who urged him on while Ratti drew back:

For the third time I have proposed to the Holy Father an expiatory and protective act in response to the sad events in Spain, as many others have suggested. The Holy Father still has not accepted that proposal. He did approve the official article prepared by the secretary of state that appeared in *OR* yesterday evening, "The Holy See and the Religious Situation in Spain."[5]

This sensation of uncertainty, not to say confusion, finds confirmation in the long letter Pius XI sent to the Spanish bishops that same month. In it the pope confessed that "We did not understand that the Spanish Civil War would be so protracted and ferocious." He seemed disarmed once again on 25 August with Pacelli: "Call out to the world for prayers? Prayers directed at whom? How and in what sense?"[6]

In those same days, the British diplomat Sir D'Arcy Osborne initiated a series of requests destined to continue throughout the conflict, in which he asked the pope to "use his influence to restrain the Nationalists and prevent acts of violence and brutality" – given that, as recently reported in *L'Osservatore Romano*, "whichever side wins in Spain, its government will not be recognized on a par with other European governments if its supporters are guilty of atrocities." The pope, however, "replied indignantly to the suggestion that Nationalists could be compared to the assassins and iconoclasts against whom they were fighting."[7] The Basque clergy complicated the situation still more and called to Rome for help from the first weeks of the conflict. For the time being, all that came from St Peter's were calls to stop the violence and killing; as Pius XI put it to a group of French Franciscans on 4 September: "the horrible fratricide, the sacrilege, the horrible torment and destruction."[8]

It was not until 14 September that the pope made a decisive statement. It came during an address to 500 Spanish refugees; Pacelli, as is well known, would refer to them as "martyrs of the faith," victims of a minority that had rebelled against God and the Church. The pope used similar terminology in protesting the anti-clerical slaughter: "All that which is most human, most divine; sacred persons, things, and institutions; invaluable and irreplaceable treasures of faith and Christian piety and of civilization and art . . . indeed even the sacred and solemn silence of the tomb; all this has been attacked, disfigured, and destroyed."[9]

This was his first public statement on the Spanish Civil War; the text was prepared by Pacelli,[10] translated into Spanish and read by the pope, who on this occasion stuck to the written text rather than improvising. Francoist propaganda obviously made the most of the address and published it widely, leaving out the references to Nationalist excesses and also the appeal for charity with which the pope concluded. In that conclusion he used language of intense spirituality in reference to the perpetrators just denounced: "Love them, love them with a special love, compassionate and charitable, love them. We cannot do otherwise, pray for them." This sort of charity cannot have pleased the Nationalists much, and in fact they censored it in their press.

Pius XI to Pacelli: "No, cardinal, not that"

Commitment of Basque Catholics to the democratic ideal, even if only among a minority fringe, put the Vatican in a difficult situation, particularly with regard to those priests who favored the autonomist cause and were shot in October and November 1936.

It was in these same weeks that a sort of surrogate Spanish Civil War was taking place in what was in a sense the background to the conflict, namely France of the Popular Front. Beyond the Pyrenees, the Spanish Civil War engaged and in some cases overwhelmed the full political spectrum, including Catholics. News of the Francoist *limpieza* and photos of armed rebels blessed by Catholic priests tempered the indignation felt regarding persecution of the clergy. There emerged a democratic Catholic position perhaps best expressed in the words on 8 October of the exile Luigi Sturzo; he asked the Church, as it was not a party to the conflict, not to undertake any sort of crusade or holy war. Or again in the words of Bernanos: "There are certainly too many Catholics in France who approve of and glorify the terrorist methods employed with brutal efficiency in Spain and also in Austria."[11] Or yet again in the pages of *Esprit*: "No, neither Catholics, nor men of the Church, nor the ecclesiastical authorities were justified in throwing their support behind this illegal and bloody revolt."[12]

This humanitarian revulsion may have played a role in delaying recognition of the future Spanish *caudillo* and so may explain why, in spite of the persecution of his Church during the terrible summer of 1936, the pope waited as long as he did to issue a statement approving of the rebel junta, though of course he also continued to be blocked by the maintenance of relations with the legitimate Republican government. With the approval of Pius XI, Pacelli continued to urge his Francoist cardinal of the first hour – the bishop of Toledo, who had openly sided with the rebels from the first days of the *pronunciamiento* – to achieve some sort of moderation of Francoist excesses, especially with regard to the Basque Catholics, who had opposed the advance of the armed rebels from spring 1937. Gomá in fact refused a proposal that Pacelli had sent to him on 10 February 1937 for an episcopal document on the whole situation, as he deemed it too ambiguous and non-committal. The Spanish cardinal wanted a clear statement to the bishops supporting a crusade. Pacelli took note and carefully put off making any clear choice.[13]

It was Franco himself who came quickly to the point when he encountered Cardinal Gomá on 10 May 1937 and asked that the Vatican cease vacillating and make a tangible gesture – for example, a collective pastoral favoring the Nationalists. Gomá enthusiastically took up the proposal, in spite of the firm opposition of Vidal i Barraquer, and obtained the endorsement of almost all the Spanish bishops. On 25 June, Gomá informed the secretary of state of the imminent publication of an episcopal letter on 1 July 1937. Although calm in tone and avoiding rhetorical excess, the "collective letter of the Spanish bishops to bishops throughout the world" represented a clear choice in favor of the Nationalist movement, in which, "whatever may be the human defects, we can identify an effort to consolidate the traditional Spanish and Christian spirit."[14] But the pope remained resistant and rejected the repeated request of Pacelli to publish the document in the *Acta Apostolicae Sedis*: "No, cardinal, not that."[15]

At the end of 1936, Pius XI proposed that Galeazzo Ciano, Mussolini's foreign minister, be enlisted to bring Franco to a more reasonable position relative to the Basques; he said as much in an audience with Pacelli on 20 December: "Since if we say: you are Catholics, Catholics, Catholics. They will continue to reply: we are Basques, Basques, Basques. We need certain information and guarantees; we don't want to be the ones to pull the chestnuts out of the fire. Then we will be able to say to the good Basques: we ask much of you."[16]

The pope, however, continued to be tormented by the urge to remain impartial during these weeks and to engage the other side in a possible negotiation. Just two days later, he wondered if there might be some "father or preacher" able to invoke the threat of communism and so dislodge the stubborn republicanism of the Basques:

> We need to make the Basques understand that, even if they are obliged to sacrifice some of their autonomist goals, it might be well to make that sacrifice rather than fall victim to the reds, to sacrifice far more

to the Bolsheviks by turning the Basque region into a fulcrum for Bolshevik propaganda and so a danger to all the West. We need to explore what effect the possible involvement of the Holy See might have on the people there.[17]

Meanwhile, Cardinal Gomá worked ably and discreetly on behalf of Franco, both among the representatives of the Secretariat of State, such as Pizzardo and Tardini, and, encountering less resistance, with the superior general of the Jesuits. The cardinal's efforts paid off, and already on 19 December 1936 the Holy See appointed Gomá himself as its delegate to Franco's Junta of National Defense, the first sign of improving relationships with the future *caudillo*. Pacelli in fact sent him the Vatican's regards and wished him a "rapid and total" victory.

Franco, however, did not achieve victory in the Basque regions thanks to the improbable mediation of the Vatican, but rather by force of arms employed in a way that stunned a world still not accustomed to the aerial bombardment of defenseless populations. When, on 26 April 1937, Guernica was destroyed by the Nazi *Luftwaffe*, even French Catholic opinion was outraged and expressed compassion for the victims. After having criticized "the indifference of too many Christians in the face of the suffering of their Basque brothers," *L'aube*, together with *Vie Catholique*, encouraged readers to sign an appeal drafted by Mounier – and supported by figures of the caliber of Mauriac, Maritain, Madaule, Gabriel Marcel, Claude Bourdet, and others – "that the world be spared the merciless massacre of Christian populations." Accused by the French right of siding with international masonry, these Catholic papers defended their orthodoxy by citing at length Pius XI's statements on peace.[18]

In those tragic days following Easter, twenty Basque priests wrote to the pope asking that the horror of Guernica be publicly condemned, and two of them were received in Rome by a frosty Pacelli. These were only a few of the protests directed to the Holy See, but, with the collapse of the Republican defenses at the end of the spring, military resolution of the "Basque problem" sped up the *rapprochement* between the Vatican and Franco. During the summer and autumn of 1937 Negrín's Republican government sought to repair relations with the Church by re-establishing a minimum of religious freedom. To this end, several attempts at mediation were undertaken: Josep María Trias i Peitx, general secretary of the Democratic Union of Catalonia, a progressive Christian democratic party, met with Jacques Maritain, Marc Sangnier, and, with some difficulty, Cardinal Vidal i Barraquer, who hoped for the intervention of Cardinal Verdier.

The cardinal of Paris who at first seemed interested in seeking media-tion with the Basque government, subsequently declared instead his agreement with Gomá. In spite of his apparent liberalism, Verdier had in fact communicated to the Spanish primate his approval of the collective letter of the Spanish episcopate in a note dated 7 September 1937.[19]

Monsignor Antoniutti's fascination with Franco

Monsignor Ildebrando Antoniutti arrived in Spain on 25 July 1937, sent on an official mission to coordinate aid for Basque children who had been sent abroad, especially to Russia; it was a humanitar-ian mission close to the pope's heart and in which he took a per-sonal interest. He discussed it often with Pacelli, expressing concern and special insistence and making available large sums of money. Nonetheless, Antoniutti's primary task was to lay the groundwork for official recognition of the Franco regime, a regime for which he felt great sympathy.

Antoniutti was openly fascist, a position already made clear during his previous mission to Poland. He was a minor figure in the complex galaxy orchestrated by Cardinal Gomá, and, while he was not really up to the task assigned him, we explore Antoniutti's mission in some detail just the same, as the documentation of those first steps is now available.

At the end of July, even before being officially appointed as chargé d'affaires (a mission carefully documented in a two-volume diary), Antoniutti sent the secretary of state a lyrical account of his private meeting with Franco:

> The building's decor retains its ecclesiastical tone. A great crucifix dominates the entrance against the background of a national flag on which is written: *Por Dios y por la patria*. Religious paintings and portraits of bishops adorn the walls of the corridors and rooms through which soldiers and official pass with a martial air.
>
> The *generalissimo*, wearing his country uniform, received me in the great throne room. Here too there is a great crucifix on one side and a portrait of his holiness on the other. He came forward and kissed my ring . . . the svelte and agile figure of the general, his distinguished carriage, his gracious manners, his soft and calm voice disguised the warrior who has dominated Nationalist Spain. He described to me the evolution of the counter-attack: it is not a military movement but a religious one; it is a crusade to revitalize among the Spanish the ancient

93

and glorious Catholic traditions . . . When peace is re-established, we shall see much greater ruin wrought by the reds than is currently imagined . . . the general speaks with fervor; his large eyes and voice betray a strong inner sentiment. "No one – relayed the chargé d'affaires – has followed the events in Spain with greater concern than the holy father . . . now his holiness has sent me in his name to aid the return of many babies who were sent abroad and to help with other charitable initiatives to help the many victims of the war."[20]

The passionate defender of Catholic civilization and *hispanidad* was unable, however, even with a starstruck listener like Antoniutti, to hide his fierce hatred for the Basques, priests included: "The general told me that the military is sorely offended by these priests, and many must be punished."

On 4 August 1937 Franco was pleased by the formal recognition of his chargé d'affaires to the Holy See, the marqués di Aycinena. The Vatican had given Antoniutti the task of encouraging the general to take a more humanitarian approach and so facilitate return of those Basque children who had been evacuated in the face of the advancing Nationalist troops. Franco seemed touched by "this new proof of the Holy Father's benevolence" and commented to Antoniutti: "These children were torn from their homes and sent abroad under the flag of Moscow; it will be a great consolation for me to see them repatriated under the flag of the pope."[21]

Judging from Pacelli's notes of 15 August, the pope was much less enthusiastic than his chargé d'affaires:

He received with complacency the latest confirmation of General Franco's profoundly religious sentiments. Nor did he disguise his concern and skepticism for the tolerance those authorities have shown regarding certain erroneous doctrines and directives and the ease with which the much praised Generalissimo will lead Spain back to its religious traditions.[22]

The Francoist press accused the secretary of state of having come up with the idea for the address to the Spanish refugees. Pacelli replied with "displeasure and surprise," not so much "for my own poor self, who is of no importance," but rather for the inferences "relative to the Holy Father . . . who inspired by goodness and sentiment wrote himself the entire address to the refugees delivered at Castelgandolfo," offering a great example of compassion. To describe it as a "*discurso de vocablos de hielo* was not only false and unjust, but irreverent and ungrateful."[23]

94

On 23 September, Pacelli warned the Holy See's chargé d'affaires about Franco's sympathies for Nazism and his dangerous racist ideology, encouraging greater vigilance on Antoniutti's part. But nothing seemed to cool the monsignor's enthusiasm. On 9 October, after having met with Franco on the occasion of his official accreditation, Antoniutti sent a true paean to Franco, going so far as to laud the Spanish arms that had already saved Christianity once in the waters of Lepanto:

> Referring to the Feast of the Holy Rosary, the most Spanish of all holidays, and to the Battle of Lepanto, he added that the soldiers of the new Spain fought for those same ideals of the crusades, for God and country and in defense of Catholic civilization which is also Spanish civilization. This gesture, much hoped for by him and all Spaniards who fought to return the country to its Catholic traditions, had a special place is his Catholic and soldier's heart . . . and he claimed that this day was the finest his government had so far enjoyed . . . and he asked me to tell the pope that his only ambition is to free Spain of communism, the enemy of religion and the fatherland, and to establish a new order based on Christian doctrine.
>
> I must say that I am heartened in my mission by the fact that I am dealing with people who openly declare their Catholic faith.

In their discussion Franco seemed to make many concessions regarding the Basque clergy and emphasized the strategic nature of his ties to Germany: "Certain demonstrations of sympathy are directed at Germany as ally and not at its system of government . . . we must recognize the great debt we owe to Germany who came to our aid in this difficult moment of our national history; we have to take this into account."

Both the Spanish and French press read this accreditation for what it really was, the official recognition of Franco; as far as the newspapers were concerned, the Holy See had chosen sides. And yet, on 6 December 1937, Pacelli once again recommended to Antoniutti greater reserve in his relations with Franco:

> The august pope, while expressing his paternal pleasure regarding noble proposals of future relations between the Spanish state and the Church . . . after reading what your excellency wrote regarding the meeting with Franco, has ordered me to communicate to you that, in spite of the declarations of the general himself, it is not without "profound sadness" that he has learned of the distressing attitude of certain elements in the falangist party, and especially the mission of young

falangists sent to Germany to study German organization . . . a true danger for the Spain of tomorrow.

On Christmas Day 1937, Pacelli was praised by the pope for these invitations to caution and for his zeal in reminding the Francoist government "of the great dangers that it faces if it does not rapidly curb Nazi propaganda."

Recognition of the Franco government

During the consistorial allocution of 13 December, Pius XI resisted making a pronouncement on Spain, just as he had done over the previous months, and issued this controversial statement: "We perceive . . . that which is happening in Russia and that which is taking place in Germany as posing great dangers to Christian civilization. Meanwhile in Spain which is so dear to us, debate continues amidst sadness and a thousand tests; we hope for better days there."[24] Can we interpret these words of the pope as expressing hope for a Francoist victory? Or do they reflect instead a bid for a role as mediator between the two parties, as the French foreign minister seems to have thought. Speaking to the American ambassador in Paris a few weeks later, he said that he was certain that "the pope was ready to offer his mediation at any moment."[25] And the fact remains that, once the final obstacle to the abrogation of the anti-clerical laws of 1932 was overcome on 24 April 1938, Pacelli could telegraph Antoniutti:

> Given that the Holy Father has decided to nominate an apostolic nuncio to the national government in the person of Monsignor Gaetano Cicognani, previously apostolic nuncio to Austria, we request your evaluation. In recognition of the services rendered by you, the Holy Father is pleased to assign you to the important apostolic delegation in Canada. In transmitting to General Franco this benevolent resolution of the Holy Father, we ask that you also communicate the Holy Father's recommendation that the advancing troops avoid as much as possible destruction and killing, both out of a Christian sentiment of humanity and civilization and in the national interest.[26]

The trade-off of recognition for a more humanitarian approach, then, was a constant in the Vatican's approach. Requests like that sent by Pacelli on 14 August 1937 were frequent: "According to news we have received . . . the red government is prepared to exchange priests held in the Catalonian prisons for . . . a similar number of civilian prisoners held by the Nationalists. Please raise the issue with General Franco and explore those measures he deems possible and opportune."[27]

We find yet another index among the coded telegrams sent from Rome between 27 December 1937 and 16 June 1938: the largest number were messages from the pope asking for acts of clemency, commutation of death sentences, prisoner exchanges, and a reduction of the bombings of Barcelona in March, though the Paris nuncio on 22 March 1938 did suggest greater public condemnation of the bombings of Barcelona, rather than relying on silent condemnation, if only on humanitarian grounds.[28] Or again in early June, when the French and British governments called once more for the Vatican to intervene, the Holy See replied that it "had constantly exercised its influence over Franco to prevent indiscriminate bombing," though in order for that influence to have any effect it must be applied quietly and in a way that would be compromised by its joining with "other governments in these sorts of initiatives."[29]

The first weeks of winter 1937–8, as we have seen, were taken up with the failed attempt at mediation by Cardinals Verdier and Vidal i Barraquer. Shortly afterward the pope would suffer the indignity of seeing his *Mit brennender Sorge*, an encyclical close to his heart, suppressed by the Franco government. On 16 May 1938 a nuncio from the Holy See was finally appointed to the Franco government – not Monsignor Antoniutti, as Cardinal Gomá would have liked, but Monsignor Gaetano Cicognani, who would remain in Madrid till 1953.

While recognition of Franco's government undoubtedly aided the Nationalist cause, it did not signal the Holy See's encouragement of an alignment between Franco and the Axis. Indeed, it seems that the much hoped-for official presence at Burgos was used as much as possible to avoid just that development. That position helps to explain, for example, the great tension created by the Spanish–German accord signed in Burgos on 24 January 1939. In a meeting with José Yanguas Messía, Franco's ambassador to the Holy See, Maglione emphasized the pope's great indignation:

> His Holiness ardently desires that Generalissimo Franco and his government understand the pope's great displeasure over the recently signed Spanish–German cultural accord. It is an accord that obviously opens the door to Nazi ideological propaganda, filled as it is with a

pagan spirit, in a country so profoundly Catholic as Spain. The Holy Father considers this accord of exceptional gravity and expresses his great alarm and profound bitterness over what he views as a humiliation of the Spanish Catholic conscience.[30]

In order to avoid a rupture with the Vatican, Franco did not ratify the accord.

This was an important episode, the first serious dispute with Franco over his cultural affinity with Hitler (as opposed to their military cooperation). The pope, debilitated by his illness, emphasized this point and underlined the danger for youth given the planned exchanges with German schools and universities. These concerns were underestimated by the minister of education, Pedro Sáinz Rodríguez, a fervent and mystic Catholic who sponsored a reform of secondary education imbued with Catholic spirit and monarchism, tied to Spanish tradition and hostile to Germanophile falangist tendencies. Nuncio Cicognani invested no little effort and ability in emphasizing the danger of this pact – much more than a symbolic gesture – and indeed succeeded in seeing it postponed indefinitely. The pope played a passionate role, though the archive of the Cicognani nunciature is not yet available, and so we do not have access to the unpublished documents on this affair that would help to clarify his position.[31]

The Spanish Republic was ultimately defeated in April 1939, two months after Pius XI's death. On 16 April the new pope, Pius XII, delivered a radio message to Spain: "It is with great jubilation that we turn to you, beloved children of Catholic Spain, to express our paternal congratulations for the gifts of peace and victory with which God has crowned the Christian heroism of your faith and charity, displayed in your great and generous suffering."[32] Pius XII's emphatic blessing of Franco's victorious forces did much to dispel the diffidence he had inspired as secretary of state, when many of Franco's followers believed, probably incorrectly, that throughout the Civil War he had been the author of that moderate Vatican policy so obviously in contrast to the enthusiasm of the Spanish bishops.

In fact, all members of the Secretariat of State, though to differing degrees, expressed great caution on the question of supporting Franco in the early years of the Civil War. The newly available documentation, though incomplete regarding Spain, offers stark confirmation of Pius XI's hostility toward Franco, a leader for whom he felt no sympathy at all and from whom he felt ever more distant as the Nationalists moved ever closer to Hitler's Germany.[33]

Against secularism: the condemnation of Mexico

Proof that communism remained a deeply felt threat, one that dated back before its emergence in the heart of Europe, came from Mexico, a country that already at the turn of the century had declared anti-clericalism to be one of its constitutive elements. The specter of communism in Mexico in fact took the form of revolutionary radicalism and freemasonry, elements present in the first governments of the century and that reappeared in other moments in the country's history. At the beginning of the twentieth century, only a minority of the population – 70 per cent of which consisted of peasants – was anti-clerical, but it was an influential minority concentrated in the ruling class, as revealed by the historian who has studied the phenomenon most carefully.[34] Between 1914 and 1915, the attack on the Church was severe; the clergy was persecuted; all religious cults were banned; and Catholic schools were closed. It was in fact an anti-clericalism deriving not from Marxism and communism but rather from a deep-rooted hatred of the Church's excessive power; Pius XI, however, read Mexican anti-clericalism as a communist phenomenon.

During the presidency of Venustiano Carranza, the constitution of 1917 legalized this anti-Catholic fury that denied the Church all rights and activities. In an act of resistance, Catholics founded a "National League for the Defense of Religious Freedom." The Holy See attempted to keep a representative in Mexico in the person of Monsignor Filippi, but the apostolic delegate was expelled during the first year of Pius XI's papacy. In December 1924, a subsequent accord allowed for the sending of a second representative, Monsignor Serafino Cimino. But that was also the moment when President Plutarco Elías Calles came to power, a fierce opponent of the Church who responded to Catholic mobilization with a series of repressive laws. The conflict intensified as the government applied these laws, and Catholics resorted at times to violent resistance. In 1925, following a number of serious incidents, several Mexican bishops traveled to visit the pope, who in turn spoke of the Mexican situation in his consistorial allocution of 14 December 1925.[35]

At the beginning of the following year another harsh law was passed, and the pope responded with an apostolic letter to the Mexican episcopacy accusing the Mexican government of conducting "an ever more fierce war against the Catholic religion." He condemned the "schismatic sect," a reference to the National Church promoted by the government, and called on Catholics not to form a political party, but to engage in "religious, moral, intellectual, economic, and social action."[36]

Calles's response was harsher still, inspiring, on 31 July in Oaxaca, the *Revolución Cristera* (or *Cristiada*), the first armed Catholic revolt. Many priests fell between 1926 and 1929, as the movement led by the Catholic League took up arms. Its militants were known as *cristeros*, after their battle cry, "*Viva Cristo Rey*," and the crosses they wore; they came to form an armed militia numbering tens of thousands. The pope issued an encyclical praising the martyrs who had perished in the conflict and comparing them to the victims of the French Revolution, whom he had beatified a month previously in conjunction with condemnation of Action Française. The pope openly praised the Catholic resistance in Mexico, and the fact that he never publicly criticized the violence was interpreted as tacit approval.

Pius XI signed a first important accord in 1929, following installation of the new president, Emilio Portes Gil, in 1928. The compromise, which recognized the legitimacy of religious cults, satisfied neither the hard-line *cristeros*, who felt their sacrifice insufficiently rewarded, nor many government and masonic elements, who saw it as an excessive concession. The conflict continued, though less violently than before, and the pope regretted the failure to respect the accord in the encyclical *Acerba animi anxietudo* of 29 September 1932; in that document he called on Catholics to "defend the sacred rights of the Church," certainly not with violence but through Catholic Action. The government, however, read this as an incitement to revolt, and so for a third time the apostolic delegate, in this case Leopoldo Ruiz y Flóres, was expelled. The 1929 accord, the so-called *Arreglos*, was just the sort of compromise that found a place in the pope's politics of concordats, a measure accepted as a *modus vivendi* in order to avoid situations that might otherwise become ungovernable.

The policies of agricultural reform and literacy pursued by President Lázaro Cárdenas in the 1930s failed to meet the political and social expectations of the forces supporting the Mexican Catholic Church; and so the tensions of the previous decade persisted, if in a less acute form. Pius XI, in fact, followed the entire affair with great attention, including its most controversial and violent aspects.

The pope issued his encyclical *Firmissimam constantiam* in the same month, March 1937, as the encyclicals against communism and Nazism. In it he condemned the Mexican legislation. In a sense he also declared the armed resistance illegitimate, while limiting himself to a criticism of its effectiveness and pointing out that, other considerations aside, it had no chance of success. Events would prove Rome's estimation to be correct.

All of the pope's addresses linked the events in Mexico to those in Spain and Russia, as if they were all part of a coordinated plan on the part of the Communist International. Following a well-worn path, communism was seen as "intrinsically perverse" and bent on the violent persecution of the Church. And so the particular Mexican case, characterized by an anti-clericalism of heterodox origins, was put down entirely to a sort of meta-historical force of communism.

— 5 —

NAZISM AS PUBLIC ENEMY NUMBER ONE: PIUS XI AND HITLER

The nuncio should reply in no uncertain terms: anomalous situations call for anomalous remedies, Hitler is both head of state and head of the government.

Pius XI to Nuncio Orsenigo, 28 February 1936

Catholics and the rise of Hitler

Holy Father! As a daughter of the Hebrew people and, thanks to the grace of God, a daughter of the Catholic Church for the past eleven years, I am compelled to describe to the father of Christianity that which is worrying millions of Germans. Over the past weeks in Germany we have witnessed events and behavior that amount to a total disregard of justice and humanity, not to mention love of one's neighbor. For years now the National Socialist leaders have preached hatred of the Jews. Now that they have seized power and armed their followers – which include notable criminal elements – they are harvesting the fruit of the hatred they have sown . . . Their boycott – which denies individuals the possibility to engage in economic activities, denies them the dignity of citizens, and denies them their homeland – has led many to commit suicide. I myself know of five cases; and I am convinced that the phenomenon is widespread and will claim many more victims. One may claim that these unfortunates lacked the moral strength to endure their fate. But if the responsibility lies largely at the feet of those who pushed them to this act, it also falls to those who remain silent. All that which has happened and which is happening daily is carried out by a government that describes itself as "Christian." Not only the Jews but also thousands of faithful Catholics in Germany and, I believe, the entire world have been waiting

102

for weeks in the hope that the Church of Christ would make itself heard in condemning this abuse of the name of Jesus Christ.[1]

This is the first part of a letter sent to the pope by Edith Stein, a searing prophesy regarding the responsibility of those who remained silent, first of all the Church. It was an appeal unheeded. We know of its existence from the autobiography of the future saint,[2] and it has been possible to consult the letter itself since the opening in 2003 of the archives on Germany. It is a warning that weighs heavily on the memory of the Catholic Church to the present day.

Edith Stein's voice was joined by those of many others. It must not have seemed a particularly authoritative voice, coming as it did from a Jewish woman who had converted from atheism, a philosopher and mystic about to enter a Carmelite monastery – even if she was "a woman known throughout Catholic Germany and well regarded for her faith, the sanctity of her behavior, and for her learning,"[3] as the abbot of Beuron, Raphael Walzer, described her in a note that accompanied Stein's letter to the pope. Pacelli replied that he would certainly show it to the pope. But at that point the trail ends; nor are there further traces in the files of the Secretariat of State, save for the record of her book on Saint Thomas, sent as a gift to the pope.[4]

The letter Stein sent to Pius XI in April 1933 testifies to the fact that protests against the persecution of the German Jews were lodged immediately. In addition to Stein's letter, the files include the protests of Rabbi Zaccaria Schwarz and other Jewish "high notables." For Nazi anti-Semitism struck the Jews immediately, as soon as the *Ermächtigungsgesetz* was approved giving Hitler full powers without need to consult parliament. The boycott of economic activities and the expulsion from public offices of all non-Aryans started on 1 April 1933. The slow and inexorable escalation that would lead to the Nuremberg Laws of 1935, *Kristallnacht* of 1938, and the Final Solution of the 1940s had begun.

In spite of the growing electoral successes of the National Socialists, the German bishops continued to express their opposition, prohibiting Catholics from joining Hitler's party and Nazi militiamen from participating in religious ceremonies, including funerals and weddings, dressed in the party uniform. Documents from the Berlin nunciature provide ample testimony and note Hitler's growing annoyance; eventually he sent Göring to Rome to protest.[5] Yet in spite of episcopal opposition, support for Hitler increased even among Catholics. As the Berlin nuncio Cesare Orsenigo wrote: "the large number of transgressions leads us to wonder about the efficacy of episcopal injunctions among a population so fascinated with new ideas."[6] On 16 March 1933 the same nuncio reported on comments from the newspapers of 14 March regarding a coming together of Catholics and Hitler:

> I have to state that until now the relationship between the Center and the new government has not been at all tense. The Center continues its usual practices without encountering explicit opposition . . . While this does not represent the peace trumpeted by some newspapers, it does represent a promising truce. So the victors would like to see removed those obstacles that continue to prevent Catholics from participating in the new order with a clear conscience.[7]

On 26 April 1933 Hitler received a delegation of bishops, whom he reassured regarding his esteem for the Catholic Church and Christianity in general: without its solid base, "the German state is inconceivable both in its history and in its recent development."[8] According to the long audience the nuncio had with Pacelli, the German chancellor claimed to have developed a solid conviction:

> From his study of history he has come to the conclusion that Christianity, as embodied in the Christian churches of the past centuries, no longer has the strength and conviction to battle on its own the forces opposed to the state and to Christianity, and that since the Reformation it has lost the power to combat liberalism, socialism, Bolshevism solely with spiritual weapons. To his mind, it is in Spain that these ideas are borne out, as it hovers on the brink of Bolshevism, a threat also in Poland and Romania. At this point he referred to the audacity of Bolshevism in Germany, recalling the Reichstag fire and the 300,000 kilograms of stolen explosives of which only 30,000 have been recovered.[9]

Hitler declared himself a convinced supporter of the "profound sense of the Christian religion," sought to avoid conflicts between the various Christian denominations, and guaranteed the rights and liberty of the churches: "so they do not have to worry about their freedom." He emphasized the new Germany's interest in confessional schools: "As a statesman I have to say that I need men of faith. Dark clouds gather over Poland. We need soldiers who are believers because they make excellent soldiers . . . and so we will keep the confessional schools . . . naturally it is important that there also be teachers who are believers."[10] For this reason the Catholic youth organizations would remain intact, "providing they strive in their sphere to combat Marxism."[11]

His intransigent anti-Semitism was, moreover, another proof of his following the centuries-long teachings of the Church. Thanks to Hitler, the Church would finally be protected from the dangerous influence of the Jews:

> With regard to the Jewish question, he asserted that he considers the Jews to pose a threat; he recalled the attitude of the Church up to the year 1500 and deplored the fact that liberalism had overlooked this danger. He concluded that he views the members of that race as a threat to the state and to the Church and so he feels that, acting as he is, he renders a great service to Christianity.[12]

The nuncio and the bishops were reassured by Hitler's conciliatory gestures, focusing more on the evidence of a common sentiment than on the practical issues. That focus recalled the intersection of anti-Semitism and anti-Judaism that had profoundly marked the history of the Church, an intersection that made it difficult to distinguish the racial problem from the religious one, as both the German bishops and Rome claimed they wanted to do.

The famous sermons delivered by the cardinal of Munich for Advent reveal this inner conflict. They repeated the traditional distinction between the people of Israel before and after the coming of Christ: "If racial science, inherently neutral with regard to religion, incites instead a war against religion and undermines the foundations of Christianity . . . which is in turn condemned for its original link to pre-Christian Judaism, if stones are thrown against our Lord and Savior Himself . . . then the bishop cannot remain silent."[13]

Yet in practice, even Faulhaber had failed to take a clear position in reaction to the first measures taken against the Jews – a boycott of their economic activities and banishment from teaching posts and public offices. The bishops held that protection of the Jews was not for them a priority. And so, in April 1933, Cardinal Faulhaber stated that the Jews knew perfectly well how to protect themselves on their own, and that to expose oneself in support of them would give the government a good excuse *"um die Judenhetze in eine Jesuitenhetze umzubiegen"*:

> The measures taken against the Jews are not Christian, and every Christian, not simply every priest, should oppose them. The Catholic hierarchy, however, faces much more important problems. For Christianity in our country, schools, the maintenance of Christian

associations, and sterilization are still more important issues given that the Jews can defend themselves on their own. So we should avoid giving the government a reason turn its hatred against the Jews into hatred against the Jesuits.[14]

In spite of the fact that the episcopacy was internally divided on how to respond, the regime's anti-Semitism in the early 1930s "was taken as a given, considered part of an inevitable context, and so not amenable to opposition."[15]

It was institutional and governmental legitimacy that made things difficult for the Church. The fact that anti-Semitism was enshrined in the law of the state meant that any protest on the part of the Church could constitute meddling in the internal affairs of the state. On 8 April, Orsenigo telegraphed Pacelli: "The anti-Jewish battle took on government status yesterday. Intervention by the representative of the Holy See would constitute a protest against a law of the government." To de-legitimate the government amounted to striking a blow against Germany. The nuncio added that, given that "the Holy See did not formally protest against the anti-German propaganda of recent years, it cannot now give the impression of being more sensitive to the Jewish cause than to the German one."[16]

This is the first expression of the primary argument that would inspire the caution of many Vatican elements: to attack Hitler was to attack a legal government and the country it governed. In that regard, several years later the pope would start with the same premise and, communicating with his nuncio, come to precisely the opposite conclusion: "The nuncio should reply in no uncertain terms: anomalous situations call for anomalous remedies, Hitler is both head of state and head of the government, so he cannot be treated as having limited responsibility, like a king or a simple republican president."[17] There is good reason to question whether Nuncio Cesare Orsenigo was up to the difficult task he faced.[18] His first statements in this regard sound like a "preventive self-defense":

> The nuncio seems to avoid seeking a solution to these difficulties. He prefers immediately to alert the Holy See that eventual attempts to remove "state obstacles" are impossible and we should prepare for the worst. He seems concerned mostly to protect his own work, to avoid exposing himself to accusations of diplomatic incapacity, perhaps also to avoid the possibility of being replaced. He fears finding himself at the center of a conflict from which there is no escape.[19]

106

Beyond his personal limitations, what is most striking about Orsenigo's many reports to Pacelli is not so much his acquiescence relative to the German authorities, but rather a sort of vagueness, at once metaphor and metonym for the difficulties of the Church (and so not only his own) to judge, act, indeed even understand the importance of the evolution of events; that vagueness was evident first of all between 1930 and 1933, a period that witnessed the dissolution of German political Catholicism and then the rise to power of Hitler. One can clearly read the difficulty encountered in understanding the extraordinary and unprecedented events and interpreting them within the usual vocabulary of Vatican diplomacy, concerned first of all to maintain diplomatic relations and so unable to understand the exceptional nature of the "illegal legality."

In spite of Orsenigo's fidelity, thoroughness, and attention to detail, qualities valued by the pope, who specifically chose him for this post, we can nonetheless detect certain personal failings. More than once the pope had to instruct him to take a firmer line with the Nazis. It is hard not to compare him with his predecessor, Eugenio Pacelli, who was thrust by the Curia into the heart of a Europe at war.[20] In the heat of the moment, Pacelli, always diplomatic and prudent, quickly understood the crucial events taking place and intuitively worked on several different levels, making an alliance with the left in order not to marginalize the Catholics and their party. He became the champion of German unity without falling into the arms of the Nationalists, achieving important gains with his astute policy of the concordat. He displayed an ability and decisiveness not in keeping with his cautious and uncertain character and perhaps owing to an entourage of active *consiglieri* and informants who were well integrated into German political life – figures such as Matthias Erzberger. It was an entourage faithful to the rich political tradition of German Catholicism, the democratic and confessional tradition of the *Zentrum*, the oldest Catholic political party (model and inspiration for Luigi Sturzo's Popular Party).

As nuncio, Orsenigo inspired the opposite reaction; the tight network of relationships left behind by Pacelli was replaced by an inability to evaluate and communicate with the German interlocutors, who tended instead to obfuscate Orsenigo's ability to evaluate events and the issues they raised.[21] The silence of Vatican documents on the horror of *Kristallnacht* is striking. In his 15 November report, which arrived at the Secretariat of State on 19 November, Orsenigo described it simply as "anti-Semitic vandalism"; nor is there even a reference in the "Pacelli notebooks." According to the prefect of the Secret Archive, Sergio Pagano: "The Secretariat of State interpreted the Orsenigo report as closely related to actions taken against the Jews in Italy, and generally speaking the racial question in Germany was viewed in tandem with the racial question in Italy.[22] *Kristallnacht* was dealt with implicitly in the audiences referring to the Italian racial laws. Nor was it much help that, from the moment of his arrival, the new nuncio seemed victim of a solitude that rendered him little more than a gauge of the new and undeniable successes of the regime among Catholics, especially young Catholics, who welcomed the end of the old and drawn-out history of parliamentary politics. Hitler showed himself ever more conciliatory toward Catholicism while Bolshevism seemed ever more threatening.[23]

The tradition of Catholic anti-Judaism

Racism was of course firmly condemned; not so anti-Semitism, and still less anti-Judaism. From October 1933 to January–February 1934, for example, bishops and the Catholic press, not only in Germany, attacked the positions put forward in the *Mythus des XX. Jahrhunderts* by Alfred Rosenberg, leading Nazi theorist on anti-Semitism and proponent of a racist neo-paganism that ultimately targeted Christ Himself for His Jewishness. In another example, Cardinal Faulhaber of Munich, in his famous defense of the Old Testament delivered during Advent 1933, and to which we have already referred, confirmed that Catholic tradition of the previous half-century according to which religious, spiritual, and ethical anti-Semitism was legitimate and opportune; however, he condemned racist anti-Semitism.

The distinction is a subtle one. The anti-Jewish roots of anti-Semitism are continuously intertwined in the history of the Church, one conditioning the other, and it is truly difficult, if not impossible, to determine at each moment the degree to which anti-Semitism derived from the Church or from sources outside it – though it was of course always a current much influenced by the tradition of deicide.[24]

In 1928, five and a half years before the polemic with Rosenberg, Pius XI made the first significant and formal condemnation of anti-Semitism on the part of the Church. It occurred in the context of the suppression of the Amici Israel association and included explicit reference to anti-Semitism (as even *Mit brennender Sorge* did not).

Hubert Wolf has recently reconstructed the affair using documents from the Holy Office.[25] That reconstruction reveals a serious and political split within the Church; the climate of the late 1920s saw old prejudices existing side by side with calls for change and a decision in one direction balanced by one in the other. So, for example, condemnation of Action Française was followed by that of Amici Israel on 28 March 1928; the latter included the condemnation of anti-Semitism but not reform of the Good Friday liturgy, as proposed by the suppressed society, so that it would no longer include the famous and controversial phrase *"perfidis Judaeis."*

The Amici Israel association came into existence in February 1926. In opposition to the anti-Semitic spirit of Maurras, it sought to promote a new and loving attitude to Israel and the Jews, to leave off speaking of the people of the deicide. It was a new sentiment that sought to capture the heart of the ecclesiastic hierarchy, and in fact, after just one year of existence, it counted eighteen cardinals among its members as well as 200 archbishops and about 2,000 priests.

On 25 March 1928, the Congregation for the Doctrine of the Faith issued a decree ordering the suppression of the association[26] following its proposal to revise the Good Friday prayer by eliminating the term *"perfidis,"* applied to the Jews accused of deicide. The pope asked the Sacred Congregation of Rites to come up with a reform, and he put Schuster in charge of the issue. The reaction, however, was severe; opponents claimed that if they started reforming the liturgy there would be no stopping the process. Merry del Val, secretary of the Holy Office, registered his firmly contrary *Votum* on 7 March:

> This request put forward by the so-called Amici Israel strikes me as completely unacceptable, indeed even rash. We are dealing with ancient prayers and rites of the liturgy of the Church, a liturgy inspired and consecrated for centuries that includes condemnation of the rebellion and betrayal perpetrated by the chosen people who were at once unfaithful and deicide . . . I would hope that these Amici Israel would not fall into a trap laid by the Jews themselves, who insinuate themselves throughout modern society and seek with whatever means to minimize the memory of their history and take advantage of the good will of Christians.[27]

On 8 March the pope accepted the findings of the Holy Office, though the *Votum* caused him a "feeling of pain."[28] He asked that justification for the decree be presented with great care in order to avoid accusations of anti-Semitism, but admitted that he could not approve "initiatives contrary to the universal liturgical tradition." He expressly asked that the following passage be added: "Just as the Holy See condemns hatred and animosity between peoples, so must it above all condemn hatred against a people already chosen by God, namely that hatred that today is commonly referred to as anti-Semitism."[29] It was a clear resolution, even if, as has been noted, "the condemnation of anti-Semitism was not so global as it seemed at first sight. It was in fact hatred that was condemned, as emerges when entering into the merits of both the doctrinal and ideological bases and political motivations for anti-Semitism."[30] As Father Enrico Rosa would further specify in the pages of *Civiltà Cattolica* and in reference to the resolution against anti-Semitism, "condemned, yes, but in its Christian form and spirit"; he returned in fact to the usual distinction between a good and a bad anti-Semitism.[31]

Returning to Germany in 1933, we can certainly imagine that hesitation on the part of the Catholic hierarchy derived in part from a defensive instinct. The bishops were worried that, in addition to striking Bolshevism and Judaism, the new regime would attack Catholics as well, and this fear encouraged them quickly to conclude a concordat. It was a concordat that, as compared with that signed with Mussolini, served not so much to achieve the goals of the Church but, in the words of Pacelli, to avoid greater evils.

The Jewish question – into which the Church agreed not to enter insofar as that might represent meddling in the internal affairs of another state – was dealt with only in a secret addendum, the so-called *kurze Notiz* specifically requested by Pius XI to protect Jews who had converted to Catholicism. He wanted them to be treated exactly like other Catholics and so exempt from the anti-Semitic laws. The German position on this point was also resolute: the racial question must not be confused with the religious one, as religion could not replace or cancel out one's Hebrew race and blood. This was a crucial point and one that would arise again when the Vatican condemned the Italian racial laws of summer–fall 1938.

Meanwhile, German failure to fulfill the spirit of the concordat was evident almost immediately. So, while Hitler enjoyed international recognition, the Vatican could only hope to avoid open persecution: "In those first few months after the Nazis came to power, the Holy See and the German Catholic Church strove to protect their position in Germany by soliciting guarantees from the regime, that quickly proved illusory, by means of a concordat with the whole of the Reich, an agreement they had sought in vain over the past decade."[32]

As we have already seen, in the months after Hitler's seizure of power, a major source of distress for the Church was the enthusiasm with which Catholic youth joined the Nazi movement, with the full consent of their parents. The Catholic associations found it increasingly difficult to resist the rapid Nazification of German society, as evidenced in the alarm sounded by Orsenigo on 26 February 1934 regarding the private negotiations of Catholic schools with the Hitler youth. Catholic parents, concerned about what the future might hold, were more and more inclined to transfer their children to state associations. Orsenigo reported on the conversation of Cardinal Karl Schulte of Cologne with the Chancellor and its presumed positive outcome:

> The cardinal applauded the positive developments: their meeting was dignified and calm and the exchange courteous, although the situation remains uncertain. The cardinal and bishop of Berlin are pessimistic and hope that the concordat will save essential religious freedoms. Brutal methods, the weakness of Catholic families worried about the economic future, and the lack of freedom of the press all make the situation a delicate one.[33]

The greatest worry was about youth and the Nazi education program; already at the beginning of the 1930s the Church had expressed alarm. And this was the sole issue that inspired true indignation and repeated appeals from 1933 to 1934. Orsenigo's reports described the pantheistic relationship between the Hitler youth and nature. Nudism in the forests, displays of the body, and all sorts of promiscuity were condemned and likened to communist education programs – indeed, there was even fear that the one might be infecting the other. The situation worried the bishops and so struck the nuncio that he suggested a parallel with the dissolute sexual morality of Bolshevik youth. Also striking was the unprecedented reference in Orsenigo's reports to women, uninhibited as they participated in Hitler's parades. It was nearly the only criticism that Orsenigo raised relative to these demonstrations: women unashamed to display themselves in public. Among the many corporations and other organizations that took part in the inauguration of the Reichstag, "there was also a contingent of girls who, however, received no special applause. Indeed, two ministers who were standing next to me, [Franz] von Papen and [Wilhelm] Frick, declared their opposition to women taking part in these public demonstrations"[34] – a first sign that the reassurance of traditional and conservative values would be a more complicated issue than the Church might have liked.

German protestants

The sigh of relief issued by the Catholic episcopacy in the first period of Hitler's rule and its alignment with the Nazi regime once it had come to power can usefully be compared with the still more acquiescent attitude of the protestant churches. As the Reich's bishop of the German Evangelical Church and state bishop of the Evangelical Church of the old Prussian Union (the most important evangelical group), Ludwig Müller held the dominant position in that church. On 21 January 1934 he announced:

> I feel obliged to declare that the National Socialists have not contradicted my own convictions in any way by introducing the Aryan concept into the law on religion. If a Jew should come to me to be baptized, I would baptize him, but if he should tell me that it is his burning desire to become a pastor I would reply that that is impossible. I would reply to him: very well, but be then a missionary among the Jews, for it is impossible that we should have among our community a pastor of foreign blood.[35]

The protestant church of the Third Reich did not allow individuals who were not full-blooded Aryans to hold any ecclesiastical positions. In those same years, when voices like that of Stein or the Jesuit Muckermann were calling for a stronger condemnation from the Catholic Church, the German Evangelical Church faced this dilemma in a more dramatic and radical fashion, as, with the exception of a few intensely spiritual and resistant minorities in the so-called Confessing Church, it became a faithful and attentive ally of Hitler. The Confederation of Evangelical Churches, torn between allegiance to the Reich and rebellion, between defense of the institution and prophetic witness, solidified its alliance with Hitler.[36] The so-called synchronization of the German protestant churches with Hitler's National Socialist regime took place in January 1934.

The Führer was especially pleased by the loyalty of "his" protestant church and suggested to Catholics that this was a good example of dedication to the fatherland. The Italian example of harmony achieved between fascism and the Church was frequently cited, and Orsenigo's correspondence reports frequent calls to follow the example of both the Lutheran brothers and the Italian Catholics. On 27 October 1934, the Berlin nuncio reported on a meeting with Interior Minister Frick, at which the latter complained that, unlike the protestant churches, the Catholic ones did not fly the National Socialist flag but only the papal one: "I replied that this was a detail (*sic!*) for the bishops to decide, and as he had cited the example of fascist Italy I assured him that in Italy only in old and exceptional cases, for example the Milan cathedral, were flags flown over churches there. The impression I took away from the meeting was that the minister had expressed a serious desire for agreement and pacification."[37]

Yet, with a few isolated exceptions, not even the dissident protestant church was able to make an effective protest. With regard to Catholic indignation over the Rosenberg text, the protestants did not share the same concerns: "Protestantism has left the task of exposing the imprecision and false judgments of Rosenberg to the realm of mere theology and depends on the good sense of the laity, which should be able to recognize the immorality of Rosenberg's assertions and their incompatibility with Christianity."[38]

It is interesting to follow the details of the crisis in the protestant world through the eyes of a special observer who informs us of its day-to-day development, and in particular lets us know in an indirect and masked way the thoughts of the Holy See on the German situation. That source is the feigned correspondence of Federico Alessandrini, who in fact never left Rome and wrote under the pseudonym of "Renano"; he would later be vice-director of *L'Osservatore Romano*, and we have already discussed his relations with Pius XI in chapter 1. Those articles are a true mine of information on the climate in the Vatican as, prior to being printed, they were reviewed by the Secretariat of State and had to respond to the demands of Pacelli himself; they represent a sort of Vatican news agency from which information was sent out to the Catholic press. At times between the lines and at times directly, those articles denounced the ideological premises of Nazism, starting with the mysticism of Rosenberg, as well as describing the oppression of Catholics and protestants and the horrors of the Night of the Long Knives. It was a way to skirt around Nazi censorship. And in fact the correspondent Renano was long sought in Germany, until it was understood that he actually resided in the secrecy of the Vatican itself.

This well-informed and mythic correspondent, presumably reporting from those cities witnessing the most crucial developments of the 1930s, in fact derived his information from a careful reading of the local press, as he himself would later recount in his memoirs:

My information was complete and indisputable. For example, with regard to Germany and Nazism, I received not only the major Berlin papers but also those from the other major German cities and the

113

organs of the various Nazi leaders that assiduously reported on their undertakings and speeches . . . the office acquired a variety of material, up-to-date and interesting information on the most pressing issues of the day . . . and so were born the various "pieces" published in Catholic papers between 1933 and 1939 in the form of dispatches from Madrid, Vienna, and Berlin.[39]

In an article from 31 January 1934, the presumed correspondent Renano wrote relative to the racist declarations of Müller:

> It would be interesting to know what ideas the "bishop" of the Reich holds on the spread of Christianity from Palestine throughout the world . . . Müller's words are very serious, not only for their dogmatic content but also given the moment when they were delivered: 600 pastors supported by various bishops in the *Länder* of southern Germany are rebelling against the bishop of the Reich because of his adaptability to Hitler's ideology and rejecting his fulminations . . . On 25 January Chancellor Hitler convened the bishops of the *Länder* and informed them that dissent in the Evangelical Church could do harm to the Third Reich, especially as regards the foreign press.[40]

In another article, from 4 January 1934, regarding new "theological ideas" proposed by Professor Bergman of the University of Leipzig – "I believe in the God of the German religion; I believe in Germany, the trainer of men" – Renano abandoned any pretense of restraint: "We have here then a form of ultranationalist mysticism, a materialism that can be matched only by that of Bolshevism . . . an ultra-nationalism that is symptomatic of the materialist anti-Christian methodology of the German neo-pagans."[41]

The insistent denunciation in these articles of the irreconcilable differences between Hitler's conception and the evangelical spirit takes on special value when we consider that they were approved by the Secretariat of State. These are just a few examples that can be found among the many dispatches. And, while they do not suffice to counter the charge of silence on the part of the Church, they reveal that that silence was not total. It was not a deafening silence, as we can detect whispered protests.

The protestant who raised a protest analogous to that of Stein was Dietrich Bonhöffer, imprisoned at Tegel and then hanged on 9 April 1945, a month before the end of the war, for his role in the attempted assassination of Hitler. In 1933 he wrote "The Church and the Jewish question," calling for an intervention to protest the first persecutions. In 1934 the protestant churches persisted in the illusion that, by means of a concordat, like that signed by the Catholics, they could gain protection and advantages. Following Internal Minister Frick's injunction to cease spreading tension within those churches, Bonhöffer instead wrote that "he hoped this time the pastors would have the courage to rise up against the state." He felt a sort of asphyxiation; from 1929 to at least 1934 he had hoped to go to India and meet Gandhi, sure that "there is more Christianity in their 'paganism' than in all of the Reich's Church." Then, experiencing ever greater disillusionment over the caution, fear, concessions, and outright collusion of the protestant churches with the persecution of the Jews, he launched the famous anathema that would mark the theology of the twentieth century: "Only those who raise their voices in defense of the Jews have the right also to sing the Gregorian chant."[42] Like Stein, he stated that our destiny is not separable from that of the Jews. A rejection of the Jews by the West would be equivalent, according to Bonhöffer, to a rejection of Christ, because Jesus Christ was Himself a Jew.

The encyclical against Nazism: *Mit brennender Sorge*

In January 1937 Pius XI was very ill and bedridden. On Sunday 17th he received at his bedside a group of German cardinals who had met the previous day with Pacelli. It was an important meeting during which, in that strange and moving context, they discussed how to respond to Hitler's ever more aggressive attacks. The German cardinals included Bertram (Breslau, then a German city), Faulhaber (Munich), Schulte (Cologne), and two of the bishops most opposed to the regime: Konrad von Preysing from Berlin and Clemens August von Galen from Münster. In spite of Bertram's request, and following specific instructions from the pope, Monsignor Berning, the archbishop of Osnabrück, who had failed to resign from his post as counselor of the Prussian state as the Vatican had requested, was not invited. The German cardinals were much struck by that meeting with the aging and sick pope: "The prelates were profoundly impressed, especially by his words regarding his illness and the illumination he had received while praying during his many hours of suffering. He had penetrated more deeply the mystery of the cross and the usefulness of suffering for the good of the mystical body of Christ that is the Church."[43]

There were already telling signs of the growing distance between the Vatican and Germany before 1937, but it was in the period

115

between the encyclical to "shout from the rooftops," the *Mit brennender Sorge* (March 1937), and the famous missing encyclical that we can reconstruct important elements of the conflict between Pius XI and Hitler. A careful reading of the file on Germany for 1937 and 1938 reveals that the pope was issuing ever greater signs of a diplomatic break.[44] The details of protocol themselves – the exchange of greetings, invitations, and receptions – followed an intense rhythm that would be interesting to reconstruct in its various subtleties. The nuncio was upbraided at times for being too laudatory. The New Year's message dwelt more on issues of peace than had those of previous years, and personal wishes sent to the chancellor were more sober. Regarding the dinner traditionally hosted by the nunciature on the anniversary of the pope's incoronation and to which the chancellor and other government officials were normally invited, the nuncio received the following communication from Rome on 31 December 1937: "Given the current sad situation, the Holy Father prefers that your excellence refrain from giving the dinner."[45]

There were naturally much stronger protests, but these help us to understand better the different views of the pope and his nuncio. The pope, for example, refused to receive the German minister of justice during his visit to Rome. In January 1936 he expressed his outrage to Ambassador von Bergen, listing the many and growing threats Nazism posed to the Church and to non-Aryans. He explained that he did not believe that all of that would save the world from communism and added that "he could no longer restrain himself."[46]

Beginning in October 1934, Alois Hudal, rector of the German College of Our Lady of the Souls, had planned a doctrinal condemnation, a sort of syllabus against the "three modern heresies" – racism, nationalism, and totalitarianism. In April 1936 a commission was formed to draft the text, but the Holy Office and Pacelli decided not to make it public. It can be consulted today in the archive of the Holy Office.[47] It is a sort of principled condemnation of modern heresy, a doctrinal condemnation that would probably not have had the same sort of impact as a pastoral and diplomatic protest. It may be for this reason that the pope opted instead for a true syllabus; Rosenberg's *Mythus des XX. Jahrhunderts*, moreover, had already been placed on the Index in 1933. The most interesting aspects of this planned doctrinal condemnation were those relating to the concept of heresy that underlay it and a more explicit reference to the debate over racial theory. It was perhaps to sharpen the condemnation and give it more weight that after a few months Pius XI chose not to address these generic "modern heresies" but rather to issue the three encyclicals that came out almost simultaneously in March 1937: *Mit brennender Sorge* against Nazism, *Divini Redemptoris* against communism, and *Firmissimam constantiam* on the Mexican situation.

Although the archival material made available to historians is by now complete, there remain many unanswered questions regarding the drafting of *Mit brennender Sorge*. To begin with, there is little evidence of the relationship between the doctrinal condemnation planned by the Holy Office and the encyclical; it is almost as if the two pronouncements were unrelated.[48] The fact is that the available documents fail to resolve many questions. The various drafts of the encyclical are in the Germany file, yet there is no reference to a discussion that we know took place. In the records of the audiences – the Pacelli notebooks – for March and April 1937, there is no trace at all of discussion about the encyclical. Indeed, there are many missing days: after 26 February they jump to 4 March and then to 18 March, and then again to 27 March, 3 April, and 10 April. Only on 13 April do we finally read: "It is a great consolation to the Holy Father knowing that the encyclical will bring comfort to the good children of Germany; His Holiness thanks them for their prayers and counts on them for the future (*sic!*)."[49]

Not much. How is it possible that there are no references in the audiences to an important document about which the pope cared dearly and which, moreover, Pacelli helped to draft? Where have those pages gone? And where are the discussions that surely took place, and the preparatory documents for the encyclical itself? Perhaps the references in the audiences were removed by Pacelli himself. What one does find are many hand-written notes by Pacelli in the file that contains the draft of the encyclical; in these the secretary of state identifies the corrections with which Pius XI agreed and those that he rejected.[50] The Jesuit Angelo Martini wrote the first reliable and serious study of *Mit brennender Sorge*. His reconstruction of the events, based on documents that he was able to consult in the 1950s and 1960s but which have become generally available to scholars only recently, describes a general consensus among the cardinals, Pacelli, and the pope.[51] In fact we know now there were significant differences.

As we have already mentioned, prior to *Mit brennender Sorge* the pope met, on 17 January, with the German cardinals Bertram, Faulhaber, and Schulte and the bishops Konrad von Preysing and Clemens August von Galen. Bertram and especially Faulhaber wanted to avoid conflict – it was perhaps for this reason that Pacelli assigned the task of drafting the German text to the latter – and suggested a simple letter from the pope to Hitler and the German bishops. For Cardinal Faulhaber of Munich, the pastoral letter from the Holy Father should not be polemical and for that reason should not even mention National Socialism or the Nazi Party – a sort of doctrine of peace. The first draft in fact maintained this pastoral spirit, intentionally generic and calculated not to anger Hitler. Yet already in the second version, twice as long, the tone became sharp and accusatory. The most significant changes were attributed to Pacelli, a resoluteness that contradicts his previous concern to avoid forceful positions that would threaten the concordat.[52]

It is hard to know when and to what degree the pope's own desire to express a firm and unequivocal position, one that abandoned the diplomatic goal of saving the concordat and took on instead the form of a biblical condemnation, may have played a role. The first part of the encyclical, focusing on the concordat, can be attributed to Pacelli, while in the second part it fell to Cardinal Faulhaber to interpret the instructions of Pius XI, namely to place the condemnation of totalitarianism in "a spiritual light." The text drafted by Faulhaber and constantly checked by Pacelli was stronger than either of these cardinals would have liked. And yet it was indeed a text largely written by them even if in large part reflecting the spirit of Ratti.[53] Martini himself recalled that Faulhaber claimed to have reproduced the spiritual inspiration personally suggested by the pope.

The clear references to the Old Testament likely reflect the spiritual moment through which the pope was living at the time. In those very weeks, he received on 22 March the French Cardinal Baudrillart, who recalled: "Even in his greatest suffering, when the pain abated, if he could not sleep, he felt tranquil and his mind was active. And so he thought of the three encyclicals that he wanted to write. He drafted them in his head; then he had them read – at times he dictated – and in this way the work was done."[54]

The use of biblical passages in the encyclical would seem to confirm this observation: "He that dwelleth in heaven shall laugh at them" (Psalms 2.4); ". . . God, the Creator of the universe, King and Legislator of all nations before whose immensity they are 'as a drop of a bucket'" (Isaiah 40.15); "the Spirit breatheth where he will" (John 3.8); ". . . of stones He is able to raise men to prepare the way to his designs" (Matt. 3.9; Luke 3.8). Citations from the Old and New Testament are rich and full of meaning – the use of Isaiah to minimize national pride: "all nations . . . are 'as a drop of a bucket.'" One can read in them a pride in faith and a profound passion. The

118

centrality of Christ was not invoked in this case to advance one cult or another in the service of Church policy, as had been the case with the cult of the Kingdom of Christ and the *Quas primas* of 11 December 1926, a syllabus that had both religious value and socio-political purpose. Rather Christ is invoked in this case to combat the pride of nations and as the only true remedy for idolatry. Under no circumstances could the Church be made subordinate to national interests. It represented a profound intuition, one already present in the condemnation of Action Française and linked in a deep way to a precise idea of the Church as spiritually autonomous from any sort of nationalism.

Several well-known excerpts from the encyclical against Nazism, as for example that on the "true faith in God," demonstrate that at the core of the encyclical was a rejection of the "religious" and idolatrous nature of Nazism: "Beware, Venerable Brethren, of that growing abuse, in speech as in writing, of the name of God as though it were a meaningless label, to be affixed to any creation, more or less arbitrary, of human speculation"; ". . . race and blood . . . False coins of this sort do not deserve Christian currency"; "Human laws in flagrant contradiction with the natural law are vitiated with a taint which no force, no power can mend."[55]

The German reaction was fierce but, before discussing the persecution of German Catholics, beginning with those who helped the Vatican print and distribute the encyclical, we should explore the heavy-handed diplomatic response. On 12 April, the German Ambassador von Bergen sent Pacelli a strong note of protest against the encyclical, accusing the Church of having discarded the concordat and also failing to recognize that National Socialism had saved Germany from Bolshevism.[56] Pacelli's response of 30 April extended to many pages; it was full of sophisticated diplomatic arguments in a tone and style diametrically opposed to that of Ratti. Comparing the two documents, it is difficult to agree with Martini, who identified unity of style and content in *Mit brennender Sorge* and Pacelli's reply. The argumentation, the style, and the spirit were entirely different. The question that remains to be answered, however, is whether Pius XI and Pacelli were serving complementary but different functions or whether the greater resoluteness of the one simply conflicted with the other's inclination to compromise.

Every passage of Pacelli's long reply suggests that the conflict between the Holy See and Germany represents a temporary break, that it is nothing more than an "illness" for which a rapid, radical, and certain cure is needed. Taking into account the addressees, one cannot conclude that its purpose is political, and the accusation that it is "an attempt to mobilize the world against Germany is unjustified":

> The religious purpose is clear and far from any political tendency . . . The Holy See does not fail to recognize the great importance of those intrinsically healthy and vital political formations that defend against the threat of atheist Bolshevism . . . It has never missed an opportunity to consolidate the spiritual front against Bolshevism . . . but that cannot constitute a tolerance without limits. Nothing could be more false than the idea that Bolshevism can be fought with a force that is not spiritual . . . Dignity and necessary impartiality . . . compel the Holy Father, in combating the madness that is Bolshevism, not to close his eyes at the same time to similar errors that begin to take hold among other political and ideological currents.[57]

Pacelli rejected the accusation of endangering the concordat, citing instead the repeated German violations and describing the attitude of the Holy See as one of unlimited patience – "held by many to have been excessive" – in the hopes of grasping at the smallest opportunities for mediation.

Whatever paternity we assign to the encyclical, its most important result was not political-diplomatic but theological-pastoral, and on that level it marked a change. Both Nazism and Bolshevism were condemned, and for the first time the priority was not to present a united front against Bolshevism. It is not a coincidence that the policy of the Holy See against Hitler was repeatedly accused of weakening the anti-Bolshevik front.

Warned from many sides not to risk weakening that front, the pope came instead to conceive of a new relationship between politics and religion, a sort of urgent anti-idolatry that should take precedence over any other political considerations, even that, still important, of combating Bolshevism. "No-one fights Bolshevism better than Hitler" had been the *leitmotiv* of the first half of the 1930s. However, in the eyes of Pius XI, the merits of National Socialism in this regard, till then unchallenged, no longer served as a justification.

This partial shift in the pope's position owed more to spiritual than to political considerations, as his fear of the Bolshevik threat had not declined. And here is the most interesting point: the fact that the pope wanted to make a religious attack rather than a political one was not intended as a *deminutio*, but as just the opposite, namely a reinforcement of the condemnation. Pacelli, instead, in his long reply to von Bergen defending the encyclical, repeatedly emphasizes the religious and perfectly apolitical spirit of the document in order to soften and relativize the condemnation.

Mit brennender Sorge then seems a much more passionate and spiritually inspired encyclical than the *Divini Redemptoris* against communism, which only seems harsher: communism is described as "intrinsically perverse," without the possibility of appeal or redemption, an "absolute evil." But it is a more cerebral encyclical, more doctrinal, and a less passionate document. The force of religious condemnation is what would characterize the repeated pronouncements of the pope in his final years; and that in turn indirectly strengthened his political position, as we will see more clearly in the still harsher condemnation of the Christmas 1937 allocution.

The international campaign in support of the encyclical

The secretary of state's reply suggests a belief that there were still reasonable elements in the German government and contradicts the direct attack of *Mit brennender Sorge*. And yet direct attack it was, in its mode of delivery even before its content, in every way calculated to infuriate the Nazis: it was prepared in secret and came as a complete surprise; it was spread in a grassroots campaign (not one priest refused to read it as part of his sermon); and it had an extraordinary impact on international opinion. Its preparation and launch had all the marks of a clandestine action. Directives from the Secretariat of State on 10 March instructed "that the encyclical be made known to the faithful as far as possible contemporaneously and that packages be carried by a safe route and with the greatest possible care."[58] *Mit brennender Sorge*, which Pacelli and Faulhaber hoped would be a pastoral letter from the pope to Hitler shown only to the German bishops, became instead the touchstone for an international campaign against the Nazis.

Even the various currents of the Italian Church achieved a degree of consensus around the encyclical, though they would divide again in a year's time over Mussolini's alliance with Hitler and the racial laws. *Mit brennender Sorge* served as a catalyst, perhaps the last before the disruption that came with the end of Ratti's papacy, and testified to the possibility that the Holy See might take a decisive position; in this way it was a warning also for Italy. Ten days after its delivery, Agostino Gemelli expressed to Francesco Olgiati, his closest confidant, admiration for the effective way the pope had spread his message: "You have followed the question of the Holy

Father's letter to the Germans. He managed to have it read in all the churches without any warning."[59]

Initial caution was replaced by a campaign for international solidarity around the encyclical that did not let up until the pope's death. It was a true international grassroots campaign, which maintained the spirit of surprise, aggression, speed, and internationalism that characterized its initial publication and represented a new attitude to replace the defensive one taken by the Catholic Church up to that time in the face of Nazism. It was a propaganda campaign directed by a Pacelli who was neither reticent nor indecisive, as revealed by his authoritative circular to the nuncios and other papal representatives instructing that the encyclical be circulated and read. On 15–16 May he sent the following instructions: "In light of the ever greater persecution of the Church in Germany, the Holy Father requests that papal representatives maintain their distance from German diplomats and refrain from inviting them to dinners or receptions and from attending same."[60]

On 24 April 1937, Cicognani, the nuncio to Austria, reported that Edmund Glaise von Horstenau, the Austrian foreign minister, had met with Hitler, who was furious about the encyclical. The minister objected that so much hostility toward the Holy See threatened the good relationship between Germany and Austria: "These observations set Hitler off, and he spoke and gestured violently, inveighing against the encyclical and describing Kaas as a traitor against Germany. 'I will not put the bishops in prison, but I will drown the Catholic Church in ignominy and shame by opening the secret archives of the monasteries and revealing the filth that lies hidden there.'"[61]

On 22 August the apostolic delegate to the United States mentioned the intention of the American episcopacy to make a pronouncement, though they hesitated in case the move might be premature or inopportune. Only on 26 September did they move forward, with the proviso that the pronouncement should include no personal attacks (a constant concern of the American bishops). From England, the cardinal of Westminster issued a call for solidarity with the Holy Father on 9 September, and the Secretariat of State requested that it be released to the press. The same held for France. In Italy, the patriarch of Venice asked Pizzardi to communicate the good wishes of the episcopacy of Venetia to the German one. Participation was strongest among the Latin countries, even though the appeal was issued to all countries and provides insight into changing situations in different contexts. So, for example, the apostolic delegate in Japan reported on the increasingly positive light in which the Japanese political world viewed Hitler's regime.[62]

In this international solidarity campaign, Pacelli warned against German duplicity and falseness. On 6 August, he wrote: "While in Germany the authorities show no hesitation in striking ecclesiastic targets, abroad the representatives of the Third Reich seek to demonstrate their respect for the Church . . . Church dignitaries should not be deceived if in some places German authorities show them kindness . . . We must be especially vigilant and maintain a dignified reserve in relation to the agents of the Third Reich."[63]

In Germany, reprisals were heavy-handed and frequent: presses closed, the sequestering of diocesan archives, threats against individuals. On 19 June 1937, regarding compensation for the expropriated episcopal presses, the pope chose among various proposals to use funds from Peter's pence. A thick dossier entitled "Expropriations from Episcopal Curia and Religious Institutions" refers to the sequestering of documents from diocesan archives in Trier, Dresden, Frauenburg, and Cologne – all prestigious seats – in order to reveal "the filth that lies hidden there," as Hitler had threatened. On 10 June 1937, the secret police, on orders from Berlin, invaded episcopal curia there, seizing and taking away many documents. *L'Osservatore Romano* reported at length on the incident on 22 June, while Nuncio Orsenigo wrote:

> Among the material found were many signed requests for permission to read books placed on the Index, especially Alfred Rosenberg's *Mythus des XX. Jahrhunderts*, which many were required to read. The appeals came mostly from humble civil servants and some included political observations. Now these people are very worried and lament the fact that the episcopal curia preserved these documents.[64]

The bishop of Berlin, Konrad von Preysing, and the archbishop of Breslau, Adolf Bertram, took it upon themselves to burn documents relating to delicate affairs involving priests. Orsenigo wrote: "In response to their questions, I replied that these were issues that each bishop must resolve on his own, taking into account the seriousness of the archival material." Next to this text, in the unmistakable handwriting of Pacelli, one reads: "The Holy Father judges this a weak response . . . He instructs that you respond instead that they burn <u>without question</u> all that which might cause problems . . . You are fully authorized to raise protests, in this regard as in all other cases, both in the present and the future."[65]

There were other minor but significant cases that clearly revealed the different sensibilities of Pacelli and the pope. On 24 September 1937, Carlo Colli, auditor of the nunciature, criticized the suspension of the missionary periodical *Weltmission*: "The motivation for this sad act remains a mystery; Joseph van der Velden, vice president of the Sacred Congregation for the Propagation of the Faith, has not even made the fact public, perhaps out of fear of incurring still greater sanctions that might go so far as to include a ban on collecting contributions for the Catholic missions."[66]

A note from 29 September, possibly in Tardini's hand, reads: "The Holy Father is of the opinion that you should respond: cite the motivation as well. If the gathering of donations should be curtailed, the Holy Father is prepared to contribute some of his own. What else can be done?" Pacelli responded on 2 October:

> Now that we have sought to get the ban rescinded, it seems to me that we should wait to see the results of that attempt. Moreover, the action is known and the motivation not as mysterious as Monsignor Colli suggests. It is simply Nazi racial theory, described in many publications, and so nothing more or less than the ideology of National Socialism, alas much promoted of late. I do not think then that publication of that motivation will make much impression in Germany. The damage might be greater than the hoped-for advantage. It might, though, be worth concentrating on publishing information about it in other countries.[67]

Beyond Pacelli's irony and impatience with the lack of acumen on the part of the auditor (who had already shown limited intuition in the past), the above passage is a good example of the secretary of state's way of operating.

Between May and June 1937, the Nazi regime carried out many of its threats and exacted revenge, though not quite with the same violence as immediately following publication of the encyclical, when it closed down the presses that had printed the document. Over the following two months the National Socialists carried out a true persecution of the Church, including the most feared and underhanded move, namely carrying out the threat to create scandal by requisitioning the ecclesiastical archives in order to uncover clerical immorality.[68]

On 27 May, the bishop of Berlin exposed and declared false Nazi manipulation and anti-religious propaganda in making accusations of immorality against the clergy.[69] The next day Goebbels justified the regime's move, explaining that the trials for immorality would involve an enormous number of priests and so testify to widespread decadence among the clergy:

> This represents a serious threat for the physical and spiritual health of German youth, which, rather, badly needs to undergo a process of regeneration . . . Moreover, the publicity given to these trials does not represent a war against the Church but is instead made necessary by the slanderous suggestion that many priests are being held in prison for religious reasons. The publicity is a reaction to the Church's attempt to aid its guilty members in evading German justice, even attempting to depict them as martyrs.[70]

The tone, spirit, and Christological passion of the encyclical found new expression several months later in the pope's allocution of December 1937. In the name of faith rather than politics, Pius XI declared that his protest "could not have been more explicit or more fervid before all the world" and that his concern was exclusively religious and not political. He laid out then that altered relation between faith and politics, between religion and history, which required not mediation and negotiation but rather a profound re-examination in light of those exceptional times; it was as though taking a step backward to start off again from spiritual roots.

The German bishops

Publication of the encyclical and its distribution revealed that even the German episcopacy no longer presented a united front; it betrayed instead a complexity and range of positions deriving from a profound and agonizing crisis of consciousness. The exhaustive German documentary sources[71] reveal not only different positions but also uncertainty and well describe the internal dynamic at work. Konrad von Preysing, appointed bishop of Berlin in October 1937, asked Cardinal Bertram for a radical change of position, proposing abandonment of secret diplomatic negotiations with the Nazi hierarchy and a strong public condemnation, making the Catholic Church then the point of reference for that popular indignation and mobilization so feared by the regime.[72] A distinct difference of views began to emerge when compared with the majority of the episcopacy. Von Preysing and his cousin von Galen did not share the idea that one could still distinguish a minority Nazi fanatical fringe that might be isolated, though there were differences between the two as well, owing to the Berlin bishop's diffidence relative to von Galen's conservatism and anti-parliamentary positions. The impact of *Mit brennender Sorge* had been encouraging, in spite of the persecutions that followed, and the two bishops hoped to see the campaign constructed around the encyclical pursued, both domestically and internationally.

In April 1937 von Galen sought to convince the episcopacy to draft a pastoral letter following up on the encyclical. In two separate memoranda he called for respect of the natural rights of the individual and freedom of conscience in the face of state authority. The pastoral letter did not come to pass, and Bertram in fact complained that the bishop of Münster lacked political tact; noble conservative that he was, he seemed to imagine he could command other bishops "as if they were his peasants in Westphalia." With regard to the famous meeting in Rome in January 1937, we have already noted Bertram's disagreement with Pacelli over the non-inclusion of the bishop of Osnabrück, Monsignor Wilhelm Berning, whom Pius XI did not want at the meeting because he had refused to resign from his post as counselor of the Prussian state. On that occasion, Bertram also regretted the inclusion instead of von Galen who, in his opinion, "is a valorous speaker and combatant with a high public profile; but for our purposes these are not decisive qualities, much as I admire his authentically Westphalian courage."[73] Their positions were obviously far apart. Moreover, when Faulhaber met with the newly elected Pius XII in March 1939, he repeated that, in response to the many attacks on the Church, the bishops would do well to behave as if they were unaware of them.

But let us return to von Galen's meeting with Pius XI in January 1937, when the bishop said regarding Nazism: "We are dealing with an adversary who has no understanding of truth and faith. When they refer to God, it is not our God but something diabolical."[74] That statement constitutes the core and theological root of *Mit brenneder Sorge*, Pius XI's encyclical against Nazism, which alludes to "sacrilege" and "the defense of God's rights in the teeth of an aggressive paganism" – the latter clearly a reference to the Nazis. As Giovanni Miccoli has suggested, the pope was probably also thinking of authoritative figures in German Catholicism and those in the Roman Curia who may have supported them, namely those in the Church who were not sufficiently opposed to totalitarianism: "The vast documentation available attests clearly to the vacillating and uncertain positions of the bishops, with regard to both the immediate situation and longer-term prospects. That uncertainty in the development of divergent judgments also owed much to the desire to maintain unity among the bishopric."[75]

It is interesting to compare the intransigence of von Galen with that of Pius XI as vigorously expressed in the last years of his life. For Ratti it was the totalitarian nature of the Church that must prevail in its battle against the totalitarianisms with which it came into conflict. That profound conflict became intolerable when those totalitarianisms took on the trappings of secular religion and so inevitably sought to capture also the conscience of their subjects. In von Galen's formulation, as expressed in his three famous sermons from summer 1941, the theological argument seems to take precedence over the ecclesiological and relies directly on natural rights and the primacy of conscience. In spite of his traditionalism, it is not defense of the Church and the Catholic community that inspires his condemnation but rather the rights of the individual and of all men.

All the bishops shared an attachment to the nation, patriotic loyalty, and a rootedness in their individual countryside, cities, and Länder.[76] It was a loyalty that they often hoped would serve to lighten the persecution of the Church in the name of national solidarity. Loyalty to the homeland was a source of great embarrassment for the episcopacy and generally for the German Catholic community; on the one hand their national loyalty was recognized while on the other their protests against Nazism raised suspicion of defeatism and betrayal. Such was the difficult spot in which the bishops found themselves, between the need to offer reassurances of their loyalty to the nation while at the same time opposing Nazism, not only to defend the German Church but on behalf of all the German people. Driven by the overriding need to survive among divergent tactics, memories of the Kulturkampf, and uncertainty and concern about the regime's reaction, the German episcopacy wrestled with these dilemmas but failed to find a solution.

Edith Stein's appeal

Is this war of extermination against Jewish blood not an outrage against the holiness and humanity of our Savior, against the blessed virgin, and the apostles? Is it not absolutely contrary to the behavior of our Lord and Redeemer who even on the cross prayed for His persecutors? And is it not a black mark on this Holy Year that should instead be a year of peace and reconciliation?

All of us who watch the current German situation as faithful children of the Church fear for the image of the Church should its silence continue any longer. We are also convinced that this silence will not

127

in the long run pacify the current German government. The war against Catholicism is carried out more quietly and in a less brutal way than that against the Jews, but it is not for that less systematic.[77]

In April 1933, less than three months after Hitler's seizure of power, Edith Stein wrote this letter to Pius XI; we have already cited the first section at the beginning of the chapter. This second section refers not only to her discouragement over the silence of the Church but also to her "spiritual double identity" as both Jew and Christian, a condition that allows Stein to view with special lucidity the spiritual links of their common origin. Her life was the existential incarnation and lived testimony, to the point of martyrdom, of that fact upon which Pius XI would insist to his last breath, namely that "we are spiritually all Semites."

The contradiction experienced by the German bishops and discussed above, namely between being Germans and being Catholic pastors, was lived in a still more profound and interior way by Stein. This was of course a function of her Jewish and Christian roots, but also of her complex national identity, as she grew up in a Polish Jewish family near the German border. Regarding the decision of her Germanophile cousins to leave their native city when it became Polish after the plebiscite of 20 March 1920, Stein wrote: "My relatives could not and would not think of remaining there; they sold the family seat and left their homeland."[78] That homeland lay in Upper Silesia, a region at the heart of fierce debates following the German defeat in the First World War. Those debates were resolved by plebiscites that provoked violence between Germans and Poles, while Papal Nuncio Achille Ratti looked on helplessly, as we saw in chapter 1. He was also saddened on that occasion both by the behavior of the German bishops and by the Polish model of Catholicism, which sacrificed so much of its identity to nationality.

The Stein family, like the vast majority of Polish Jews, strongly identified with the German people. Edith herself volunteered in 1915 for the Red Cross, like many other heroic and patriotic Jews in the First World War. Born as she was in the border city of Breslau, she would always belong to two peoples, the Jewish and the German, while harboring a special admiration for the courage and the spirituality of the Poles. Of Jewish blood and Catholic faith, Edith Stein embodied an identity that it would be too banal to describe as simply multiple. Her existential and religious roots in fact would give shape and substance to her philosophical reflections on the ideas of community, people, and state.

Stein was far from the idealism of Hegel and instead followed Husserl's phenomenology and his idea of a community that would never be absorbed into the state; it was an idea that avoided the risks of totalitarian regression implicit in the concept of *Volk*, an easy degeneration in the tradition of German thought. In April 1933, when Stein wrote the above text, Martin Heidegger, who had been appointed rector of the University of Freiburg, moved closer to National Socialism, as is well known. Stein went in the other direction and relativized all public spheres in order to celebrate the personal dimension and its spiritual irreducibility. Following the tradition of Tönnies, Husserl, and Scheler, she considered the community as a locus of solidarity and responsibility, an antidote against both the ethical state and atomized individualism. It was not blood but the spirituality of a people that unites a nation, that constitutes its identity; the most germane examples in this regard were the Jewish and Polish peoples.[79]

Religion, the foundation and connective tissue for community, became for Stein the antidote against all absolutization. The more profound motivation for writing the pope, then, was not simply moral indignation but a theological and religious distinction. As has been correctly noted, Stein was not simply protesting against the violation of human rights carried out on a vast scale in Nazi Germany, but also against the attempt to discredit the source that had historically determined those rights, namely the Judeo-Christian religion:

> You cannot imagine how important it is for me every morning, when I go to chapel and raise my gaze to the crucifix and the effigy of the Madonna, to repeat to myself that they and I share the same blood . . . You cannot imagine what it means to me to be a daughter of the chosen people, to belong to Christ not only spiritually but also by descent.[80]

In other words, she understood that "the Nazi battle is not only against Judaism, but also against Catholic Christianity," Christianity that posed a danger insofar as "it is organized into a single centralized organic structure: the Catholic Church."[81]

Stein's letter is an extraordinary document. We don't know if it influenced the pope – there is no evidence in the archive[82] – but it was in any case much in line with Pius XI's thought toward the end of his life. The importance of her condemnation is not so much historical, political, or even moral, but rather profoundly theological and spiritual, the product of a combination of thought and experience of the sort perhaps to be found only in the life of a woman. Her cry of pain, her statement of historic truth, springs from her strength and the need to express an inner truth deriving from her own biography. She sought after truth, in her philosophy as in her life and till her martyrdom. (It was her Carmelite superior who approved her transfer to Holland, where she was captured by the Nazis.)

The theological core of Stein's condemnation was that the Nazis could not present themselves as Christians, that it was the pope's moral duty to declare that anti-Semites cannot call themselves Christians. But, as we know, there is a gap between mysticism and politics, as the rhythms and pressures of interiority are not the same as those of political decision-making, even the decision-making of popes and the institutions they represent.

Edith Stein was made a saint by John Paul II. Not only do her words then resonate for their particularly intense interiority and heroic courage, but, with the confirmation of such high institutional legitimization, her mystical condemnation continues through the ages.

— 6 —

"ANOTHER CROSS THAT IS NOT THE CROSS OF CHRIST": PIUS XI, MUSSOLINI, HITLER

Sad events are transpiring, very sad events, both near and far. Among those sad events is this: it is found to be neither inappropriate nor poorly timed to erect in Rome on the day of the Holy Cross another cross that is not the cross of Christ.

Regarding Hitler's visit to Italy in May 1938

Face to face with Mussolini

Solidification of the Italo-German alliance over the course of 1937 embittered the relationship between the Vatican and fascism. The growing hostility of the Holy See toward Germany was sufficiently obvious to be used by Italian diplomacy in the difficult path to alliance with Hitler. That year was in fact one of active "revitalization" of Italo-German relations. Foreign Minister Ciano's visit of June 1936 established Italo-German cooperation, solemnly proclaimed by Mussolini in Milan on 1 November when he spoke for the first time of a Rome–Berlin "axis." Signs of concern in Catholic circles close to fascism were evident by spring 1937. Even Father Tacchi-Venturi, always ready to grasp at the faintest signs of accord with the regime, now worried over the relationship between *il Duce* and the German leader, whom he considered "oblique" and "without scruples."

In September 1937 the pope expressed his irritation over Mussolini's visit to Hitler. The diaries of Ciano and Bottai offer ample testimony, as does the newly available documentation regarding 3 September 1937:

A meeting with Father Tomasetti on the question of Nazareth. He went to the Senate, where Senators Federzoni, Montresor, Balbino Giuliano, and others told him they had learned that the Holy Father is beside himself when speaking of Germany and now also of the Italian rapprochement and Mussolini's trip to Germany. All of this is the fault of France, which has pushed Italy into Germany's arms. Italy was prepared to make many concessions, for example regarding Tunisia. Now France threatens war, and Mussolini is going to Germany in order to give the impression that the two nations are united and so avoid war by striking fear in France. Father Tomasetti has sought via Donna Rachele [crossed out and corrected as Edvige] to convince Mussolini to counsel moderation when in Germany; Mussolini expects to better the situation with his trip. Father Tomasetti tried to calm the senators, suggesting that appropriate explanations could improve things.[1]

On 14 September 1937, Ambassador Pignatti wrote: "It was Father Tomasetti (who learned about it from Cardinal La Puma) who chattered about the Holy Father's anger over Mussolini's trip to Germany. But after all the good that Mussolini has done this anger is misplaced. The trip is intended to avoid war, not foment it."[2]

The Nuremberg Rally of September 1937 relaunched Rosenberg's theses as the "official religion" of the National Socialist state and so created further basis for conflict. On this occasion condemnation took the form of an important article by Pacelli, published in *L'Osservatore Romano* on 15 September and entitled "After the Nuremberg Rally." The article was translated into all languages and sent to the nuncios so that it could be distributed in the various national presses; it was an international campaign of the sort pursued with *Mit brennender Sorge*. Pacelli himself referred to this article, pleased that the pope thought it excellent and had said it "merited an A+."[3] The Nuremberg Rally, according to Pacelli's editorial, "exposes the progress of the 'Nordic brand' of neo-paganism, an ideology now used in the training of teachers and so permeating not only the party and state offices, but the schools as well. The conclusion we come to is a hard one: any attempt at pacification would seem to be vain."[4] The critique of Rosenberg's theses and concern over their influence on the younger generations, dating from the early 1930s and discussed in the previous chapter, re-emerged at this point.[5]

One of many examples of the increased rhythm of Italo-German interaction can be found in Goebbels's diary, where he complains of the constant travel to and fro, the large number of receptions for Italians in 1937, and the frequent trips to Rome taken by members of the Nazi Party. Documents from the "Germania" file in the Vatican Secret Archive refer to some of these visits and offer information on the way in which the Vatican too became a subject of the Rome–Berlin initiative. To take an example from Goebbels, there is mention of a meeting held in March 1937 with the Italian Professor Guido Manacorda, a Catholic fascist who frequently counseled the pope and, when unable to meet with him, various members of the Curia. We have already encountered him when he sought to alert the secretary of state about excessive indulgence on the part of a segment of French Catholicism regarding the Popular Front.

Manacorda had close ties to the German world – he was a professor of German language and literature – and, like many fascists, feared a break between the Holy See and Germany. He worked hard to achieve an understanding between the Vatican and National Socialism and discussed this problem at length with Father Gemelli, "who fully shares my evaluation of the current situation in Germany." On 20 March 1937 he sent a report from Florence to the Secretariat of State:

> I have returned from a busy trip to Germany with many documents. I met with the Führer, Goebbels, Frank, Rosenberg, the nuncio, our representatives in Berlin and Munich, and many Catholics of all ranks. My conclusion is that the religious problem is at a critical point, and without a rapid and decisive intervention the most serious consequences are inevitable and possibly imminent.[6]

For this reason he requested an audience with the pope during Easter week, "as I am coming to Rome to meet with the head of the government." The pope, however, avoided the meeting: "Manacorda means well, but he is a bit shady, one of those who tries to play a double game while claiming to be an excellent Catholic. Like many others, he is nothing more than a tool for observation and presentation. Write to him that the pope is not well."[7] And so he did not get his audience.

Manacorda's comments seem incredible under the circumstances and reveal his excessive trust: "I have never as at this moment found them to be more willing to negotiate and understand, the Führer above all of course but also including the most fanatical."[8] According to the professor, an immediate and absolute truce was possible, and he offered himself as intermediary between the pope and Hitler; it was for this reason that he requested an audience with the Holy Father on 1 April. Manacorda's recent visits must have changed his mind, as less than two years previously, on 12 June 1935, the Florentine professor had delivered an alarming analysis to Monsignor Celso Costantini that defined the Nazi ideology as pagan and perversely invasive.

This obvious contradiction finds its explanation in the alarm created among Catholic fascists by the possible break between Germany and the Holy See. Manacorda's effort, extreme, illusory, and coming too late, resembled other attempts – some sincere, others clearly manipulative – to lessen the risk of a break between Pius XI and Nazism that would have had dangerous repercussions on relations also with fascism. The sharp and total conflict initiated with *Mit brennender Sorge* was, however, irreversible. Many more or less significant events speak to the confusion and discrepancy that existed between the pope, who preferred a more decisive line, the German episcopacy, internally divided, and Pacelli, who, fearing harsher reactions, sought a more cautious *modus operandi*. These differences may not represent entirely distinct approaches, but they do speak in any case to a profound sense of disorientation and uncertainty.[9]

The case of Cardinal George Mundelein

"Perhaps you will ask how it is that a nation of 60 million intelligent people will submit in fear and servitude to an alien, an Austrian paper hanger, and a poor one at that, and a few associates like Goebbels and Göring, who dictate every move of the people's lives?"[10] In a speech given on 18 May, the cardinal of Chicago, George Mundelein, issued this clear and raw assessment of the Austrian paper hanger. The case of the American cardinal is well known and considered a prime example of prudence and concession, of Pacelli's caution and his divergence from Pius XI.

The newly released documentation confirms the pope's unconditional support for the American cardinal, consistent with his words of praise in *L'Osservatore Romano* on 19–20 July. In the face of indignant reaction from Germany, even Pacelli failed to criticize the words of the American bishop, though he used more moderate language. Management of what soon became the "Mundelein affair" was essentially left in his hands, and while diplomatic he was also firm:

> The Holy See cannot correct or deplore the speech of the most excellent Mundelein. That would represent an act of weakness and only

contribute to the arrogance of the National Socialists and Hitler, who in his self-delusion believes that all the world must bow before him. Though indeed that part of the speech in which the cardinal refers to the German head of state was unfortunate.[10]

Pacelli then, who offered words of conciliation and expressions of affection for the German people to Ambassador von Bergen, was nonetheless firm in refusing to criticize the American cardinal, even though he several times regretted the latter's forthright style, much different than his own and unusual among the Curia. From that point forward, the Holy See recommended that expressions of solidarity with the German Church not include personal attacks and injurious language. On many occasions, the usual dignified and polite style, never too direct or aggressive, was put forward as the most appropriate. The style of the American cardinal was not approved of, but Pacelli gave signs that he shared his assessments – "in the past two years these outrages can only be compared with those of the Bolsheviks" – even though he thought it unfortunate that those assessments had been made public.[12]

The Mundelein affair "led to an acute phase, a true war against the Church," according to the Italian ambassador Count Bonifacio Pignatti on 21 June, who also referred to a "suspension of normal relations" between Germany and the Vatican:

> It is certain, moreover, that any further reaction on the part of the German clergy will lead to a complete break, even open fighting in the streets and squares, and the Vatican will not be able to rely on foreign reaction, which counts for nothing in Germany, or on the youth of Catholic families, as it too has been drawn into the National Socialist movement.[13]

In a report a few days later, the Italian ambassador to the Holy See referred to confidential sources according to whom there was great worry among the Catholics, while government circles expressed confidence: "According to confidential sources, Hitler has affirmed the need to avoid confessional wars and his determination that the German people not be divided into two separate religious parties."[14]

On 22 August 1937 Monsignor Cicognani wrote from Washington of a possible "statement from this episcopacy," though still in a stage of pure hypothesis, as "no one wants to worsen the situation," but if it could be useful the American bishops were prepared to make the gesture. The reply of the Secretariat of State on 26 September 1937, evidently based on the belief that the situation could still be salvaged, emphasized the need that the form and tone of the statement be irreproachable, so as not to expose the Church to still harsher reactions. It concluded: "An initiative of this sort could be very useful, providing that the eventual message does not include personal attacks which, justified though they may be, would probably serve only to harm the cause."[15]

Judging from references appearing in the Chicago press in the first days of 1938, Cardinal Mundelein broadly interpreted some of the points raised in recent public statements of Pius XI. He in fact "called on the Catholic Church to rally behind the working man and his problems as a practical antidote for various isms of the day – communism, atheism, and others," and proposed to the faithful a radical vision of Roosevelt's New Deal:

> It does not help to listen to lectures on communism, to discuss it academically. If we want to accomplish anything we must offer something practical.
> The trouble with us in the past has been that we were too often drawn into an alliance with the wrong side ... Of course there is danger of communism. But don't let others use it as a cloak to cover corrupt practices when they cry out against communism and they themselves practice social injustice, when they fight against minimum wage and we find girls and women trying to live on 10 and 15 cents an hour. It is here that Catholic action should come in.[16]

While the pope had shown himself open to dialog with the communists, he seems not to have shared these more extreme positions, positions that in the US had inspired a heated discussion – or so in any case relayed Pacelli relative to the audience of 15 February, after commenting on the article "Catholics and Communists" that had appeared in *Croix*: "The Papal acts are not simply condemnations of communism, but also seek remedies. Write, with due respect, in *L'Osservatore Romano*, and then write a note of clarification to Cardinal Mundelein. It is not enough to read what the popes have written; one must also do what they say."[17]

Mit brennender Sorge reinforced the Vatican's relations with North American democracy after 1935, by means of both Cardinal Mundelein's friendship with President Roosevelt and Pacelli's important American trip in 1936.

The *Anschluß* and the pope's reprimand
of the cardinal of Vienna

On 12 March 1938 German troops invaded Austria. The next day the archbishop of Vienna, Theodor Innitzer, published a declaration of loyalty to Hitler, followed just two more days later by a warm meeting between the two. On 18 March the Austrian bishops called on Catholics to vote in favor of the plebiscite for annexation to Germany. The Vatican, informed of none of this ahead of time, reacted immediately. Already on 14 March, Ambassador Charles-Roux informed the Quai d'Orsay:

> Monsignor Tardini tells me that the Vatican had nothing to do with the appeal made by the cardinal archbishop of Vienna to his parishioners and indeed only learned about it after the fact . . . The Vatican holds that its own attitude in the face of the suppression of Austria must take into account the need not to place the Catholic Church in danger.[18]

The Secretariat of State immediately informed diplomats assigned to the Vatican that the Holy See had not been informed and learned about this development only from the newspapers. Moreover, according to the French ambassador to the Holy See, the official position of the Vatican on the suppression of Austria had to take into account the fact that the open and immediate alignment of the Austrian bishopric with the National Socialists was in part a function of the heavy oppression that had fallen on Vienna following the invasion. Other international observers in Vienna in those days noted as much. The American chargé d'affaires in Austria, for example, commented:

> Many priests have been arrested. The bishop of Graz has been two days in prison, and the prince bishop of Salzburg was placed under house arrest for three days. Cardinal Innitzer, at the insistence of Seyss-Inquart, called in person upon Hitler in the Hotel Imperial and had a fifteen minute interview with him. Subsequently a statement appeared in the press on 16 March which stated that the cardinal had expressed his joy to Hitler at the "reunion" of German Austria with the Reich and the will of the Austrian Catholics to work with all their strength at the German reconstruction. The nuncio tells me in confidence that while Cardinal Innitzer did sign a statement, the text of the one which appeared was not that which he had approved.[19]

German pressure did not justify the enthusiasm of Cardinal Innitzer, who, described by Nuncio Cicognani himself as "weak man," proved incapable of resisting forces much greater than himself. And in fact on 18 March the Austrian bishops, without consulting the Vatican, called on Catholics to vote in favor of the plebiscite for annexation to the greater German Reich. Priests were applauding the demise of most Catholic Austria. This was too much, and this time Rome could not avoid taking a public position that clearly censured the Austrian bishops.

The Pacelli notebooks contain several drafts of this censure. The text was worked over several times, and only one draft survives in a clean version, a process of revision that betrays the anxiety of the secretary of state in the face of a truly difficult situation. The final version, presented at the 1 April audience, is written in a tortured style but leaves no room for doubt:

> Following on the various and often tendentious (indeed, even on the part of individuals from whom one would not expect as much) interpretations of the noted declaration of the Austrian bishopric, we are authorized to communicate, as a point of fact and leaving aside all political considerations [this was added afterward], that, insofar as it was formulated and endorsed without any previous understanding or subsequent approval from the Holy See, responsibility devolves fully on said bishopric.[20]

The pope was very concerned about the actions of Innitzer and the Austrian bishops; he learned about them "not without a degree of fear" and convened the archbishop of Vienna to Rome. Pacelli's notes, combined with the ample documentation from the nunciature in Vienna, testify to the pope's profound irritation over the position of the Austrian cardinal; so from 5 April 1938 we read:

> If we are to speak of resignation, the Holy Father, though it is a hard thing, will accept it under the circumstances. Inform Monsignor Hudal to tell the cardinal (the cardinal has announced that he will arrive in Rome this evening at 7:40 and leave again tomorrow morning around 10) not to make gratuitous observations: even a child, summoned by the pope, would not say that he is leaving immediately afterward. The Holy Father is sadly surprised: "a son of the Church, summoned by the pope, replies that he is coming, but only for a few hours?"[21]

The pope would probably have preferred harsher measures, and Pacelli sought via Monsignor Hudal, rector of Santa Maria dell'Anima, to avoid the worst. On the audience of the following day, Pacelli wrote: "Innitzer's visit. I presented the Holy Father with my planned declaration. (Telegraph Orsenigo that he advance the idea that the only solution is a resignation *eius quid est*; the Holy Father has made it clear that such is the core of his thought.)"[22]

The Holy See's initiative announced to the world its opposition to the sudden alignment of the Austrian bishops. The French Embassy underlined that the statement Innitzer was obliged to issue in Rome "constituted a complete denial of the previous statements made by the Austrian bishopric," namely the recommendation that the faithful vote in favor of the plebiscite of 10 April; now "the Austrian faithful are no longer bound to vote 'yes.'"[23]

Even after the plebiscite of 10 April 1938 that reduced Austria to a province of the Nazi Reich, the Holy See sought to maintain its distance from the cowardly behavior of the Austrian Catholic hierarchy; as Pacelli remarked to the American ambassador to London, Joseph Kennedy, "Their unexpected declaration ... did not receive any approval either previously or afterwards from the Holy See." Pacelli's condemnation was circumstantial:

> Under this [political] pressure as a matter of fact the bishops have overlooked to quote in the text of the declaration the fundamental principles of the freedom of the practice of Christian religion, of the respect of the rights of the Church, and of the abolishment of the anti-Christian propaganda, a clause that in view of the persecution in Germany could have appeared quite natural.[24]

Within a few weeks, the Vatican saw its fears fully realized, as the "de-Christianization measures" taken in Austria confirmed, in the words of the French chargé d'affaires to the Holy See, "the pointlessness of the servile attitude taken by the Austrian bishopric regarding Nazism": alas, "religious persecution" was freely practiced without encountering among the Austrian bishopric that energetic and courageous resistance "of which the German bishopric has offered the example."[25]

The true persecution taking place in those months was instead that against the Jews, carried out in particularly hateful fashion and inspiring no public reaction of note. This was demonstrated by a 10 June article by Enrico Rosche in *L'Osservatore Romano* in which, while condemning the brutality of the methods used against the Jews, he nonetheless concedes, in keeping with German propaganda, that the measures are to some extent justified, as the Jews "had taken over the best positions in all fields, and not always by legitimate means." The Holy See had other priorities than the defense of Austrian

Jews, while Austrian Catholicism, profoundly marked by its nearness to the Nazi spirit, showed itself essentially fragile. Even before the *Anschluß*, Austrian Catholicism was seen as strong in numbers but not particularly autonomous, powerful, or solid, as noted repeatedly in the reports from Orsenigo, the nuncio in Germany; on 31 January 1938 he wrote:

> Unfortunately, the Austrian clergy appears to be poorly prepared for resistance on the economic front, either morally, given its history of dependable government subsidies, or economically, given its already stretched finances and the lack of a tradition among the population to support their own clergy. Many Austrian dioceses already receive regular stipends from Germany.[26]

In the disorientation that followed suppression of the Austrian state, proposals like that of Monsignor Alois Hudal were put forward. The Austrian Hudal sympathized openly with the Nazis; he had been photographed together with Hitler during the latter's visit to Rome in spite of the pope's bans on participation. Hudal's ambitions had often been frustrated, as he repeatedly sought to play a mediating role with the German world; he likely became involved in the Austrian affair in order to fill just such a role. He wanted to celebrate a mass of thanksgiving in the Roman church of Santa Maria dell'Anima, a Te Deum of thanks for the *Anschluß*. He was prevented from doing so – as described in Pacelli's account of the 16 April 1938 audience – by express orders from the pope:

> Monsignor Tardini, and not I, should call Hudal and tell him sweetly, taking the broadest perspective but according to ever stricter necessity, coming finally to the point: the Holy Father does not want this. It is up to him to do this and to put things in order. It would be very disconcerting for many people. We must be coherent. Tell him, moreover, that the Holy Father insists that we are not keeping our distance; rather it is he who has broken with policy must put it right.[27]

Why did the pope ask that Tardini and not Pacelli block Hudal's rash liturgical initiative? One can imagine that Tardini was considered more appropriate than Pacelli because of his lower rank and either because he was more persuasive than Pacelli or else because the secretary of state, in whom Pius XI seems never to have lost the faith, was too good a friend of the Nazi-sympathizing monsignor. Hudal was an ambiguous figure who played an important role after the war in hiding Nazi criminals before they could calmly escape to

South America; according to Sister Pascalina, he supplied the material to Rolf Hochhuth that he used to write *The Deputy*. Hudal returned in July from a trip to Austria, where he had been received by Reichskomissar Josef Bürkel and "was met by Pacelli, who was very 'pessimistic' but at the same time open to finding a *'modus vivendi'* with the German authorities."

"Kill Innitzer"

You have lost almost everything in the last month. You have lost your Catholic circles and your Christian unions. But in spite of all this you will join together with your priests in new unions. I know well that for the past six months many of you have not approved of the behavior of the priests; but perhaps you have not fully grasped the responsibility that Catholic priests bear at this moment. Whatever should happen, I know that you represent Catholic youth inspired by idealism.[28]

On 7 October 1938 the Reuters agency made public the contents of this speech, delivered the day before by the archbishop of Vienna from the pulpit of his cathedral. It was an impassioned sermon that sought to galvanize the Austrian Catholics' sense of belonging, an appeal to their religious identity in opposition to the National Socialists, and came just a few days before the process was begun in Munich that would soon afterward see Hitler's troops marching into Wenceslas Square, and so the unleashing of full-scale nationalist fervor in the victorious Reich.

In the course of just a few months, the Austrian Church had passed much more quickly through phases that took several years in Italy and Germany, from a position of more or less convinced support of the dictatorial regimes of Mussolini and Hitler to one of disillusionment, if not open hostility. In Vienna this transition was lived in dramatic fashion by Cardinal Innitzer, who, as we have seen, from the start did not hesitate to offer the backing of the Church to Hitler.

Following this sermon that attacked the Führer and spoke to Catholic pride, the cardinal was acclaimed in the streets of the ex-capital by Catholic youth. Nazi reaction was fierce. The correspondent of *The Times* sent a vivid report to his readers:

Vienna last night was the scene of fierce anti-religious rioting as a result of the critical comments on the National-Socialist regime made by the Archbishop, Cardinal Innitzer, in the pulpit of St. Stephen's Cathedral on the previous night.

141

Thousands of anti-Catholics, many wearing Nazi emblems and official party uniforms, gathered in the square outside the Cathedral and demonstrated against the Cardinal, whose conciliatory attitude toward the Nazis at the time of the *Anschluß* appears already to have been forgotten. At 8:30 p.m. they stormed his Palace . . . They threw stones through the windows, shouting "Give us the black dog," "Kill Innitzer," "We will tear Innitzer apart," "Leave nothing to send to Dachau."[29]

Police who were present made no effort to prevent the sacking of the archbishop's palace. The correspondent witnessed the protesters climbing ladders into the palace and saw them "smash the beautiful cut-glass chandeliers and wall fittings and throw pictures and books through the windows. All were heaped on to the bonfire."[30] Monsignor Jacob Weinbacher, Innitzer's secretary, was lucky to escape lynching, though his hands were badly injured, and another less fortunate priest from the cathedral was tossed from a window. A note from the Secretariat of State confirmed the seriousness of the event, "much more dangerous than it appeared from the official announcements":

The life of the cardinal himself was seriously endangered, as he was personally attacked and hit . . . The rioters expressed a bestial hatred of him . . . The fire raging in the objects gathered in the square was so great that the crowd was forced to retreat . . . Viennese Catholics are desperate after these events that can only be compared to those that have occurred in Bolshevik Spain.[31]

When Pius XI learned of the devastation in Vienna from Tardini on 9 October 1938, he commented that "even Cardinal Innitzer has come to recognize the evil intentions of that government and declares himself content to be treated like the pope." He ordered, moreover, that "it be made known to the world that the archbishop of Vienna is opposed to Nazism." Five days later he confided to Tardini: "Poor Cardinal Innitzer, I feel for him! I am truly sorry for him! Look at how he is repaid." At the previous day's audience he had commented on a note from Orsenigo that referred to a phrase from Innitzer's speech: "Christ is our Führer," subsequently repeated by young Catholics outside the church: "Our cardinal is several times unhappy! First *Heil Hitler* and then . . . ," a recollection of Innitzer's initially warm welcome for the Führer.[32]

In Rome there were those who did not share the pope's sentiments and would have liked to help Hitler complete his project. Such was Hudal, who in this same period sent two long memos to Pacelli in which he insisted on the need to smooth over relations with the German Reich, toward which "the Church must abandon its purely negative opposition in favor of an active ecclesiastical policy." He also proposed that an apostolic delegate be appointed to Vienna for purely religious purposes as soon as possible (he may have been thinking of himself) to supplement Innitzer, who was obviously inadequate. Pacelli showed these proposals, which also included the appointment of an apostolic delegate for the German Sudetenland, to Monsignor Ludwig Kaas, former president of the Zentrum and Pacelli's close collaborator when he was nuncio in Germany. Kaas disagreed with almost all of the proposals, which in any case came too late, but nonetheless believed that a *modus vivendi* with Germany should be found. He let it be understood, however, that the main obstacle was Pius XI himself, hated by Hitler: "Many believe that under the current pope all negotiation is out of the question because of the Führer's antipathy."[33]

Pacelli's response to Hudal's proposals of 15 November was purely formal:[34] the secretary of state was not optimistic, but once again was convinced that there was no other alternative to seeking conciliation with Germany. Philippe Chenaux, the historian who has most carefully reconstructed the relationship between Pacelli and Hudal, correctly concludes: "While it is an exaggeration to speak of a 'Pacellian approach' for Hudal, it is nonetheless the case that the Austrian prelate's ideas on conciliation . . . may have reassured Pius XI's secretary of state in his ideas regarding the need to come to a truce for the sake of spiritual peace."[35]

The Holy See and the alliance between Rome and Berlin

Following the annexation of Austria by Germany in March 1938, the tortured relationship between Hitler and Mussolini arrived at a crucial juncture. Mussolini's openness to the *Anschluß*, though tinged with disappointment, convinced Germany to block the residual Italian tendencies favoring a possible *rapprochement* with London and Paris.[36] Improved relations with the Holy See would certainly have facilitated the alliance with Mussolini upon which, according to Richard Weizsäcker, Hitler had decided on 2 April.[37] After *Kristallnacht*, Mussolini presumably told Ciano that, if something similar were to happen to German Catholics, the axis would not have held. During the year between the *Anschluß* and the Munich Conference, the religious question became for the Germans a means to gauge and render more alluring the alliance, while for the Italians it served as a brake. The Vatican found itself the unintended object of a diplomatic contest between the two dictators in which Hitler's visit to Rome, capital of both the fascist empire and world Catholicism, played an important role.

On the occasion of Hitler's visit, Pius XI famously described the swastika as "a cross inimical to the cross of Christ." That phrase symbolized the pope's opposition to Hitler and was emblematic of his disdain for an event – Hitler's trip to Italy – that was heavier on symbolism than political substance: "Sad events are transpiring, very sad events, both near and far. Among those sad events is this: it is found to be neither inappropriate nor poorly timed to erect in Rome on the day of the Holy Cross another cross that is not the cross of Christ."[38]

During Hitler's stay in Rome, while the lights of the city shone brightly and fireworks celebrated the event, the Vatican remained in complete darkness. Its museums were firmly shut as a sign of disrespect for a leader who famously enjoyed Italian art. The pope made a point of leaving Rome for Castelgandolfo, where, as reported in *L'Osservatore Romano*, he could breathe better air.[39]

The existing historiography, perhaps so as not to minimize the dramatic nature of the pope's frigid attitude, has tended to overlook the fact that Hitler too showed absolutely no interest in a meeting. That disinformation seems to have characterized not only contemporary historians; apparently the papal nuncio to Paris, Valerio Valeri, noted a discrepancy in the Rome correspondence of the Catholic paper *La Croix*, which referred at the same time to fascist protests against Pius XI's refusal to meet with the Führer and to the fact that the pope would have received Hitler had he simply been asked. The pope would in any case have agreed to meet with the Führer had he not been offended by Hitler's failure to ask, as is clear from the exchanges between the Secretariat of State and the Italian Embassy:

> This morning – wrote Ciano to the Berlin Embassy on 19 April – I spoke with the secretary of state about a possible meeting between the Führer and the pope. The cardinal was very reserved. He did say, however, that he was convinced that the Führer would never make the public declaration expected of him by the pope. I observed that if the Führer were to show serious interest in visiting the Holy Father, perhaps the pope would concede in the end, to demonstrate his spirit of conciliation. Cardinal Pacelli gave me the impression that he shared my evaluation.[40]

According to the Italian foreign minister, judging in any case from his archives, the pope had let it be understood by the Italian authorities that he would have received "*o Furiere*" – his title was Italianized in this way by the adoring Neapolitan crowds – if he had made the request "in the appropriate fashion."[41] The papal secretary, Confalonieri, confirmed this conditional openness: "There is talk of an eventual meeting between Hitler and the pope, but it is obvious that in order for that to happen clear a gesture must be made that demonstrates to the world and to the Church the beginning of a change in policy. Pointless."[42]

There was a great deal of pretense on both the Italian and the German side prior to the visit. Even the men closest to Hitler signaled a hardly credible *rapprochement*. So, for example, on 19 March Count Magistrati, the Italian chargé d'affaires to Berlin, referred to a conversation with Marshal Göring:

> Göring recognizes the importance of the religious question, especially at this moment. And Hitler too wants religious pacification – "he looks forward and not back" – and so is considering a general amnesty. For the Vatican the moment is at hand for a "great and definitive chance" to achieve an agreement with the Reich. But, in order for that to happen, the Holy See must accept the *Anschluß* and convince Austrian Catholics to accept it as well. Göring has praised Cardinal Innitzer's second "appeal." The marshal also points out that the trials against religious have been suspended for months now following Hitler's orders. Nor does he plan further hostilities in the future. Göring rules out the possibility of a meeting between Hitler and the pope. He recalls, though, with a certain warmth the audience granted him by the Holy Father in 1933, even though he had the impression that the pope saw little difference between National Socialism and communism.[43]

Pacelli, well equipped to recognize the manipulative nature of these openings, did not give up and continued to see the possibility of gaining some advantage. In particular he envisioned relaunching drawn-out negotiations on multiple fronts: the education of youth, pastoral freedom, the defense of Catholic Action, the end of the anti-Catholic campaign, and finally response to the many notes sent by the Holy See regarding violation of the concordat.[44]

Mussolini hoped to use the double role of the eternal city to increase his negotiating leverage vis-à-vis Berlin, while not overly annoying the pope. To this end he made statements that seemed to lend him distance from Hitler, but only succeeded in irritating Pius

XI. False affirmations of good will were mixed in with real threats, so that it was difficult to identify a coherent position. Germany seemed instead to issue inconsistent signs of mollification that alternated with harsh attacks. It was a war of dissimulation. One could imagine a degree of support from Mussolini, but the hope that he might influence the Führer and lead him to more moderate positions was quickly dispelled – indeed, coincident with Hitler's arrival in Rome. Mussolini's mediator on this occasion was again Tacchi-Venturi, and there is interesting documentation on his role in this period, just as it began to wane.[45]

The pope was irritated by the fluctuations of Mussolini, who forwarded to him Hitler's threats, while the fascist press sang his praises. From the audience of 8 January 1938 we read:

> Write to Father Tacchi-Venturi on behalf of the Holy Father. "The Holy Father is unable to reconcile what he reads in *il Duce*'s press, in particular *Il Messaggero*, and would be grateful should he make this known as soon as possible to *il Duce*. And send along the ambassador (the Holy Father himself wanted to summon him). The pope speaks in this fashion, as everybody knows. The head of the government wanted to see Tacchi-Venturi in order to praise the positions of the Holy Father; but then witness all that is written in the press. Say in the name of the Holy Father that he is sadly surprised to see himself treated in that way in the press that calls itself fascist and, as is well known, gets clearance from the top. The Holy Father asks if we are serious or not. If this principle has any meaning, the Holy Father prohibits such behavior. We can accept invective, but not ridicule."[46]

It is a confusing report in specifics, if clear in overall emphasis. The meaning of the penultimate phrase is unclear: "If this principle has any meaning, the Holy Father prohibits such behavior." What principle and what exactly is prohibited? The letter Pacelli sent to Tacchi-Venturi on 8 January 1938 so that it could be read to Mussolini translated this message, as always, into less confrontational language, though without losing its meaning:

> His Holiness was especially pained today by articles on the visit to Rome by the chancellor of the German Reich that appeared in papers, like *Il Messaggero* of this morning, that call themselves fascist. He does not understand how the fulsome statements of Mussolini can be reconciled with the positions taken by a press that is well known to take orders from above.[47]

146

The pope's requirements were put into a letter of 10 January sent to Tacchi-Venturi after much correction by Pacelli.[48] Together with the copy of Pacelli's letter is another addressed to *il Duce* in which the Jesuit Tacchi-Venturi softens the Vatican position still more:

> The Holy Father did me the honor yesterday evening of assigning me the task of informing you that he thanks you for the assurances you have transmitted through my offices regarding Catholic Action, which is to say that things will remain in the peaceful status quo in which we currently find them. His Holiness added that if there are any problems, not so much with Catholic Action as with this or that lay member, please to let him know through myself or other channels.[49]

The Jesuit sought to emphasize the possible moves that Mussolini might make in the context of what appeared to be an irreparable break between Germany and the Holy See. On 17 March he wrote to Mussolini: "The Holy Father was very pleased to learn that your excellency will take whatever measures he can to insure that religious persecution cease in Germany and not be implemented in Austria. But you are already informed in this regard from the letter of the secretary of state that I myself sent to you yesterday evening."[50]

Pacelli's elaboration weakened the pope's message, and Tacchi-Venturi's relation softened it still further. Both betrayed a general embarrassment and the growing fear that a break between the pope and Hitler would also damage his relations with Mussolini.

Mussolini suggests that Hitler be excommunicated

On the eve of Hitler's visit to Rome, Mussolini made the surprising suggestion to Pius XI that he excommunicate the German dictator:

> The head of government (Mussolini) told Father Tacchi-Venturi in a private meeting (Thursday, 7 April 1938) that more energetic measures needed to be taken with Hitler, not immediately but waiting for the opportune moment to take those measures, for example excommunication. He added that one should not imagine that the Hitler movement is a temporary phenomenon that will pass, as this man has accomplished great things for Germany. The only way to stop him is with war, but we wish to avoid war. He well understands that this more energetic measure taken by the Holy See would please persons whom the Holy See does not like, but that does not lessen the need.[51]

How to interpret this document? It is indeed surprising, if entirely wrapped up in a context that might offer some sort of explanation. Preparations were under way for the festivities to mark Hitler's arrival, while the pope made no effort to hide his indignation. The relationship between fascism and the Vatican was at a low point and would not improve following imminent introduction of the racial laws. Mussolini's proposal, then, might represent a ham-fisted attempt to gain the pope's sympathy at a moment when the latter was on a collision course with Hitler. Or it might even be an accusation that the Catholic Church was not doing all it could to prevent Europe and the world from falling into the abyss that opened before them. A more forced reading might detect an attempt to employ the Holy See in a plan that sought to avoid closing off other possible avenues of cooperation (especially in the context of the agreements crafted by Dino Grandi at Easter): "persons whom the Holy See does not like" refers more than likely to Jews and masons.

It is difficult, however, to make out the design of a truly alternative policy, one that contradicts the entire context. Certainly the events of April must have played a role, in particular Mussolini's irritation over the Alto Adige question. In which case the proposal may be nothing more than a gratuitous verbal outbreak – as so often with *il Duce* – an idle threat with no real political significance. What renders the proposal shocking and indeed incredible, even as a mere hypothesis, is that it comes in the midst of negotiations for the Italo-German alliance, negotiations that did, however, follow the usual stop-and-go pattern revealed in all the work of Renzo De Felice. The issue in any case remains a serious one, as this would have been a personal excommunication and not a condemnation of the principles or philosophy of Nazism, as had occurred in the case of Alfred Rosenberg's ideas when his *Mythus des XX. Jahrhunderts* was placed on the Index (for which there exists ample documentation in the archives of the Congregation for the Doctrine of the Faith).

All the available documentation speaks to the psychological and cultural diffidence that characterized the relationship between Hitler and Mussolini, a relationship characterized by continual sparring and acts of disrespect – a contest in which the sense of who held the upper hand switched back and forth.[52] But this proposal does not fit the usual stereotype. The Jesuit Tacchi-Venturi was not facetious like *il Duce* and certainly had no interest in falsifying a request of this sort, one to which in any case there is also reference among Pacelli's audiences.[53] Beyond its place among the many anecdotes of the regime, this document is interesting for the level of uncertainty and confusion that it reveals on the part of Mussolini in those crucial months. The report of the Italian nuncio Borgongini Duca regarding a meeting he had with Ciano on 30 April makes this clearer still:

> Minister Ciano did not convey his thoughts to me, but I was left with the impression that he too was not enthusiastic about German policy and deplored the persecution of the Church. He asked me what impression Göring's declarations to Count Magistrati had made in the Vatican, and I replied that those declarations could not make any impression at all as they were immediately contradicted by the positions taken by Hitler. He added that Göring is more conciliatory than Hitler, who is unlikely to change direction. Count Ciano did express his personal approval of the moderate positions taken by the Church in not adopting extreme sanctions (excommunication, breaking off of diplomatic relations, and the like).
>
> He may have said these things to me in order to extract some sort of reaction on my part, but I simply replied that the Holy See did not want to be responsible for eliminating the last hope of negotiation and added nothing more.
>
> I seemed to detect in Count Ciano's words a cooling on Mussolini's part toward Germany and perhaps the fact that he would not disapprove of those extreme sanctions.[54]

Discussion of extreme sanctions that might be taken against Hitler, for example excommunication, did moreover take place in Mussolini's circle, even if only superficially, and they were probably limited to deterrents and deviations. The religious question and papal intransigence certainly created problems for some fascist hierarchs and inspired an almost desperate attempt to shore up the German ally. The most difficult role, as evidenced by his meeting with Borgongini Duca and a series of embarrassing moments, was that played by Ciano, who could not afford to see relations with either Germany or the Vatican deteriorate. A month and a half later, on 15 June, in another discussion with the Italian nuncio, the minister of foreign affairs affirmed that "he had always sought to do whatever possible to advance the requests coming from the Holy See and regretted failure in this regard on one issue only, that of establishing peace between the Church and Germany":

> "There must be a way to come to an understanding, and I should be happy to offer my services. The Catholic Church is losing ground daily in Germany." . . . And he asked repeatedly if, in the face of such a debacle, it might not be the moment to back off a bit . . . from the position of absolute intransigence. On the other hand, in order to avoid

isolation, the Italian government finds itself of necessity firmly behind the Rome–Berlin axis . . . I added: "What does your excellency believe should be done in a practical sense? You know that one can not reason with unreasonable people, people lacking even a smidgeon of conscience." He replied: "And still I believe that they will negotiate. In any case I wouldn't know what sort of practical suggestion to make, but felt the need confidentially to express my state of mind and offer any help that I can."[55]

On 2 July Nuncio Borgongini Duca was received by Bottai in order to convey for the umpteenth time criticism of the immodest "gymnastic practices of girls in school." This was a recurrent concern of the pope, and while it seems a minor issue compared to the major political ones of the day, excessive exposure of the body, especially the female body, was disapproved of from the moment the Nazis took power and is the subject of interesting discussion and documentation. In the meeting between Bottai, now minister of national education, and the nuncio, Bottai described his recent visit to Cologne:

"Speaking yesterday evening with Mussolini, I commented that you cannot imagine what they are capable of doing when you consider that, in the presence of the minister of national education of a Catholic country, their minister of education (if I understood Rust correctly) delivered a one and a half hour speech in which he announced that it was time to be done with the religion of Jesus, who was in any case a bastard (that was precisely his sacrilegious blasphemy). He described a careful program of de-Christianization. I attended rites in honor of water, fire, and earth, and while for Italians blasphemy makes the blood curdle, these rites are instead ridiculous; still I worry about the great harm they do to the young and wonder where all of this will take us. Enough, I concluded, let us put our faith in God." I communicated to him that these practices were identical to those of the Bolsheviks . . . He asked me if the Holy Father was in pain.[56]

The meeting concluded on a coarse note, with comments in Roman dialect on the "ever worse" gymnastic practices in Italy. Although a minor episode, the fact that such important topics – in essence the contrast between pagan religion and the Semitic roots of Christianity and the education of youth – can conclude in a "good Roman laugh" offers a disconcerting picture of the way in which important figures on the political-ecclesiastical scene used the "religious question" at such a tragic moment. We find another pathetic attempt to maintain distance from Hitler on religious issues in the critical comments of Roberto Farinacci at the Nuremberg Rally of September 1938.

Farinacci on that occasion countered the pope's attack on the recent fascist racial manifesto by invoking the pope's non-infallibility regarding scientific and terrestrial topics; just as the Church had erred in the case of Galileo, so was it mistaken regarding racial theory. Even the usually accommodating Orsenigo, so inclined to accept the official versions and to find any sort of conciliation, raised doubts about Farinacci's criticism and his true loyalty to the spirit of Nuremberg.[57]

The impression that one derives from this series of awkward and half-hearted attempts to use the hostility of the Holy See against Germany in order to limit or condition the alliance with Italy is one of great uncertainty and limited conviction. It was a confusion that in any case led to the seemingly irresistible decision to proceed with the meeting with Hitler. The Vatican, and especially the pope, was used by Mussolini as a last attempt, a sort of charm to ward off the unavoidable and disastrous alliance with Nazism, an alliance for which Mussolini attempted by means of his pathetic request for the excommunication of Hitler to render Pius XI partially responsible.

"SPIRITUALLY WE ARE ALL SEMITES"

And I am ashamed . . . ashamed to be Italian. And tell that, father [Tacchi-Venturi], to Mussolini himself. I am ashamed not as pope but as an Italian! The Italian people have become a herd of stupid sheep. I will speak out, without fear. I am forced to by the concordat, but even more so by my conscience.

From an audience with Tardini, 28 October 1938

The missing encyclical on racism and anti-Semitism

The pope's summer of 1938 in Castelgandolfo was a long one. He had left Rome for the Castelli Romani already at the beginning of May in order to avoid Hitler, and he stayed there till late autumn. Those were months of intense work during which he delivered his strongest speeches against racist separatism. One of these was attended by the American Jesuit John LaFarge, who had arrived in Rome in early June and joined the many faithful who, along with the teaching faculty of the Gregoriana, attended the papal general audience. It was LaFarge whom the pope asked to draft the text of a new and harsher encyclical against racism and anti-Semitism.

A number of elements led to the decision to issue an encyclical still stronger than *Mit brennender Sorge*: a still stinging recollection of the Führer's visit, symbol of the accord between the pope's native Italy and Nazism; preparations for the Italian racial laws that were its first bitter fruit; and friction over Catholic Action. And so in that same summer of 1938, as the Evian Conference failed and the Jews, ever more alone, headed toward catastrophe, Pius XI finally decided to go beyond a simple condemnation of generic racism. Hence the famous encyclical that never saw the light of day.

A few days after having listened to Pius XI at Castelgandolfo, LaFarge received to his great surprise a summons from the pope, who had read and admired his book entitled *Interracial Justice* attacking racism against blacks in the United States. Here is LaFarge's description, taken from his 1954 autobiography, of that meeting on 22 June:

> The Holy Father received me graciously. Apparently he had just returned from a walk and his white cane rested on a ledge behind him. I found he wished to talk to me on the question of racialism, which had now become a burning issue in Italy and in Germany. He said he was continually revolving the matter in his mind, and was deeply impressed by the fact that racialism and nationalism were fundamentally the same. He had read my book *Interracial Justice* and liked the title of it. " 'Interracial Justice,' *c'est bon!*" he said, pronouncing the title as if it were French. He said he thought my book was the best thing written on the topic, comparing it with some European literature. Naturally, this was a big lift to me. Apparently what appealed to him in my little effort was the spiritual and moral treatment of the topic, and the fact that I did bring into synthesis the Catholic doctrine and the natural law and the pertinent facts, as well as some practical methods for dealing with the question.[1]

Full of praise for his work, on 22 June Pius XI assigned the stunned American Jesuit the task of writing the text of an encyclical: " '*Say simply,*' he told me, '*what you would say if you yourself were pope.*' "[2]

The choice of an American Jesuit holding open and democratic ideas, an expert on racism but a complete outsider relative to the Curia and to Italian and German issues, speaks to the pope's solitude and to what he himself described as a revelation: "He told me that God had sent me to him, as he was looking for a man to write on this topic." It was a decision to which he had come after months of profound reflection: "He then outlined the topic, its method of treatment, and discussed the underlying principles."[3]

As compared with *Mit brennender Sorge*, the novelty of the lost encyclical lay in its explicit condemnation of anti-Semitism, a term that had not appeared in the official documents of the Holy See, with the exception of the decree of the Holy Office from 25 March 1928 dissolving the "Friends of Israel." That decree, discussed in chapter 5, condemned "the hatred against a people chosen by God, hatred that today is commonly referred to as anti-Semitism." It focused more on hatred than on anti-Semitism and always maintained the distinction between an evil anti-Semitism linked to the idea of race and a good one relating to Jewish practices. The fact of addressing directly the issue of anti-Semitism in the encyclical and without this sort of parsing was important and new. The French scholars Georges Passelecq and Bernard Suchecky, while they do a fine job of reconstructing the narrative of the lost encyclical, nonetheless underestimate this novelty. It is again Miccoli who sets it out clearly:

> It is almost impossible to imagine that the solid linking of racism and anti-Semitism – expressed with clear and penetrating efficiency in the project (a linking, moreover, highly unusual in Vatican documents) – could have derived from an independent initiative of one of the drafters. LaFarge confirms as much in his entry on "racism" that appeared posthumously in 1967 in volume XII of the *New Catholic Encyclopedia*. The encyclical was intended to deal with racism and especially anti-Semitism. It was meant to deal with them together. This was something entirely new; insofar as, according to the pope, the condemnation of racist doctrines had become universal, did that condemnation then apply to anti-Semitism as well?[4]

We need not trace the tortured drafting of the encyclical. LaFarge did not feel up to the task and requested assistance from the Jesuit superior general Ledóchowski, who assigned two other Jesuits to work with him: Gustav Gundlach, a German forced to live in Rome following his harsh condemnations on Vatican Radio of the pro-Nazi positions taken by Cardinal Innitzer of Vienna, and Father Gustave Desbuquois, director of Action Populaire, the Jesuit group operating in the outskirts of Paris and an active part of that French social Catholicism that sponsored the *Semaines sociales*. This small group worked in strict secrecy in Paris until, following several drafts (there are three versions, one in each of the mother tongues of the three Jesuits: French, German, and English), the Jesuit superior general wrote to LaFarge on 1 September that he could return to the US while assigning to Desbuquois the task of sending the text by a "secure route."

LaFarge, however, did not leave immediately but instead returned to Rome to meet with Ledóchowski, presumably to deliver to him the text of the encyclical so that it could be presented to the pope, before embarking for America on 1 October. And yet the pope received the text only four months later, on 21 January 1939, after having made insistent requests. Twenty days later Pius XI died. What happened during those four months? Based on the reconstructions that have been made, to which research we refer, it appears that

Ledóchowski intentionally delayed, holding up delivery to Pius XI, who was seriously ill and not expected to survive much longer. For Gundlach, who assigns no responsibility to LaFarge, this is more than a suspicion:

> If one considers, in addition, that it took the boss [Ledóchowski] two weeks to submit the business to the person mentioned [Father Rosa], and that he has since remained completely silent, one begins to have strange ideas. A person unconnected with the affair might see in all this an attempt to sabotage, through dilatory action, and for tactical and diplomatic reasons, the mission with which you were directly entrusted by Mr Fisher [Pius XI].[5]

As we have seen, Ledóchowski, the Polish Jesuit superior general, was fiercely anti-communist and harbored scant sympathy for the Jews. He had been a strenuous supporter of the encyclical against communism, *Divini Redemptoris*, and in all likelihood boycotted that in defense of the Jews. The choice to have it revised by Father Rosa, to whom he had sent the text, is itself significant. This Jesuit had in fact for twenty years published in *Civiltà Cattolica* articles on Jews that were so harsh as to be used by fascist propaganda in defending Mussolini's racial laws against Vatican criticism. LaFarge, on Gundlach's advice, informed the pope that he had delivered the encyclical to the superior general and, according to testimony from the American Jesuit Father Abbott, it was this note that led Pius XI to request, via Tardini, its immediate delivery – delivery that finally took place on 21 January.

The story of the lost encyclical has become something of a Vatican spy story and as such has generated a lot of interest. Just the same, it is a serious and important issue insofar as it is yet another confirmation of a changed attitude on the part of the pope that evolved over the last years of his life; indeed, it is one of its most significant indicators. It was not then a hasty reaction or improvisation, but rather exactly the opposite, in some sense a distillation of the pope's thought that he wanted to sanction in a formal encyclical dedicated for the first time explicitly to the issue of anti-Semitism. It was a gesture that in the climate of those months would have intensified in unpredictable ways the conflict not only with Nazi Germany but also with Italy and its racial laws.

The recently opened archives seem not to contain any trace of the planned encyclical, though one can find documents there from those months that testify to more than one initiative on the part of Pius XI to aid victims of the persecution. By summer 1938 the Holy See had already monitored for years the spread of anti-Semitic policies in the heart of Christian Europe. Among the many examples we could cite is that of Monsignor Aldo Laghi, the chargé d'affaires to Switzerland, who referred at length to the activities of the First World Jewish Congress held in Geneva from 8 to 14 August 1936 and at which the first steps of this new plague were denounced:

> Nazi oppression of the Jews becomes every day more serious in Germany. The measures and laws adopted defy any juridical concept accepted in the civilized world. The persecution not only deprives German Jews of all rights and destroys them economically but also seeks to spread the anti-Semitic poison in all the countries of the world.[6]

In the judgment of the French Embassy to the Vatican, the Holy See at the end of January 1938 was fully aware of the extent of anti-Semitic policies in European states: from the discrimination recently introduced in Romania "following the example of the Third Reich," to the boycott of Jewish merchants in Poland, to the purge "of part of the once dominant Jewish element in the Counsels of the USSR," and finally to the "anti-Semitic campaign undertaken by a number of Italian papers." These developments distressed the Church, which was "clearly opposed to anti-Semitism, as it sees there combined the racism it condemns, the hateful nationalism it rejects, and a spirit of intolerance that might target also Catholicism." The expansion of the anti-Semitic movement, moreover, "was a sign of the growing influence of Hitler," even among Catholics.[7] And so, for example, on 7 December 1938, the archbishop of Westminster, while thanking the pope for having taken an interest in converted Jews who "because they do not possess pure Aryan blood have been expelled" from the territory of Hitler's Reich, relayed an acknowledgment from Lord Rothschild: "The thoughts and feelings of the Holy Father will be faithfully interpreted with declarations that he looks with human and Christian approval on every effort to show charity and offer aid to all those who are innocent victims in these sad times."[8]

In that same period, the initiatives on behalf of converted Jews accelerated. Various papal representatives, for example, were asked to help converted Jewish professionals forced to take refuge abroad. Or again, in December, an attempt was made to facilitate the expatriation of Austrian converted Jews and convince Canada to accept their immigration. The pope wrote personally to Cardinals Mundelein, Dougherty, O'Connell, and Villeneuve so that they might aid Jewish scientists, persecuted "according to those well-known laws directed against all those who are not Aryan," and further requesting "care and charity for those who belong to that which was His people [this last bit was written in Latin – literally, "the people from whom He comes," a reference that evokes the pope's "spiritually we are all Semites"] and for whom He cries on the cross itself invoking charity and forgiveness."[9] American Jews showed great appreciation for what the pope had done for their brothers, and in August 1939 the American United Jewish Appeal donated $125,000 in memory of the deceased Pius XI. On 29 December 1939, already several months into the war, Monsignor Bernard Sheil, auxiliary bishop of Chicago, cited the courageous example of Pius XI:

> No man of our time or generation has fought the fanaticism of intolerant racism with more vigor and courage than Pius XI. When cruel and tyrannical laws were decreed against your people, his fearless voice rose in indignant protest. He condemned racial intolerance and hate as contrary to God's laws, the dictates of good sense, and the wellbeing of civilization.[10]

On 15 March 1939, the same day that the Nazi flag flew over Hradcany, Gundlach wrote to his Jesuit brother who had received from Pius XI the task of preparing the encyclical; it was a troubled letter in which he confided to LaFarge that, after the death of the pope, while "we hope that the right line will be followed as in the past. We are nonetheless concerned to see diplomatic influences accorded more importance than is right":

> But it is erroneous to want, out of fear of red communism, to spare the bourgeoisie, and especially the Catholic bourgeoisie, all real sacrifices ... by holding up frightful images of communists attacking religion and the Church ... But the Church will not be able to exist honorably and successfully unless it clearly supports the challenge of the gospels and of natural law, *everywhere* and with regard to *everything* ... Today, at the same time that the newspapers are describing the fall of the rest of Czechoslovakia and Prague, we have to see clearly that this crazy business of race could become no less a danger to the world than red communism.[11]

Mussolini's racial laws

On 15 July 1938, the same day as the publication of the Italian "Manifesto of Racist Scientists," Pius XI met with the sisters of Notre Dame du Cénacle, the order with which he had been linked since his days as a priest in Milan. During that audience he referred to "having on that very day received an item of great seriousness," one that took on the form of a "true apostasy." "It is no longer a question of this or that idea that is in error, but rather the whole spirit of the doctrine is contrary to the faith in Christ": "'Catholic' means 'universal': there is no other possible translation in Italian or any other modern language. And 'Catholic Church' means 'universal Church.'"[12] The regrettable news that he had received that morning was evidently that next step of the regime on the path that led to the racial laws.

That encounter inaugurated the series of discourses against racism and nationalism Pius XI delivered during his prolonged summer 1938 stay at Castelgandolfo following his departure from Rome on the occasion of Hitler's visit (the dates of the discourses are 15 and 28 July, 21 August, and 6 and 18 September). As we have seen, this was the period during which he came to the decision to issue the encyclical against racism and anti-Semitism. They constitute his most mature reflections on exaggerated nationalism, racism, and totalitarianism. He himself recognized this fact when he said that day "that he had never thought about these issues with such precision, in such absolute terms, one might even say with such intransigence."[13] And yet in those very hours the Jesuit Angelo Brucculeri would write in *Avvenire d'Italia* that he had "no objections" to racism, and his was just one of the many voices that did not follow the lead of the pope, as one can read in the pages of *Civiltà Cattolica*.[14]

These were the days when Pius XI began instead to use progressively stronger language against Italy in a crescendo that would end only with his death. The understanding between the Church and fascism was not simply pragmatic or contextual; throughout the 1920s it stood for the hope that authentic conservative values could grow and collaborate reciprocally. Disillusionment was great, then, over not only the non-Catholicization of fascism but also Mussolini's surprising indifference regarding the maintenance of good relations with the Church. The pope felt this disillusionment deeply during the last months of his life, especially regarding the racial laws and Catholic Action.

On 16 February 1938, *il Duce* denied the existence of a Jewish question in Italy. Four months later, on 14 July, a document entitled the "Manifesto of Racist Scientists" laid out "the fascist position on the racial problem." Anti-Jewish laws followed in September and November. These were the same months during which Pius XI made his most important pronouncements against Nazism, while the Italian racial laws were condemned as violations of the concordat regarding mixed marriages. Susan Zuccotti rightly asks: "What did Pope Pius

XI and officials at the Vatican Secretariat of State do and say during these two critical periods, as they became more and more conscious of Mussolini's intentions?"[15]

On 13 April 1938 the Congregation of Seminaries and Universities, of which the pope himself was prefect, sent the Catholic rectors a circular requesting that Catholic instructors oppose the eight errors of the racial doctrine. Its distribution was limited, but the message was reinforced with an article in *L'Osservatore Romano* entitled "Examples of Racist Theories." It was in any case in that same summer of 1938 that Pius XI launched an attack that provoked Mussolini in an area in which he was especially sensitive: on 30 July the pope asked "why Italy had so disgracefully to imitate Germany . . . The Latins did not speak of race, or anything of the kind. Our Italian forefathers had better terms than these."[16] On that same day, in Forlì, *il Duce* furiously declared it absurd to suggest that fascist racism imitated the German variety. A bit later, on 18 September, he was still more explicit in attacking those who made this suggestion: "They are poor imbeciles, and I don't know whether to revile them or to pity them."

On 30 July, Galeazzo Ciano immediately convened the Italian nuncio Borgongini Duca in order to explain to him, as Ciano describes in his diary, the aims and scope of "our racism"; Ciano found an appreciative listener, so much so that he described him as "personally very anti-Semitic." The summary submitted to the Secretariat of State confirms that Borgongini Duca was in fact, unlike his pope, more than receptive to the racial laws introduced by the government and described to him:

> Monsignor, where are we headed? This morning *il Duce* called me [it must have been a telephone call, as Mussolini was in Forlì] very upset by the pope's discourse to the students of Propaganda Fide, so upset that he has replied publicly . . . The government must regulate the relationship between whites and blacks in the empire . . . Along with the question of the blacks, we must also deal with that of the Jews, for two reasons: 1. because they are being expelled everywhere and we don't want those expellees to think that Italy is some sort of promised land; 2. because it is in their doctrine, consecrated in the Talmud, that the Jew must mix with other races like oil with water, namely staying on top, in a position of power. And we seek to prevent that in Italy they take control.[17]

To the scattered arguments of *il Duce*'s son-in-law, the nuncio replied in kind that the Church had always taken care "to prevent not only sexual relations but also marriages between blacks and whites, in order to avoid the creation of half-castes that combine, as is well known, the worst of both races." He added that the words of the pope that so alarmed Mussolini needed to be interpreted as a pious religious oration without any political significance. He was reassured by Ciano that Italian racism would be much different from German racism: "He told me that Italy is a Catholic country and that, if anyone here were to say that Jesus Christ was a bastard, he would be punished as a blasphemer." The nuncio limited himself to regretting that the Reich continued to persecute Jews who had converted to Catholicism: "I explained to him my concern that Germany continued to persecute as Jews even those who were baptized and converted and so had left their people. In Italy, instead, thanks to the concordat, one could not block the marriage of a converted Jew and a Catholic."[18]

On 12 August *L'Osservatore Romano* confirmed that Borgongini's attitude was shared by the Vatican establishment, openly contradicting Pius XI and denying that the pope meant that fascism was imitating Hitler. In fact just the opposite was true, as the pope, making explicit reference to the racial laws, had often cited them as examples of Italy blindly following Germany's lead: "Italy and the Italians are a herd of sheep! We have Mussolini to thank for that!"[19]

It may have been the distinction between discrimination and persecution, advanced by the fascist government on 5 August, that motivated the positions of the Vatican paper. Alternatively, the reduced tension between the two banks of the Tiber may find explanation in a granting of greater freedom for Catholic Action in exchange for acceptance of the racial laws. On 14 August *L'Osservatore Romano* returned once more to the topic and published an article describing the excellent treatment the Jews, protected in the ghetto, had always received from the Church. Two days later Mussolini replied by sending a private note asking that the pope not address the issue in public and assuring that he in any case would treat the Jews better than the Church had.

Pius XI rejected Mussolini's proposal and, as Pacelli wrote relative to the audience of 20 August, asked Father Gemelli not to bow to these injunctions.

The next day – in that month packed with controversy – the pope also criticized Father Tacchi-Venturi for his reticence and too-easy acceptance of Mussolini's positions:

Tell Tacchi-Venturi that what must be said must be said . . . Let Father Tacchi-Venturi know that the Holy Father, angry and discontent, is worse. And say also to Mussolini that, if he wants to kill off the Holy Father, he is using efficient methods. But the Holy Father will first make it known to the world how the Catholic religion and the Holy Father have been treated in Italy. Hold firm![20]

At this point the outbursts of *il Duce* intensified, as he threatened to scratch below the surface and turn the Italians once again into anti-clericals; it was a crescendo that would grow until the death of the pope.

"Spiritually we are all Semites"

In the experience of Italian Jews, as indeed in the books and films that have recalled that dark moment in Italian history, the most agonizing memory is that of Jewish students banished from public elementary and secondary schools just as they were about to return for the new academic year. This wound on national memory has a precise date – 5 September 1938 – when, at the end of the summer vacation, the regime issued a decree entitled "Measures for the defense of the race in fascist schools."

The day after the racist decree, 6 September, the pope pronounced what may have been his clearest statement on anti-Semitism. With a trembling voice, he spoke to pilgrims from Belgian Catholic Radio on the sacrifice of Abraham; at the invitation of the pope himself, Monsignor Picard, president of the radio, carefully transcribed that discourse:

> At this point the pope could no longer control his emotions . . . and it was with tears in his eyes that he cited the passages from Saint Paul that describe our spiritual descent from Abraham . . . Listen carefully: Abraham is our patriarch, our ancestor. Anti-Semitism is not compatible with the sublime thought and reality evoked by this text. Anti-Semitism is a hateful movement with which we as Christians must have no involvement . . . Through Christ and in Christ we are the spiritually descendants of Abraham . . . Every time I read the words "the sacrifice of our father Abraham," I cannot help but be profoundly moved. Christians are not permitted to take part in anti-Semitism. We recognize that everyone has a right to self-defense and can undertake those actions necessary to protect his legitimate interests. But anti-Semitism is inadmissible. Spiritually we are all Semites.[21]

The spiritual inspiration that emphasized the common Semitic origin – the affirmation that "spiritually we are all Semites" – again

161

reinforces rather than lessens the weight of the condemnation. A theological density of this sort seems, moreover, to clash with the juridically reductive nature of the Vatican's opposition to the racial laws. And the observation regarding the protection of legitimate interests seems to put forward once again a justification for discrimination against the Jews, against whose invasiveness one can justifiably defend oneself.

The argument that underlies Pius XI's reasoning, however, recalls instead the religious roots of anti-Semitism, that anti-Judaism that had so strongly influenced the history of the persecution of the Jews and that in the statement "spiritually we are all Semites" finds its most convincing refutation. His judgment is unequivocal, at least regarding the responsibility of the Christian tradition for the persecution of the Jews. It is a judgment that becomes that much more significant in an environment that does not support it – indeed, tends to oppose it, as is clear from the summary of this audience that appeared in *L'Osservatore Romano* and remarkably neglects to cite the pope's reference to the Jews.[22] *Civiltà Cattolica* made no reference at all. Indeed, nowhere in the Italian press, Catholic included, do we find reference to these weighty theological affirmations, affirmations that were much cited in France.[23]

The path taken with the racial manifesto in July and followed by a series of declarations and measures during the summer concluded with a general anti-Jewish decree issued on 17 November 1938, entitled "Declaration for the defense of the Italian race." Pius XI expressed his concern several times in the month of October, as noted in his audiences with Tardini; for the 19th we read:

> The Holy Father approves of the idea that when Cardinal Mundelein comes to Rome the two of them will discuss the merits of an eventual initiative to help Italian Catholic Jews, who will find themselves in more difficult conditions than those who stuck to the Jewish religion. On the Jews he says: "They have acted as porters. Saint Augustine wrote as much: *studentibus nobis libros portant*. Spiritually we are all Semites." The pope insists constantly that we do what we can: "on the question of the marriage of Jews, the pope instructs that we quickly issue an official memo, as the writings and initiatives of Father Tacchi-Venturi are basically private matters."[24]

The next day he considered the publication of an official document, "so that it is clear that the Holy See has alerted the Italian government to the painful consequences of its new laws."[25] And one more day after that, in addition to the concern that the Italian government would not hesitate to violate the concordat by holding firm on mixed marriages, he ordered a reply to the telegram sent by the high rabbi of Egypt, exclaiming: "If he only knew that we too have been students of the high rabbi of Milan!"[26]

During these same months, both *Civiltà Cattolica* and *L'Osservatore Romano*, although they avoided comment on the fascist decrees, were the objects of sarcastic attack in the fascist press, which pointedly recalled the positions taken by the Jesuit journal at the end of the nineteenth century: "there is much to be learned from the fathers of the Company of Jesus . . . fascism cannot match, in either its measures or their execution, the rigor of *Civiltà Cattolica*."[27] In any case, on 5 October the fascist government prohibited Catholic journals from commenting on the racial question, even with regard to Germany.

Negotiation on the validity of mixed marriages began in October. The spirit with which Pius XI undertook these negotiations is well illustrated in Tardini's summary of the audience with Tacchi-Venturi on 24 October:

> Father Tacchi-Venturi referred to the absolute intransigence of the government regarding the "racial question." I pointed out to him that the minister of popular culture had prohibited all newspapers from taking up the attacks of *L'Osservatore Romano* against racism. This ignited the anger of the Holy Father, who said to Father Tacchi-Venturi: "But this is enormous! And I am ashamed . . . ashamed to be Italian. And tell that, father, to Mussolini himself! I am ashamed not as pope but as an Italian! The Italian people have become a herd of stupid sheep. I will speak out, without fear. I am forced to by the Concordat, but even more so by my conscience. I have no fear! I would prefer to beg in the streets. I will not even ask Mussolini to defend the Vatican. And even if the piazza fills with people, I will not be afraid! They have all become like so many Farinaccis. I am truly discouraged, both as pope and as an Italian."[28]

The Vatican proposed mediation, but Mussolini rejected the proposal; indeed on the 25th he even refused to receive Tacchi-Venturi, who wanted to deliver personally the note from the Holy See.

Nuncio Borgongini Duca suggested a compromise: based on the small number of mixed marriages in Italy, he hoped to get the regime to extend civil recognition to a few cases. But the intransigence of *il Duce* was matched by that of Pius XI and Pacelli, who in turn refused the nuncio's compromise "on principle."

On 7 November 1938 Father Tacchi-Venturi said that *il Duce* had "the impression that the Vatican is pushing Italy too far in this case, as in many others." To which the pope replied: "Remind Mussolini to think carefully about what he is doing. He must know that there are many Italians, including at high levels, who are unhappy with Mussolini. This is a *vulnus* of the concordat, and the Holy Father will not concede in any fashion."[29]

Pacelli's summary, dated 14 November and *sub secreto pontificio*, reconstructs all the proposed mediations and their failures. The decree law that forbade citizens of Aryan race from marrying persons of other races stipulated that eventual religious marriages of this sort would not be recorded in the civil registers (article 6), and this apparently violated article 34 of the concordat, according to which religious marriages had the same civil status as any other marriage.

The thick dossier on the last months of the pope's life put together by Tardini in 1941 (and discussed further below) includes the original documentation on these negotiations. A signed letter from Pius XI to Mussolini dated 4 November cites the *vulnus* and requests insertion of the following phrase: "or also in those cases where the two spouses, though 'of different races,' both practice the Catholic religion." Mussolini rejected the insertion, and the pope sent him another letter on 5 November that irritated *il Duce* even more.

A long note from Pacelli to the Italian ambassador clearly sums up the terms of the conflict, a note moreover that includes one loathsome reference, if a fairly typical one from those weeks, regarding the desire of the Church to combat "the danger of defective offspring" – an expression that, while not explicit, likely refers to children born to parents of "different races":

> For centuries the Church has maintained two canonical restrictions: one prohibits marriage between Catholics and people who are not baptized; and the other prohibits marriage between Catholics and people who are baptized but not Catholic . . . The case of two Catholics of different races, however, is a very different one. Certainly it is the practice of the Church . . . to discourage among its children marriages that pose the danger of defective offspring, and so in this regard it is willing, within the limits of divine law, to support measures taken by the civil authorities to achieve that noble end. But if, nonetheless, two Catholics of different races intend to marry . . . the Church cannot, solely on the basis of racial difference, deny its assistance.[30]

He then adds: "It is true, nonetheless, that these marriages are very rare . . . and so it is that much more unfortunate that the solemn Convention has been violated for such a small number of cases . . . it is a question of principle." On 14 November *L'Osservatore Romano* reported Pacelli's sentiments almost word for word, though in more generic terms:

> Everyone knows that the Church of Jesus Christ is Catholic, that it is universal . . . Everyone, of whatever race, is called upon to be among the children of God . . . Race has never constituted a criterion for discrimination among the faithful . . . In a process that is slow, and at times dangerous and difficult, the Church has always sought to destroy the barriers that spiritually divide humanity and to create and develop sentiments of fraternity and love.[31]

Il Duce did not even respond to the pope's letter and showed himself immoveable, deaf to the appeals of the pope, Tacchi-Venturi, and the Catholic press. *L'Osservatore Romano* led the way in this regard though, while the paper firmly defended the concordat, it did not go so far as to criticize the fascist racial laws. Pacelli complained on 4 December that the Holy See learned only from the newspapers that the text of the decree law had been approved on 10 November, and Mussolini's refusal to negotiate was a hard blow to the Vatican, not so much over the question of interracial marriage but because this represented a clear violation of the concordat. And so the Vatican hoped, at least until the end of the year, that the regime would rethink its position. Indeed, it made another attempt to revive negotiations in the last weeks of the pope's life, an attempt that became still more complicated with the attacks on Catholic Action.

There are multiple reasons for the Vatican's desperate attempts to reach an agreement with Mussolini: a concern to not worsen the situation for Catholic organizations; the fear of deteriorating diplomatic relations with Italy in a period that looked ever bleaker; and, last but not least, a sort of underlying, when not openly declared, sympathy in many Catholic sectors for a discrimination that, while it should not degenerate into persecution, nonetheless did not really merit condemnation, on either a religious or a social level.

The condemnation of totalitarianism and the conflict over Catholic Action

"Catholic means universal, not racist, nationalist, or separatist; and Catholic Action must adhere to this same spirit . . . It must be said that there is something especially objectionable in this spirit of separatism, of exaggerated nationalism that, precisely because it is not

Christian, not religious, ends up being also not humane."[32] On 21 July Pius XI spoke these words to the youth of Catholic Action and so connected the theme of universalism to that movement which he held close to his heart. And less than a week later, with a clear-eyed fixation that was decidedly not a product of senility, he repeated to the students of Propaganda Fide that the Christian way of thinking can never be "racist, nationalist, or separatist": "We do not want to introduce divisions within the human family . . . When we forget the categories, the universals . . . things go very badly in the world, as too many do not understand the universals." According to the pope, indeed, one should not use the term "human race," but rather "humankind" as the word race "is really better suited to animals."[33]

This was not an abstract and generic idea of natural rights as a function of the hierarchical design of a Christian society. According to this vision, the care of the Church must extend to all of humanity and not just to Catholics. An internal criticism of the fundamental categories of totalitarianism derived from this "new return" to what he referred to as the "universals," a return to origins. Nor is it without import that this almost desperate appeal targeted the missionary movement and Catholic Action, an organization that operated among the laity. Following the signing of the Lateran Pact, a sense of acting in a "Christian State," or in any case of a division of labor with the lay state, predominated, and so the efforts of Catholic Action were directed at "the reflowering of a Christian spirit among the people." At this later date, Catholic "universals" were "objectively in conflict with the regime."[34]

Following the first conflicts between the regime and Catholic Action in 1931, the social brief of the lay apostolate began to focus primarily on defending the spaces of the Church from the regime's invasiveness. But until the late 1930s, thanks to the continued conviction of residing in a Christian state, concern was not great, and so energies were directed toward internal development and piety. It was thought that the common ground shared with the regime on the question of Catholic education provided important guarantees:

> Certain of the values encouraged by the Church coincided with those promoted by the regime, such as respect for authority and doctrinal orthodoxy. The social dimension of the public cult showed itself primarily in relation to the need that the faithful gain a better understanding of the collective dimension of their religion and so reshape the space of their private devotions.[35]

166

It was in the context of this continual mixing and adjustment of commitment to internal development versus the need to find public expression that the 1938 conflict over the nature of Catholic Action and the ban on holding dual memberships took place. Tardini's summaries of audiences from October 1938 are interesting in this regard and describe the conflict that arose in Bergamo, where Achille Starace finally decided to remove the *Federale* (fascist authority) hostile to Catholic Action but asked in return that four former members of the Popular Party be dismissed from the board of Catholic Action. The pope had no trouble with this request and indeed wondered how it was that they had ever been appointed to the board of Catholic Action, given his objections to the Popular Party:

> He went on to say that, while the Popular Party had done some good, it had also done much that was bad. "They did not understand that fascism was going to win the political contest. Mussolini himself told me that he had initially offered the Popular Party many positions in his government." At this point His Holiness noted that, in the difficult period through which the diocese was passing, the current bishop was not up to the task, showing himself to be slow, uncertain, almost fearful. His Holiness added: "I almost wish that these younger men had some of my old age!"[36]

Starace preferred not to give away the name of the new *Federale* of Bergamo and said that he had "chosen the best candidate he had." The pope commented: "One wonders what sort of best candidate there might be among certain groups," and added:

> If they strip any more memberships, I will intervene energetically! I'll cause a scandal! I will let the world know! Taking away a membership is like taking the food out of one's mouth. And I will give food to those who have been deprived of it. And when I run out of money I will use Peter's pence. Fascism will cut a fine figure. We get old for a reason; the old enjoy a certain immunity, and I intend to use it.[37]

There was no longer simply competition between fascism and the Church over the education of youth in order to create a Christian and fascist society; it was rather precisely over this issue that their aims became incompatible. The encyclical *Non abbiamo bisogno* was issued on 29 June 1931 to protest the measures taken by the regime to limit the activities of Catholic Action and recognized that "a conception of the state which makes the rising generations belong to it entirely, without any exception, from the tenderest years up to adult life, cannot be reconciled by a Catholic either with Catholic doctrine or with the natural rights of the family." This approach risked leading to "a real pagan worship of the state," in conflict with both "the natural rights of the family" and the "supernatural rights of the Church." The same encyclical continues:

> In everything that We have said up to the present, We have not said that We wished to condemn the [fascist] party as such. Our aim has been to point out and to condemn all those things in the programme and in the activities of the party which have been found to be contrary to Catholic doctrine and Catholic practice.[38]

This distinction was not only defensive and diplomatic. Indeed, it recalled the common ground that had been explicitly described two months earlier in the encyclical *Quadragesimo anno*. In this latter document, the pope praised fascist corporativism, with its emphasis on class collaboration and the repression of socialist organizations, as a model much in keeping with Catholic social doctrines.

Oversimplifying, one might claim that in 1931[39] two hegemonic forces contested one against the other to manage the social body, but with similar goals. At the later date, by which time that contest had been won by the regime, the Church could no longer ignore two non-negotiable tenets: the defense of the rights of the Church and the defense of the inalienable rights of the individual, regardless of race. These were two points that could no longer be kept separate, two programs that Pius XI had sought to keep independent of one another but which at the end of his papacy had to be brought together or else risk betrayal of the principles of the gospel. Such also was the lesson learned by the Holy See in its interaction with Hitler's Germany – that Germany to which Mussolini seemed irresistibly attracted, as evidenced by his refusal to consider any sort of mediation over the racial laws.

Among the pope's many references to "exaggerated nationalism" in summer 1938, that directed at the French Federation of Christian Unions may have laid out in the most explicit terms his idea of totalitarianism. Nor was it an accident that those reflections were included in a discussion of France and of labor, two topics close to his heart. The meeting opened with warm salutations to our dear brothers, workers who have come from France, "this dear France for whom we have prayed never more than we do today, for whom we pray and continue to pray . . . a country that enjoys many resources of all sorts . . . the heart of the pope is always with its first daughter." After having recalled the visit of his delegation for the celebrations in Lisieux, the importance of which we have already discussed, he went on to praise the Federation of Christian Unions as a great example of an organization in which the individual is not submerged in the collectivity and so a counterweight to "the position frequently held of late that the collectivity is all and the individual nothing . . . everything to the state, nothing to the individual." Nor, however, did the Church hold the contrary position – "everything to the individual, nothing to the state" – but instead supported a "correct relationship between the collectivity and the individual":

> But there are hidden and still graver designs; and those who claim all for the collectivity make of the collectivity a divinity, and so also the individual is deified . . . a sort of deified pantheism . . . And this represents a great usurpation, for if there is a totalitarian regime – totalitarian in fact and by rights – it is the regime of the Church, as man belongs wholly to the Church, must belong to it as man is the creation of the good Lord . . . and so the Church truly has the right and obligation to lay claim to the totality of its power over individuals. Every man in his entirety belongs to the Church, because he belongs entirely to God.[40]

The collectivity does not exist separately from the individuals that make it up and must continue to be its only protagonists. These affirmations contain a more complete synthesis than do the pope's later reflections, though those later reflections do reveal continuity with ideas on the "totality-totalitarianism" of the Church as he had always understood it, even in the 1920s.

The pope's ultimate condemnation of totalitarianisms derived not from a democratic or liberal position but from disillusionment with the dictatorships that, rather than promote a greater role for the Church in society, sought to take its place, using the Church as a model and so rendering it subordinate to and dependent upon the regime. For the pope, totalitarianism represented the final outcome of that impulse deriving from the French Revolution and according to which man can live without God. Those same claims of man's autonomy from God resurfaced in the 1930s under the auspices of racism and atheism. In this regard, there was no longer any theological difference between fascist racism and communist atheism. Communism in any case had always been clear about its denial of God and had not disguised its atheism; indeed, it came to be viewed by the pope as a more passive form of atheism than Nazism. In Nazi paganism he saw a sacredness of messianism present from the outset

169

and one that cancelled out any other religious project. And so Nazism, as heir and interpreter of that atheism, responded to the need humanity felt for sacredness in those decades of the twentieth century.

And so, paradoxically, a pope who could never be described as liberal or democratic came to understand that liberalism offered greater guarantees to Christianity, not because of its ideology but because of the situation it created. Pius XI, though he never became a liberal, came to speak of individuals, not only of persons, and realized *in extremis* that Christianity could operate better within a context of individual freedoms than with the authoritarian imposition of a social model.

The Munich crisis and "warmed-over broth"

The pope's judgment of the Munich Conference could not have been clearer:

> Chamberlain provided Hitler with a golden foot-stool! The opposition was right. Precisely what Chamberlain predicted has come to pass: should anyone attempt to dominate I shall oppose him. Now that figure has shown himself – could one attempt any greater dominance? – and Chamberlain has given in.[41]

Clearly Pius XI did not share the enthusiasm of some, including some in the Curia, for the apparently avoided war. Instead he was indignant and wounded by the illusions and expectations encouraged by the resolution and reprimanded both Chamberlain and his foreign minister, Halifax, for having betrayed the British spirit of freedom. He received them on 13 January 1939 and cited the models of Thomas More and John Fisher, appealing to their sense of liberty in hopes that the English tradition would prove more resolute and not so compliant as it had shown itself at the Munich Conference of September 1938.[42]

For more than a year pressure had been put on the pope, especially by the French, to pursue a peace initiative. That pressure became a chorus and continued throughout 1938, coming to include his closest collaborators, Tardini and Pacelli, who encouraged him to launch appeals, prayers, and initiatives. The several attempts to encourage him to make a statement on Munich are described by Tardini in an article written at his behest by Federico Alessandrini.[43] The pope seemed to resist these blandishments – for appeals and requests he might have sent to Hitler and Mussolini – based on a deeply felt and justified skepticism, particularly as regards Hitler and the desire of Nazi Germany to bring to a positive conclusion the ongoing negotiations with Chamberlain. Angelo Martini has noted that no documentary proof of the pope's radical skepticism during those crucial days survives among Pacelli's papers.[44] Now that documentation has become available and testifies to the pope's thorough diffidence regarding possible bargaining or mediation with Hitler.

That conviction had evolved over time and was already evident a year earlier in an analogous situation, namely in March 1937, when Switzerland, France, and the US attempted to pressure Pius XI into leading an international mediation effort to bring an end to the Spanish Civil War:

4 March. Herriot, president of the Chamber of Deputies, told the nuncio that the Holy See would be in an even better position than Roosevelt, as Roosevelt would have a hard time with the democratic regimes. He stated: "I do not see other alternatives than an intervention by the pope or by the US president, but preferred the first of these – though of course the two alternatives are not mutually exclusive; to the contrary."[45]

The conviction that only the pope could halt the armies that were already on the move in Europe found expression again on the occasion of the *Anschluß*. On the very days that German troops were marching on the Ringstrasse in Vienna, the French ambassador to the Holy See alerted Tardini to the fact that Hitler's next move would almost certainly involve Czechoslovakia, and so "France, respecting its commitments, would go to war. And England in turn will respect its commitments to France." Tardini was skeptical – France would not be able to help the government of Prague, short of invading Germany, but "I'm not sure that all of the French people would favor that," and in any case England "does not seem to want war" – and indeed he predicted exactly what would come to pass in a little over six months. For Charles-Roux, on the other hand, the prospect of a war between the European powers created the urgent need for "a word from the Holy See to confirm and defend the principle of civil co-existence":

The ambassador said that, in France, the United States, and elsewhere, all those who recognize the Holy See as a spiritual and moral force await its authoritative voice. Otherwise, according to the ambassador, "*vous perdez*," as the forces of the left will invoke those principles that the Holy See should proclaim with all the weight of its authority. Just as after the war the Holy See sought to clarify its own concept of peace distinct from that of the socialists, so today it should uphold its doctrine of justice, charity, and law, a doctrine much loftier than that advanced by the left. And it is all the more important that it speak out now, as once the war breaks out it may be too late.[46]

In mid-June 1938, reviewing the ability of the Holy See to influence the opinion of national churches in countries already ruled by the Nazis or in danger of being overrun, the chargé d'affaires of the French embassy to the Vatican devoted special attention to what appeared, following the *Anschluß*, to be the next step in Hitler's march to the East, namely Czechoslovakia:

Most of the Sudeten Germans are Catholics. It is a surprise, then, if the 'voice of blood' speaks to them and not that of their religion; and yet such is the case. I'll recall just two recent examples. First of all, the individual and collective joining of the Sudeten Party by German religious in Czechoslovakia, in particular many seminarians, who ask "why they should be more Catholic than Bishop Innitzer." Then there is the recent appeal launched by the leader of the Catholic German Societies of Czechoslovakia, Monsignor Hilgenreiner, an organization that like the agrarians has merged with the Sudeten Party . . . If we add that Abbé Hlinka, leader of the Slovakian Catholics, has a close and emotional tie with the Hitlerites, we have to admit that, as a force for resistance against the Nazi tide in Czechoslovakia, Catholicism seems very weak indeed.[47]

Prior to his assignment to the Vatican, François Charles-Roux had been the French ambassador in Prague, where he had worked to establish better relations between Czechoslovakia and the Holy See. On 18 August 1938 he met with the sostituto, Monsignor Montini, to request a decisive intervention by the pope in favor of peace.[48] The secretary of state did not think that the Catholic Church could exert much influence on the faithful among the German minority in Czechoslovakia, and Pacelli confessed as much to the British chargé d'affaires in those very days: "In spite of the way the Church has been treated by the Nazis, he believes that most of the Sudeten Germans wish to be incorporated into Germany."[49] Tardini expressed a similar opinion two months earlier, when he confessed to Rivière the Holy See's fundamental impotence: "The Sudetens are first of all Germans and fanatic about the idea of a community of race; their religious concerns usually take second place . . . Nationalism is on the rise throughout the world, and Catholicism, universal by its very nature, may suffer as a result."[50]

Just the same, Montini immediately informed Pacelli and the pope of the French request and received an audience on the 20th, two days later. Although there is no evidence to confirm that this meeting took place, Angelo Martini has reasonably noted that Pius XI's discourse of 21 August could well reflect its content. On that Sunday in August the pope, without warning, went to the villa of Propaganda Fide, where he continued that discussion of the pagan doctrine of race begun with those same students the previous month, on 28 July, a topic that as we have seen occupied much of his discourse during that final summer: "Events, alas, confirm our claim that exaggerated nationalism is 'truly a curse,' a curse of divisions, contrasts, and the threat of war."[51]

The tension in Europe increased day by day, as did the requests that the pope help to avoid the approaching catastrophe. While Hitler issued bellicose statements at Nuremberg, Father Martin Gillet, master general of the Dominicans, wrote to Pacelli on 12 August 1938 beseeching him to convince the pope to issue his own "declaration of peace."[52] Informed of the request of his countryman, the ambassador to France added his own voice to the plea, but, in spite of this pressure, "the Holy Father, having listened and reflected, has concluded that this declaration would be neither useful nor opportune." Given his open break with Germany, he strongly doubted that intervention on his part would have any effect.

At the end of summer 1938, as the most catastrophic scenario loomed tragically imminent, the appeals to Pius XI understandably increased. The papers of Pacelli and Tardini reveal as much. Hence the notes of Tardini on 13 September: "In these difficult moments for all the world, as the threat of war increases and we await the outcome of the most recent diplomatic attempts to avoid a massacre, would an invitation to prayer from the pope not be useful? . . . If nothing else, might we not issue a *pro pace* collect for all the world?"[53]

The pope clearly rejected the possibility that he make direct contact with the eventual adversaries, both to maintain neutrality and because he had already been accused by the Germans of favoring those powers dominated by Judeo-masonic capitalism.[54] At this stage, with all room for negotiation clearly lost, it seemed pointless to him to engage in an attempt at mediation that would at best serve appearances. Fully convinced that the situation was on the verge of going out of control, there was nothing left but to pray. Such was his approach in moments of crisis; nor does it seem so much an act of surrender as, in contrast to the agitation of his aides in the Secretariat of State, a more clear-sighted understanding of the nature of the catastrophe and a desire to maintain a level of sobriety (in one so passionate as he) that makes no rhetorical concessions, either political or religious.

In the end Pius XI did respond to the request that he issue an "important" and solemn prayer. He did so over the radio in a voice breaking with emotion and offered to God his own life in exchange for peace. It was a moving testimony and not the emotional collapse of an old and sick man:

> This life which . . . the Lord has granted us and nearly renewed, we offer it with all our heart for the health and peace of the world. Let it be that the Lord of life and death take from us the immeasurable and already long gift of life or instead should choose to prolong still more the work day of His tired and ill worker.

His voice trembled over these words, yet another testimony to how his own human and personal experience intersected with the larger course of history, intensifying his own understanding of events rather than clouding them with emotion, as has been justly noted:

> It is a partial and emotional view that has read Pius XI's gesture on that evening of 29 September 1938 in a charitable and slightly hagiographic light . . . yet that gesture and the behavior of the pope reveal a clear understanding of events and of the principal actors of the drama that was playing itself out, as well as a presentiment that was unfortunately not mistaken.[55]

When Vatican radio broadcast the pope's emotional address at 9:30 a.m. on 29 September, the government leaders in Munich were already in their second session. The pope's passive resistance – to Pacelli's repeated requests that he take a more active role, for example, he replied only with silence – likely derived from his bleak outlook and did not hide a certain annoyance with those requests for a direct intervention on his part. There seemed too great an imbalance between the gravity of events and the claims of his aides. Consider his response to Tardini's request for another appeal for peace in October: "But don't you understand? This is all warmed-over broth!"[56]

Pius XI then was not a *munichois*, and unlike many of his contemporaries he was not persuaded by the signing of the agreement. On the morning of 3 October, receiving Tardini, he expressed his disapproval "that the fate of Czechoslovakia was decided by the four leaders in Munich without any of that country's representatives being present."[57] The pope, then, did not share the general enthusiasm over "peace for our time," or over the fact that Mussolini claimed credit. By Tardini's account, Achille Ratti judged Mussolini, who in those weeks "took credit for the success of the avoided war," to be little more than a *farceur*.[58]

The pope's skepticism over the Munich Agreement contrasted, moreover, with the enthusiasm expressed by the churches of Rome, where sermons seconded the hopes for peace raised by *il Duce* in Munich. In September 1938, at San Carlo del Corso, one priest intoned: "The enemies of the Church are trying to block the negotiations of the head of the government and the Führer." Those who did not rejoice over *il Duce*'s great work as peacemaker were labeled communists, as one heard in the Church of the Gesù, the Roman church of the Jesuits, whose rector was Father Tacchi-Venturi. As Andrea Riccardi noted: "the real threats to peace are the communists":[59]

> The "pacifist" victory of *il Duce* in Munich was considered an affirmation of the Catholic and moderate spirit of the regime. This was not, however, the interpretation that *il Duce* favored, taken as he was with the idea of the cultural and war-like "revolution" of the Italian people.[60]

Clearly these evaluations differed markedly from that of Pius XI, who passed harsh judgment not only on Mussolini but also on Chamberlain, whom he accused of having "provided Hitler with a golden footstool!" Indeed he told the British premier as much in person when they met on 13 January 1939.[61]

The fact that Pius XI did not join in the chorus of praise for the dismemberment of Czechoslovakia granted by the governments of London and Paris, under the illusion that they would in that way halt the forward march of Hitler toward war, was appreciated by one of the rare dissenting voices of the French press, namely Georges Bidault, in *L'aube* of 3 September:

> Amidst the great sadness into which we are plunged by the abdication of the once proud democracies, there is just one great force that brings us pride and comfort. It is the voice of the great Pope Pius XI, the only fearless voice among so much surrender . . . for his voice does not change with the winds, following the fluctuations of fear, panic, and emotion . . . it is a voice that pleads and instructs, but does not change or demean itself.[62]

As Cardinal Karel Kašpar of Prague wrote to Pacelli, "His Holiness, our most blessed father Pope Pius XI, is the only one who in these sad days has had the grace to protect us"; or Edvard Beneš, who wrote to the Holy See from London in 1943: "I cannot forget the very sympathetic attitude of His Holiness Pope Pius XI toward Czechoslovakia during the crisis of 1938 and the message he sent to me at the most critical moment in the history of my nation."[63]

— 8 —

THE END OF A PAPACY:
A SIGH OF RELIEF

For daily life is made up of small things, and great things are rare.
Such is the teaching of our Lord in heaven who rules the world and
knows the small bird who dies in the forest and the hair that falls from
our head. (Matthew 6.26; Luke 21.18)

From the last discourse written by Pius XI
before he died and never delivered

The pope pressures Gemelli

At the end of October 1938, the pope asked Pacelli to return from
his holiday in Switzerland because he needed his secretary of state.
Relations with Mussolini were tense, and the pope showed firmness
and lucidity. Yet he was weak, sick, and old, and likely finding it
difficult to control so many different affairs. It would be an exaggeration to speak of manipulation by his aides, but it is easy to see that
Pius XI no longer fully controlled the situation. Perhaps the most
tangible example in this regard is the encyclical against anti-Semitism
that he had commissioned several months before, but the text of
which was intentionally withheld from him. The Jesuit Gundlach
recalled: "Things seem to be proceeding in such a way that he gets
only what others want him to get; he is supposed still to be in good
psychological condition, to be sure, but not able to do very much on
his own."[1]

Various notes in the archives speak to the concerns of many, both
close and not so close to the pope, who sent signals to Mussolini that
the more intransigent positions taken by Ratti were his alone and the
positions of a pope no longer able to make decisions. There was a

177

climate of fear and uncertainty, and in the meetings between Ciano and Borgongini Duca the nuncio sought, and with reason, to advance positions very different from those of Pius XI.

The Catholic press, as we have seen, on several occasions failed to print the strongly worded defense of Jews included in the pope's discourses. Leading figures of the Catholic hierarchy, representatives of the Secretariat of State, and especially the Jesuits around *Civiltà Cattolica* gave very different readings of the racial laws and, whether out of conviction or opportunism, adopted a much softer and conciliatory line. A key figure in this regard was Agostino Gemelli, who was very close to the pope and had in the past always relied on that friendship to support his University of the Sacred Heart. At the end of 1938 and in the first days of 1939 Gemelli came under pressure to use his authority to moderate the conflict. His role during these weeks is revealed to us in the intense correspondence he maintained with his old friend and confidant Paolo Toffanin,[2] who was in turn well connected in fascist circles and kept Gemelli informed of the growing displeasure with the pope. Gemelli was very close to the pope and followed his illness first hand; he added a new physician to the Vatican team and was in constant contact with the Curia and its most important members.

The racial laws, moreover, affected Gemelli directly; as rector of the university in Milan, to which of course those laws applied, he found himself stuck between the need to follow the directives of the fascist hierarchs and fidelity to the Holy See. The ministers in Rome heard that the Catholic University had enrolled Jewish students for the new academic year, and Gemelli, who in spite of pressure to do so had not signed the "Manifesto of Racist Scientists," pursued a vacillating and awkward course over these weeks. On 5 November he wrote to the wife of Minister Alfieri: "The accusation that the Catholic University has enrolled Jewish students must have been made by our enemies. We have no Jews, either baptized or non-baptized. As you well know, I carefully and faithfully observe all the laws of the state, even those (like that regarding baptized Jews) that I think unjust."[3] The Franciscan Gemelli, then, only objected to the fact that the racial laws also applied to baptized Jews, but he did not hide his disapproval.

From an audience with Pacelli on 20 August, we learn that the pope was angry with Mussolini for having forbidden the Catholic press from publishing any anti-racist articles, even ones referring only to Germany, and that he asked Gemelli to side with him in resisting this intimidation:

178

Write to Gemelli regarding pressure that the publications of the Catholic University not print the pope's discourse of 28 July. "This issue is all the more serious given that it regards both a university and the words of the pope. Alas there are also other instances, but they can be summed up in the present one, given the importance of the Catholic University to the pope. See then that he takes care of this or else the Holy Father himself will do so, writing and speaking out as is fitting. We owe as much to the Church."[4]

It would prove difficult, however, for Gemelli to follow his old friend in the intransigence of his final hours.

Pressure from the regime and from important exponents of the Curia increased in the autumn, as is clear from the details surrounding the famous Bologna discourse of 9 January 1939 to commemorate William of Saliceto. At the end of that discourse, and straying from his prepared text, Gemelli spoke of the "tragic situation of the Jews":

The situation of those who, because of their blood and their religion, cannot be part of this magnificent fatherland is undoubtedly tragic and sad. Tragic as once again, as in other centuries, we see carried out that terrible sentence that the deicidal people brought down upon themselves and for which they have wandered the world unable to find peace or a homeland, while the consequences of that horrible crime continue to persecute them everywhere and in all eras.[5]

These words echo heavily with the classic terms of anti-Jewish condemnation and contribute to that characterization of Gemelli as an anti-Semite that the difficult conditions of blackmail and pressure under which he operated do little to dispel. Gemelli probably thought it useful to make a "reassuring" anti-Semitic statement in order to balance the accusations against the cardinals of Bologna – Nasalli Rocca – and Milan – Schuster – who had spoken out against the anti-Jewish discrimination on the day of the Epiphany (6 January). On that same day the nuncio to Turkey, Monsignor Angelo Roncalli (later John XXIII), preached against racism in the French Church of the Holy Spirit in Istanbul. It is impossible to believe this was sheer coincidence. More likely a signal came from Rome, but from whom? The pope himself?[6]

A letter dated 7 January 1939 from Farinacci to Mussolini would seem to confirm that pressure was applied to Father Gemelli: "I have managed to get my bishop to make an address different from the others. I hope to have persuaded Gemelli to make a similar one in Bologna." Farinacci is referring to Monsignor Giovanni Cazzani, bishop of Cremona, who according to the *ras* had spoken "calming words on the Jewish question," recalling the unavoidability of the divine curse. Farinacci goes on to explain to *il Duce* his intention to create confusion among the already disoriented Catholic ranks: "My greatest hope is to create a great ruckus among them."[7] Nor did he have any trouble in finding supporters, as fear of the unknown consequences of a conflict between the regime and the Holy See had been growing following the pope's pronouncements and alarmed many members of the Church.

It is probable then that, in addition to external political pressure, there was also pressure from within the Curia itself, as Gemelli himself revealed when he claimed that "behind the anti-Jewish statement of Bologna, there was an 'order' received from a 'high personage,'" and surely that personage was not Farinacci. Did this mysterious figure come from the world of politics or from within the Church? A letter from Toffanin suggests the latter, as he calls for an anti-Jewish statement from Gemelli "so as not to make things worse" on that very day of Epiphany, when condemnations of racism were issued from three separate pulpits.[8]

The last weeks of Pius XI

Achille Ratti would have preferred a sudden and unexpected death that found him still active and immersed in work. He was only partially successful, as his illness was long and painful, but he was fully active to the end. His last days were filled with appointments and above all expectation regarding the coincidence of important dates, which included the tenth anniversary of the Lateran Treaties and the seventeenth anniversary of his election as pope. The pope had a special attachment to Saint Andrew Avellino and kept before his bed a depiction of the saint dying at the foot of the altar; he had died suddenly while serving the Church. Pius XI looked at him from his bed during the days of his debilitating disease and prayed that he too would enjoy a similar end. His faithful secretary, the person who was closest to him in those last weeks, commented: "He hoped not to disturb anyone and that, should he not be granted an unexpected death, at least it would be quick. For this reason he never went to bed in the evening without having first put all his things in order, so as not to cause anyone distress."[9]

On 12 January 1941, Tardini gathered together in a single "position"[10] all the documents, notes, and diaries relative to the last days of the pope's life, days during which, at the limit of his strength, Pius XI sought to survive till the tenth anniversary of the concordat with the Italian state. The position – that is, the dossier that includes all of these documents – is compact and recounts the urgent narrative rhythm of those days, full of tension and rich in almost cinematic detail, a crescendo that proceeds to the death of the pope. All knew that the pope's death was imminent – his physicians, his entourage (Pacelli and Tardini first of all), and the pope himself; but it was a death that he hoped desperately to postpone till after 11 February, the tenth anniversary of the Lateran Treaties, for which he had convened the Italian bishops and to whom he intended to deliver his definitive spiritual testimony.

The documents re-create a frenetic and tense climate. The pope was getting worse but no one would say as much, least of all to Pius himself, who sought to resist his illness, hiding it and minimizing its seriousness. It was like the family of an aging, terminally ill patient that seeks to reassure and protect him, even from himself. Yet in this case it was not warm affection, like that of Confalonieri, that dominated but rather concern to block any actions dictated by his still lucid and uncontrollable will. He was not just a dying pope, one whose ever greater excesses struck fear in his entourage, but a pope fighting his final battle, externally against Mussolini and internally against his own body. At the beginning of his illness that body was hidden and protected, but at the end it emerged in its suffering form, exposed to the members of this strange extended family that surrounded him. It was a family that included physicians, members of the Curia, his closest collaborators from the Secretariat of State stationed outside his bedroom door, and his closest secretaries, who cared for his ailing body and administered communion. In comparison with successive papacies, however, a barrier remained between the exposition of his body and the faithful. The press and radio followed carefully the progress of his illness, but it was only a faint anticipation of later practices – starting with Pius XII, who was photographed in the throes of his agony – when viewing the body of the dying pope became a media event:

The pope is not well. Professor Bonanome has detected a disturbance of the prostate. The catheter (is that the right word?) is permanently attached. Professor Cesaliacherchi has noted cardiac weakness (40–44 beats), a consequence, as with the prostate pain, of a circulatory disturbance. And yet the Holy Father has dictated a communiqué that begins: "The pope is well, but as a precaution will suspend audiences in order to be ready for the celebrations on Saturday and Sunday." We altered this announcement a bit in order not to broadcast falsehoods, while still not telling the truth. Moreover, the antechamber issued the usual sheet of audiences with a long list of names. All this to give the pope the impression (but is this necessary?) that all are convinced he is well and that things proceed as normal. I ask myself if all this is a good thing. Is it a baby or a pope who is sick?[11]

Pacelli and the physicians strongly advised against organizing the celebrations; the events were important ones but too stressful given the pope's condition. Pius XI fully four times rejected the suggestions of his prudent secretary of state and sought to calm his entourage by offering reassuring scenarios: "I shall make them laugh, as we shall speak of words public and private, spoken, written, and . . . telephoned. And at that point we shall say that Saint Peter could not have dealt with these topics": "And so speaking, he looked at me, happy with what he was preparing. But as usual everything remained secret. Nobody saw it, not even his eminence Cardinal Pacelli. Just as he had done for the Christmas discourse, the pope had Monsignor Confalonieri type it up."

The pope was attentive and present to the last and concerned himself even with small details, like the organization of a cold buffet "for the cardinals and bishops after the ceremony in Saint Peter's." On that occasion a sum of money would be distributed with a prayer of suffrage, and a mass of suffrage would be celebrated for him:

> The pope spent the last days of his life busying himself with the preparations for this much anticipated commemoration. He spoke of nothing else. The 11th and 12th of February were to be days full of work and rich in consolation for him. Instead, on the 11th his corpse was transferred to Saint Peter's and on the 12th the people flowed into Saint Peter's not to celebrate Pius XI but to contemplate for a final time his beloved visage.

The documentation collected by Tardini offers "a picture of the final days of the immortal pope"; indeed, it could be published in a separate volume, as the material is introduced with comments, explanations and questions by Tardini himself, as though he were preparing a sort of critical edition of those final fearful days. He introduces his reconstruction with a eulogy for the end of temporal power:

All have come to realize that the loss of temporal power was a blessing for the papacy, that the moral prestige of the papacy has as a result increased dramatically, and that the restoration of that power would be absurd . . . These thoughts were present in the mind of Pius XI, who . . . in a sense spiritualized the terrestrial state, reducing it to a minimum . . . but being territorially and politically surrounded by a powerful Italian state . . . he sought a sort of "spiritual guarantee."

The treaty, which had resolved the Roman question, and the concordat had served to systematize the religious situation in Italy, so that "the absolute independence of the pope in the exercise of his Universal Magistracy" was guaranteed by the fact that he found himself "at the center of a truly and profoundly Catholic nation that recognized, respected, and defended the rights of the Church." It was for this reason that the pope considered the treaty and concordat indissoluble and so was in the habit of saying *aut simul stabunt aut simul cadent*. Celebration of the tenth anniversary of the conciliation, then, "would have been a normal and ordinary event," were it not for the anomalous and extraordinary circumstances of the moment, namely the break between the two signatories of the agreement: "Acute tension between His Holiness Pius XI and fascism; the special solemnity desired by the pope for this event with two meetings for the entire Italian episcopacy and two papal discourses; the sudden worsening of the pope's illness and his death that transformed the planned-for festive celebration into a ceremony of mourning."

Tardini alerted the eventual reader of his dossier to the "lively skirmishes between the pope and fascism," and the harshest criticisms were of Mussolini: "With me Mussolini has been a villain and betrayer of faith! He repeated this over and over, adding that if Mussolini did not want to participate in the celebrations he would conduct them on his own."

The dossier continues with audience notes kept by Pacelli (from 3 January to 6 February 1939), not transcribed but preserved in their original form and introduced by Tardini's observations regarding the fact that the pope was preparing his own discourses. The example he cited was the Christmas discourse, "entirely prepared by him personally, without first showing it to anyone." It included the relevant themes to which he returned in his final days: celebration of the conciliation, the racial laws as a violation of the concordat, religious persecution in Germany, and "the recent glorification in Rome itself of an enemy cross that is not the cross of Christ." The report continues:

183

Given that the twisted cross can be found in the . . . catacombs and is now the flag of the Reich, Cardinal Pacelli sent the sostituto to His Holiness, as soon as the discourse was finished, to ask him to delete this reference. The Holy Father did not want to and said that he was certain he spoke the truth. The illness deprived him of some of his tranquility, making him easily excitable. But it did not in any way diminish his clarity of vision and the courageous effort to carry out his mission.

On that occasion the pope said that he would speak of the "most noble sovereign" and his "incomparable minister." These were phrases that struck all as ironic; Mussolini understood them that way too and was mortally offended. Indeed, the Italian government immediately sent word that it would not be participating in the festivities, though in the end *il Duce* reconsidered and sent Ciano to make the necessary arrangements. Ciano described Mussolini's fury and the great lengths to which he had gone to calm him down – a futile effort, as *il Duce* was convinced that, with the appellation "incomparable, the pope intended to ridicule him." Mussolini complained that across the Tiber they always speak out "against Italy, but not against the other nations that pursue similar and even more extreme policies, including on the racial question (like Hungary!)." He charged his ambassador to deliver a note of protest listing three arguments:

> Certain Catholic circles have made ironic comments regarding words the pope has said about me.
> I deplore the pope's attack on the party, an attack about which all Europe is talking.
> Conclusion: it is Mussolini's conviction, based on information received from the police, that Catholic Action is a front for a true anti-fascist political party and blocks almost everywhere the activities of the regime, employing organizations that resemble unions (for physicians and Catholic writers). Moreover, Catholic Action's central organization should not exist, as the 1931 Accord establishes that "Catholic Action is essentially diocesan."

According to a note of Pacelli's from 6 January, this last point especially irritated the pope. He considered Mussolini's references to Catholic Action to be a personal affront, as he purposely ignored "that he had many times described Catholic Action as the apple of his eye and said that Catholic Action did not engage in politics." Pius XI returned to this argument the next day:

The same was said in '31, and Mussolini himself had to admit after the opening of the Catholic Action archives that there was nothing at all to be found. If he is annoyed at being pilloried by the foreign press, the Holy Father has more to add and at his age no longer fears the consequences. And if Mussolini does not want to take part in the festivities, we will go ahead without him.

Ten days later the difficulties seemed to have been overcome, and the Italian ambassador relayed on 19 January that the head of government was available to participate in the festivities, providing that agreement could be reached on the contents of the public discourses and that *il Duce* would also meet with the bishops convened in Rome. The pope, however, refused and was not willing to submit his discourse for prior approval by the fascist leader. The following day Pacelli explained the pope's desires:

Yes on the exchange of messages. If Mussolini sends a message, the Holy Father will respond. As to the discourses, I do not know what the pope will say. He will speak as the pope to his bishops. Tell Mussolini that the Holy Father is pleased by the reply on reaching an agreement, but that he must not let the date of the anniversary arrive without having responded to the pope's letter. The Holy Father waits and has the right to wait and see what effect the words of the king will have. The Holy Father recalls that for the Christmas discourse he invoked the help of the Lord to deal with the government figures. The pope does not want to find himself in the position of saying that Mussolini has been rude and a breaker of his word. He does not, however, agree to the bishops meeting Mussolini, as they were invited by the pope, not by Mussolini.

The pope then insisted once again that he have a reply to his letter on the racial laws.

A week before the planned festivities the role to be played by the Italian government was still not clear. The Holy See's position became still clearer, and Ambassador Pignatti received the following communiqué on 4 February:

The Holy Father recalls the actions of Pius IV, another Milanese, when the emperor hesitated to cooperate over the Council of Trent: tell the emperor that, if he does not want to host the council, we will do it ourselves, as we intend to be gentlemen and good Christians. The Holy Father regrets instead the impression that the head of government will make on the people. Speaking with the bishops, the pope cannot fail to regret the absence of the government at the commemoration held at Saint Peter's.

On 7 February it seemed that neither the king nor Mussolini would attend the celebration, the first being represented by the prince of Piedmont and the second by Galeazzo Ciano. Everyone understood the political considerations behind the glaring absence of one of the signatories of the concordat. Pignatti wrote to Pacelli on 8 February:

1. Mussolini does not want to walk to Canossa.
2. With regard to modifications of the law in defense of the race, Mussolini has said that he does not want to sabotage it.
3. Regarding the ceremony in Saint Peter's, judging from the comments of the ambassador, I think that he fears that the pope will include unfavorable remarks in his discourse and that it will be published.

From the many references and attempts to defuse tension made by the ambassador to the Holy See, by the nuncio, and by Pacelli himself, one can detect Ciano's fear that the pope's persistent opposition would create a situation like that in Germany. Ambassador Pignatti said as much; he was worried that these repeated reproaches directed at the government could create "conditions for the Church in Italy that resemble those in Germany." The entourages surrounding the pope and *il Duce* expressed similar concerns in similar language, as though in a sort of pact of mutual anxiety; the contest was between the two men, Mussolini and Pius XI. The last days were marked by a bitter fight between the two, a sort of summing up of all their disagreements transformed into a final duel that ended with the death of the pope:

> The character of the two leaders, neither willing to suffer opposition and both ready to do battle, necessarily worsened the situation. Pius XI, slow in word and gesture, cautiously put forward his carefully thought-out position and so necessarily bested Mussolini, so quick to make impulsive statements and engage in exhibitionist behavior, to alter his position or line of action.[12]

Their different psychological temperaments have often been cited by the admirers of Pius XI to highlight the fact that the intransigence of the pope in those weeks was steady and controlled, in contrast to the outbursts and fluctuating strategies of *il Duce*. The illness had sharpened the sensibilities of Pius XI, making him all the more sensitive to wrongs and injustices, though without causing him to react more emotionally:

> He had always been fearless in battle and still showed himself to be so when, at the end of 1938, he had it said that he should be left to die in peace, since at his age he no longer had any fears and could speak and act as he pleased. Yet neither the illness nor his fearlessness caused him to make an ill-considered move; indeed, he intended to use the occasion of the tenth anniversary to resolve the open problem of the racial laws.[13]

Pacelli destroys the pope's last discourse

Tardini described the manuscript of the pope's last discourse as an "extraordinarily important text." Like the missing encyclical on anti-Semitism, it would never be read, and excerpts were published only twenty years later, in an audience delivered by John XXIII on 6 February 1959 to the Italian episcopacy to commemorate the twentieth anniversary of Pius XI's death and the thirtieth anniversary of the conciliation:

> It was well that all that survived of that manuscript was hidden from the gaze of profane indiscretion. There was much wild speculation at the time regarding those final thoughts and sentiments that, for anyone who understood the great spirituality of Pius XI, could only be high and noble. However, the circumstances of those weeks, not lacking in bitterness for the pope, can well explain that he might express himself using phrases and tones that reflected a justifiable resentment.[14]

In these prudent terms, John XXIII intended to reveal finally the mystery of Pius XI's last discourse. He hoped in this way to silence the rumors regarding the contents of that discourse, which no one had ever been allowed to read and which for that reason had inspired much suspicion and fantasy: "Twenty years after the death of that great man, we can assure you that the contents of his '*novissima verba*' could not have been more simple and at the same time more edifying and moving, just as one would have expected from him."[15]

The passages cited by John XXIII were faithful to the original text. Many, however, were omitted, including the harshest ones, which depicted the fascist regime as a large and dangerous institution that spies and eavesdrops. Similarly absent were the passages warning the seminarians against speaking openly, including on the telephone.

It is not so much the omissions, however, that betray the original text (the essence of which was revealed), but rather the fact that, by dividing it up into different bits interspersed with hagiographic comments and withholding the harshest terms, one gets an entirely different impression from that produced by reading the intact text. The pope's style was softened and once again the spirit of his delivery was betrayed, so that subsequently there was much debate, at times presumptuous, regarding the authenticity of the passages cited by John XXIII.[16] In fact, it was the same text, and there were no falsifications, save that weakening which seemed almost to change the contents.

According to the trustworthy testimony of the American Jesuit Walter Abbott, the text of Pius XI's last discourse, reproduced in full here for the first time, was found on the pope's bedside table on the day of his death, next to the encyclical that never saw the light of day. It was written in pencil during that last night of lucidity in a shaky but clear hand, in one go we might imagine. It dramatically describes the historical period and the danger of totalitarianism against which he warns the clergy. The Church is under attack, threatened, and spied upon, and so he counsels great caution in speaking. His disillusionment with fascism is complete and absolute, and his tone suggests that he is on the point of a diplomatic rupture.

The text that Pius XI would have delivered, had he not died shortly before, confirms Mussolini's concerns about what the pope might say. Here are the contents of the file that includes the feared discourse:

> Manuscript of His Holiness Pius XI. Written in pencil. It is especially precious because it was the final effort of the Holy Father.
>
> Corrections by His Eminence Cardinal Pacelli. They were written in pencil in the papal apartment on 8 February by His Eminence; Pius XI wanted him to read everything before it went to the printer.
>
> Two copies of the discourse typed by Monsignor Confalonieri. His are the corrections made by hand.
>
> Two drafts not corrected.
>
> My notes regarding the withdrawal of all these documents.

Tardini listed with great care the contents of the file, as though he expected an eventual critical edition of the material. His notes follow the developments of those days step by step, as one can also gather from this other note of 17 February 1939: "This is the text of the discourse he prepared, all written in his own hand (he wrote it for the most part during the nights between 30–31 January and 31 January–1 February). He spoke to me of it in the last three audiences, of 15 and 18 January and 1 February." Tardini too refers, as had Pacelli, to the previews that the pope had confided in him regarding the caution against speaking openly, but he insists upon the absolute and total solitude in which the text was conceived and elaborated by the pope:

> As usual everything remained secret. Nobody saw it, not even his eminence Cardinal Pacelli. Just as he had done for the Christmas discourse, the pope had Monsignor Confalonieri type it up. On 8 February, by order of the Holy Father, the already typed script was shown to Pacelli, who saw it in the papal apartment and suggested a few changes; immediately afterward it was taken to the secret room of the printer.

Pacelli's corrections were minimal and did not attempt to impose a less aggressive tone. The attitude of the secretary of state in those last days, revealed by a series of small details, was one of drawn-out waiting, a sort of suspension of activity that transformed itself into resolute intervention and, for once without hesitation, decisive action when he ordered a halt to everything. As soon as the pope died, Pacelli ordered the immediate destruction of all copies of Pius XI's text, already set in type in preparation for distribution to the bishops.

As we have seen, the pope considered this anniversary to be enormously important and spoke continuously of the discourse he would deliver, offering ample previews to various of his entourage; the fact that Pacelli had it shelved without offering a synthesis or any other reference to the bishops already gathered in Rome is a clear sign that he opposed a strategy of frontal attack or a breaking off of relations. Indeed, shortly after his election as pope, he said as much to the German bishops gathered in Rome for the conclave. Tardini also noted the elimination of the text; at 12:40 p.m. on 15 February 1939 he wrote:

> Montini called me. Cardinal Pacelli had called him to issue the following orders:
>
> 1. that Monsignor Confalonieri hand over all the material he has regarding the discourse of his Holiness Father Pius XI that he had prepared for the assembly of 11 February;
> 2. that the printer destroy all he possesses relative to that same discourse (drafts, set type);
> 3. that Cardinal Pizzardo is authorized to read that discourse for his own knowledge.

13:00. I went to Confalonieri, who gave me everything he had. Another typescript and His Holiness's manuscript. He assured me he would give the appropriate instructions to the printer.

18:15. Confalonieri called to tell me that the vice-director of the print shop was himself taking care to destroy all the material that had been prepared so that there did not survive "even a line."

The day after celebrating of the anniversary of the conciliation, on 12 February, the pope had scheduled a meeting with the bishops to discuss his discourse and learn their opinion on the situation. Though typically not very collegial, he stated explicitly that he had not even prepared a separate discourse for that occasion as he was specifically interested in their opinions. He confided to Tardini that his idea was to say a few words in order to initiate a "discussion with the bishops," from whom he wanted to learn their opinions on the most pressing issues of the day: Catholic Action; religious aid in Germany, in the military, and in the colonies; and, finally, the "*vulnus* inflicted on the concordat by the ban on marriages between Aryans and non-Aryans."

The first part of the text is dedicated to the importance of the seminaries and the formation of priests, where great and small things must blend together: cooking becomes as important as thought and tidying up becomes another way to pray. It is a passage that recalls Ratti as a young priest when he perceived the synthesis of female sentiment in his mother, the female religious, and his Thérèse de Lisieux, the mediator of small things:

> Piety and study, spiritual direction and external control, discipline and cleanliness, economy and administration, library and kitchen, the teaching and administrative corps and the domestic personnel, and every great and small thing. And yes, these last as well, for daily life is made up of small things, and great things are rare. Such is the teaching of our Lord in heaven, who rules the world and knows the small bird who dies in the forest and the hair that falls from our head. (Matthew 6.26; Luke 21.18)

Following the section on the seminaries, he addressed the management of words, *ministerium verbi*, "public words and private words, private words directed to a private person or to a person holding a public office; public words spoken, written, or printed; words spoken over the telephone." The pope wanted to speak to his listeners "as an aging father to his children":

190

That which I intend to say to you and of you, we must first of all say to Ourselves and of Ourselves. You know, dear and venerable brothers, how the words of the pope are often construed. There are some, and not only in Italy, who take Our allocutions and our audiences, and alter them in a false sense [originally "mystify them" had been written here], and so, starting even from a sound statement, have Us speak incredibly foolish and absurd things. There is a press capable of saying most anything that is opposed to Us and to Our concerns, often twisting in a perverse way the recent and more distant history of the Church, arriving even at the persistent denial of any persecution in Germany and adding to that the false accusation of Our engagement in politics; just as the persecution of Nero carried with it the accusation of having burnt Rome. They arrive at true irreverence; and these things are said while our press is forbidden to contradict or correct them.

Ten years after the concordat, the fascist regime was engaged in a permanent effort to falsify the message of the Catholic Church, an effort carried out by a crowd of "observers and informers (you would do well to call them spies)" who are motivated by ignorance or, worse still, "in their foolish presumption believe and claim to know all when in fact they do not understand the Church or the Pope or a Bishop or the link of faith and charity that binds us all in the love and service of Our Lord, Jesus the King." These he refers to as pseudo-Catholics:

Dear Brothers, you must take care not only about the abuse of what you say in public but also about what you say in private, especially if you should have occasion, with paternal goodness and faith, to speak with individuals holding a government or party office, the so-called hierarchs. Combined with the necessary caution, you must have for them a certain indulgent understanding as for them it is a question of their career, in simple terms of their livelihood.

He strongly urges caution also when using the telephone ("Here is something about which Saint Peter, the first Pope, did not have to worry."): "We will come immediately to Our recommendations: do not ever speak on the telephone words that you do not want to be known. You may believe that your words are travelling to your distant correspondent, and yet at a certain point they may be noticed and intercepted."

The conclusion of the discourse is a summing up of his worries and disillusionment. With an obvious reference to the subjugation of the Italian people by fascism, he hopes for "the honor of a people aware of its dignity and human and Christian responsibility" and, thinking of the racial theories, declares that all races are "joined together and all of the same blood in the common link of the great human family":

> . . . as the Psalm says, *exultabunt ossa humiliata* . . . exult in this memorable day, which recalls when God was given back to Italy and Italy to God, fine omen of a happy future . . .
>
> . . . Prophesy . . . honor, above all, the honor of a people aware of its dignity and human and Christian responsibility; prophesy, dear and revered bones, prophesy the arrival or the return of the true Faith to all the peoples, all the nations, all the races, all joined together and all of the same blood in the common link of the great human family; prophesy, apostolic bones, order, tranquility, peace, peace, peace for all the world that instead seems seized by a homicidal and suicidal folly of weapons; peace demands that We implore the God of peace and hope to attain it. So be it!

Given the pope's passionate interest in this discourse, the fact that "not even a line" of it remained is disconcerting and highlights the isolation, human more than "political," in which he lived the last period of his life. This solitude has always been described as a function of his illness, as though the aged sick pope was obsessed with the idea that he was observed and spied upon by the regime, that he exaggerated dangers and lived under a fear of apocalyptic destruction. The examination of these texts and of the hourly developments over these last long days leaves one with multiple and contrasting impressions, but never that of a pope who has lost his clarity of thought or who acts without control. The impression one derives rather is exactly the opposite, namely that in those final days the pope relived, in a concentrated fashion, all that had been developing over the previous years, both on an internal level and in his role as pastor. It was a sort of conversion or illumination that drove him to the point of appearing in the grip of obsessive senility.

Some of the documents in Tardini's file were used by the Jesuit Martini in preparing a 1959 series of articles for *Civiltà Cattolica* that sought to contextualize the discourse of John XXIII referred to above. Those articles well capture the sense of uncertainty that pervaded diplomatic circles. Ciano was always the barometer of these concerns; at a diplomatic lunch in honor of Cardinal Mundelein at the American Embassy on 9 February, he ran into the nuncio and asked him worriedly what the pope intended to do. The nuncio replied: "I do not know, because the Holy Father does not tell anyone what he will do; but it is clear that he will do something big."

Mundelein himself interrupted to recommend to the minister, in the name of all Catholics and many non-Catholics in the United States, that Italy maintain all its commitments to the Holy See. Ciano agreed but commented: "And how will we convince Mussolini?"[17]

The last meeting with Gallarati Scotti

I was received by Pope Pius XI the last time in a private audience on 3 February 1939, just before he died ... In the midst of his battle against the doctrines of Nazism and fascism, the pope had the courage on 28 July 1938 to confront the dictatorships of Hitler in Germany and Mussolini in Italy, pointing out the irreconcilable differences between the Catholic or "universal" Church and racism and Nazism, which "were barriers raised between individuals and between peoples." In that crucial moment, he was particularly injured by Hitler's triumphal visit to Rome and the fact that on the day of the Holy Cross there was erected there "another cross that is not the cross of Christ."[18]

It was in fact just one week before Pius XI's death that he had an intense discussion with his one-time student Tommaso Gallarati Scotti, who in turn offered a detailed description of that meeting in a *Corriere della Sera* article from 19 June 1957.

The circumstances of the meeting are interesting as well, for the climate they reveal and for the religious and democratic spirit of the people involved; these included Angelo Crespi,[19] a friend of Gallarati Scotti and, while little known, an important witness to the growth of Catholic anxiety as the drama of the Church played out in the totalitarian countries. He shared with modernist circles in Milan a belief in the need for a greater internalization of faith and a reform of the Church. Anti-fascist and modernist Catholics had derived great hope from the last period of Pius XI's papacy. Ernesto Buonaiuti confessed his own feelings of emotion in the face of "a Christian spirituality above and beyond the ephemeral powers of this earth."[20] Together with Luigi Sturzo among the anti-fascist exiles in Paris and London, Crespi followed with concern the statements of Pius XI, as for example the phrase from Psalm 67 that the pope cited on the eve of the Ethiopian War: *Dissipa gentes quae bella volunt.*[21] From Crespi's many letters (unfortunately not accompanied by the replies from Gallarati Scotti) we can detect a sort of neo-Guelphian approach, and we can justly wonder if that approach does not owe something to the final positions taken by the pope:[22]

I hope to outline a rethinking of the neo-Guelphian utopia as the crowning of a philosophy of history (already written) and understood to make possible the reconciliation of democracy and Christianity that have been divorced over the past two centuries. To my mind (and not only mine) this is the necessary condition for the salvation of European civilization.[23]

As evident in all our reconstruction to this point, it would be incorrect to speak of a democratic opening on the part of Pius XI, even though he did represent a fragile thread of hope – one that vanished immediately upon his death, not only for modernist Catholics but also for those adhering to the popularist culture of Don Sturzo. Gallarati Scotti's description of his meeting with the pope a few days before the latter's death focuses on the misery of nations and evokes, if one can put it this way, a sort of spiritual reading of history. It was as though the vanity of the terrestrial authorities, the greed for power, and the pride of nations were not simply condemned and combated but rather consigned into God's hands with a sad compassion for the great sin of having substituted themselves for Him and so having committed the great sin of idolatry:

> The pope asked severely: But what is left of Europe, crushed by the great Franco-Prussian War of 1870. The empires destroyed . . . that enjoyed their era of splendor and wealth: Napoleon III, the Tuileries in flames . . . and then Germany victorious? One by one emperors, kings, princes, and generals passed by in a frightening dance of death. He did not pardon the pride of the victors: William I, Bismarck, Moltke . . . but after fifty years what has remained of their efforts? A long silence. Then the pope started up again: And even the "Iron Chancellor," even Moltke, they were put aside like old useless tools. And by whom? By the young emperor – William II – full of himself and convinced that he had a divine mission . . . "And now what does William do?" the pope demanded. "He spends his time splitting wood in the Doorn Forest." I seemed to hear in those harsh words the very blows of an axe against the trunk of a tree. Fearful, I listened to the pope's meditation that contemplated the fate of the proud in the crepuscular light of his last hours.[24]

The pope dies alone

That evening news arrived that the pope's health had suddenly deteriorated. We could be on the verge of disaster. The conclave may take place in a fundamentally hostile environment and hold unpleasant surprises. I showed Pignatti's phonogram regarding the pope's latest heart attack to *il Duce* during a meeting of the High Commission of Defense, but he shrugged his shoulders with indifference. Odd; for some time Mussolini has shown little interest in the affairs of the Church. It was not always so.[25]

Just before the pope's death, Galeazzo Ciano was concerned about the acute tension between the government and the Holy See. Certainly it was not a reassuring situation for the transition to a new papacy. The Italian foreign minister on one side and Borgongini Duca on the other were at the time actively seeking agreements or mediation or any measure that would improve the acidic relationship between the pope and *il Duce*, but with scarce results. In fact, there were no new developments in these days, as diplomatic declarations generally degenerated into allusive invocations. It is interesting nonetheless to explore the atmosphere at that time, one that resembled a house of cards as it begins to totter.

So, for example, it became clear that *il Duce* really had no interest in cultivating good relations with the Vatican. He had other priorities, as revealed by his son-in-law:

> The pope is dead. Mussolini is entirely unmoved by the news . . . I went to the Holy See to visit officially the pope's remains and was met by the cardinal dean of the diplomatic corps and by Pacelli, now camerlengo of the Holy Roman Church. I offered my condolences in the name of the government and the fascist people, stating that the deceased pope had linked his name eternally to history by means of the Lateran Pacts. They were very grateful for my comments. Accompanying me to the Sistine Chapel where the pope lay on a high catafalque, Pacelli spoke to me of the relationship between Church and state in conciliatory and hopeful terms. All we could see of the pope were his enormous white sandals and some bits of his vestments. The whole scene was highly suggestive.[26]

On 11 February the fascist Grand Council suspended its session in a sign of mourning; Starace and Farinacci were opposed to the move, but Ciano insisted and was supported by Federzoni and Balbo. Then he went to the Vatican, not as previously agreed to celebrate the Lateran Pact but rather to render homage to the corpse. The rich photographic documentation kept in the archive of the Italian nunciature includes a tense shot of Ciano devoutly praying at the corpse of the pope. Later, though, he asked that this photo not be distributed, as he feared appearing too subservient to the Church.[27] *Il Duce* agreed to attend the pope's funeral, held at Sant'Andrea della Valle in Rome on 17 February 1939; it was a much more relaxed climate, and all were looking to the future as described by Borgongini:

> I received *il Duce*, who came with Count Ciano, ten minutes before the king, and I was alone with him in the visiting room of the convent. He was in good humor and asked me when the conclave would be convened. I told him that it would probably take place toward the end of the month and took advantage of the occasion to speak to him of the universal awareness of Catholics about the irreverent outpouring of the foreign press regarding the College of Cardinals, who in this grave moment think instead only of the supreme good of the Church and of human souls.
>
> He replied to me that in his view all that demonstrated the importance the world attributes to these events and that it would be far worse if all were silent, as that would be a sign that no one cared.[28]

A look through the Italian papers, including *L'Osservatore Romano*, finds praise for the pope as a defender of Christianity, but nowhere even a reference to his hostility toward Nazism and protests against fascism. Both the Catholic and the fascist press dedicated many pages to describing his life, pages that ranged from anecdote to hagiography but included no discussion of his condemnation of totalitarianism. It was as though the climate had already changed in those days of lucid agony and a new path had already been prepared.

The solitude of Pius XI, even after his death, was total; not even the anti-fascist press managed to appreciate any of the positions he had taken. The image that survived of this papacy in the decades to come was instead the simple and stereotypical one of a pope allied to the forces of international fascism. As was to be expected, the anarchist, maximalist, and justice and liberty press painted him in the darkest shades as an accomplice of global reaction,[29] and even the communist and socialist papers failed to offer a more balanced view, preferring out of embarrassment not to hazard a clearer judgment.[30] There was some appreciation of the pope's statements against racism and totalitarianism, but he could not be forgiven his support of the war in Ethiopia and above all his recognition of Franco's Spain. Those same socialists, who supported the policy of the proffered hand put forward by the communists and subscribed to a position very different from that of the maximalists, nonetheless had difficulty escaping from a similar reasoning.[31] The only exception was the heartfelt sorrow of all the French and British press, which made broad declarations regarding what the pope had done on behalf of freedom.

In Rome, among both the Curia and the fascists, the days between the pope's death and the conclave were passed in a sort of suspended stupefaction for the sudden absence of a figure who had been at once present and engaged and at the same time a looming embarrassment. Following the initial moment of disorientation, there followed a sense of relief and peaceful reassurance, as noted by various elements of the Curia and the foreign diplomatic corps. The reactions of Charles-Roux are well known; when he returned some time after the funeral he noted a different and more relaxed air among the Roman Curia.

Yet, even though physically absent, the hardly ethereal Pius XI continued to disturb the fascists: "In certain American circles it is said that the camerlengo possesses a document written by the pope. *Il Duce* wants Pignatti to find out and, if it is true, to obtain a copy in order to 'avoid a second Filipelli memorandum!'"[32]

This was not one of the many alarmist moments in Ciano's *Diary*, but rather a true case of fear inspired by the suspicions raised by the English-language press regarding a final discourse of the pope, a discourse about which there was much conjecture – at times fantastic. One finds evidence of this, among other places, in the visits that the foreign minister made to the nuncio in Italy. On 13 February 1939, Borgongini Duca wrote to Monsignor Vincenzo Santoro (of the Secretariat of the College of Cardinals):

> Yesterday evening the ambassador told me that Foreign Minister Ciano was distressed by news of an article in a foreign paper (he didn't say which) according to which the bishops present in Rome on Saturday morning received a document that was "devastating for fascism" and which the revered and late lamented pope would have delivered himself had he still been alive, but which instead was distributed after his death.[33]

The two monsignors had in fact noted with alarm an envelope passed to each bishop. But as it turned out they contained reimbursements for travel costs to bishops who had arrived from all corners of Italy; even at death's door the pope had not lost his practical side. They did not know that Pacelli had destroyed the text so that it would not be made public.

The air of mystery that surrounded those final days would endure, as we have seen, and even encouraged suspicion that the pope had been poisoned on Mussolini's orders and via his mistress's father, the physician Doctor Petacci.[34] This far-fetched theory has no documentary support but is indicative of the atmosphere to which we have referred. The question of the missing discourse, moreover, would rise up from time to time, a specter hard to transcend.[35] Any mystery surrounding the pope's death, moreover, fed the climate of suspicion inspired by the positions he took at the end of his life, positions that were as alarming and incomprehensible for many diplomatic observers as they were for many members of the Church. One of these was Monsignor Pietro Ciriaci, nuncio to Portugal; in a discussion with the Italian ambassador in December 1938 he had the following to say:

> The leaders of the hierarchy have fallen under the influence of Jews and masons, which explains the current sympathy for the left and the fact that, rather than taking care of our own interests, we are wasting time with the defense of the rights of man and of Jews. This is the real cause of the current situation in the Churches of Italy, France, Germany, and Spain.[36]

Arguments of this sort, together with the wild speculations mentioned above, miss the point, namely the simple fact that Pius XI understood ever more clearly the threat Europe faced; his historical and political intuition of an imminent "leap into evil" urged decisive and prompt action.[37]

His successor sought instead to cancel out with remarkable speed any trace of Pius XI's intransigence. The very way in which Pius XII destroyed Ratti's last discourse stands as a metaphor for the more relaxed relations that the new pope would establish with Italy and Germany. As soon as he was elected, Pacelli chose not to exploit the possibilities implicit in this moment of transition, but rather attempted to heal the strains both with Mussolini – as we have seen, the cordiality he showed the fascist hierarchs during the funeral was much appreciated – and with the German authorities. He quickly sent signs of reconciliation to the latter when he said to the German cardinals gathered for the conclave that the attitude of the Holy See relative to Germany would have to be softened.

In the crucial months between the death of Pius XI and the outbreak of the war, a papacy that, in the words of Luigi Salvatorelli, seemed on the verge of finding full expression was instead interrupted and its project discarded. This is not the place to address the silences of Pius XII, as the outbreak of the war would completely change the scenario, reducing the space for maneuver and possibly counseling greater caution. In any case, that question takes us to scenarios beyond the present work. Pius XII's "principle of caution" did indeed find a solid justification after the start of the war. One need only cite the increased persecution of Jews and Catholics following every condemnation by the Vatican, as in the best-known case of Holland, whence Edith Stein herself was deported. Before then, however, between 1939 and 1940, it might have been possible not to "waste" the last efforts of Pius XI, namely the clear-eyed choice to prefer a break with Nazism rather than a slow and agonizing suffocation.

To have followed such a path while there was still room to maneuver, moreover, would have provided the German episcopacy with a more solid doctrinal and pastoral position; but with the outbreak of the war the German Church found itself impelled by the demands of patriotism. The conflict between loyalty to Germany, to the hierarchy, and to one's own conscience found tragic expression in the courageous figure of Clemens August von Galen, the bishop of Münster.[38] On 26 May 1941 he once again felt the need to denounce publicly the horrors of Nazism, as expressed in this letter written to Monsignor Berning, who was meant to preside over the meeting of west German bishops on 9 June in Paderborn:

> If we accept these things without a public protest, when will we feel the need to take a public position? . . . Each time I have calmed my conscience with the thought that, if Cardinal Bertram and other bishops, who are my superiors in age, experience, and virtue, are not troubled by the situation and content themselves with ineffective written protests . . . then it would be arrogant and unseemly . . . for me to step forward with a public statement and possibly provoke still more brutal measures against the Church. Yet I no longer succeed in calming my conscience with these "*ex autoritate*" arguments. I think instead of Saint Thomas More and his "*ex autoritate*" behavior.[39]

And, in fact, the lion of Münster – so called for the courageous way he faced repeated death threats from Hitler and Goebbels – broke his silence and raised a cry of protest in the famous sermons of summer 1941 that had such a profound effect on the population:

> Against the superior physical power of the Gestapo every German citizen is entirely without protection or defence . . . None of us is safe . . . I am aware of the fact: this can happen also to me, today or some other day. And because then I shall not be able to speak in public any longer, I will speak publicly today, publicly I will warn against the continuance in a course which I am firmly convinced will bring down

God's judgment on men and must lead to disaster and ruin for our people and our country . . . It is not only for the sake of the Church's rights but also out of love for our people and in grave concern for our country that we beg, we appeal, we demand: justice! . . . And therefore I raise my voice in the name of the upright German people, in the name of the majesty of justice, in the interests of peace and the solidarity of the home front; therefore as a German, an honourable citizen, a representative of the Christian religion, a Catholic bishop, I exclaim: we demand justice![40]

Von Galen's stunning exhortations generated an extraordinary level of consensus and interest; Pius XII expressed his gratitude, even though he did not or could not share von Galen's intransigence. The correspondence between von Galen and Pius XII,[41] between an "imprisoned" bishop whose diocese was suffering bombardment and a pope no less a prisoner in Rome, was at once affectionate and intense. During those terrible years of war, a saddened pope seemed to be asking that his combative archbishop maintain that hard opposition in which he, as pope, was unable to engage. A sense of complicity suffused their relationship as they played complementary roles, roles reminiscent of those played by Pius XII and his predecessor. On 30 September 1941, the pope wrote in a letter to von Preysing:

On this road of sorrows that we traverse together with the German Catholics, the three sermons of von Galen have brought us a degree of comfort and satisfaction not experienced in some time. The bishop has chosen well the moment to make this courageous move . . . These three sermons by the bishop of Münster and the pastoral letter of the entire bishopric demonstrate how much can still be accomplished within the Reich by means of a frank and vigorous intervention. We must emphasize this for, just as the German Church depends ever more on your public actions, so the general political situation . . . imposes ever greater caution on the head of the Universal Church when making public statements. It is then unnecessary that we explicitly reassure you and your brothers of our constant support when, as with the case of Bishop von Galen, you make courageous and irreprehensible statements in support of God and His Holy Church.[42]

We encounter here a tormented Pacelli, sincerely pleased by the intransigence of his bishop but betrayed by a sort of regret. The bishop had chosen well the moment to make his courageous declarations, and Pacelli even admits that a clear and strong statement might have a positive effect and mobilize people. Indeed von Galen's sermons and his campaign against the euthanasia of the mentally ill inspired popular enthusiasm and achieved concrete results. And yet, the successor to Pius XI concludes, similarly forceful words cannot come from the Throne of Saint Peter.

Without wishing to issue anachronistic condemnations or absolute judgments, we can nonetheless imagine that, at the end of summer 1941, when "another cross that is not the cross of Christ" dominated almost all of continental Europe and Hitler's troops were invading the Soviet Union, Pius XII may have regretted that he had not followed the lead offered by Pius XI at the end of his papacy, when there was still space for maneuver and before Europe descended into a catastrophic abyss.

DOCUMENTARY APPENDIX

Edith Stein's letter to Pius XI[1]

Holy Father! As a daughter of the Hebrew people and, thanks to the grace of God, a daughter of the Catholic Church for the past eleven years, I am compelled to describe to the father of Christianity that which is worrying millions of Germans. Over the past weeks in Germany we have witnessed events and behavior that amount to a total disregard of justice and humanity, not to mention love of one's neighbor. For years now the National Socialist leaders have preached hatred of the Jews. Now that they have seized power and armed their followers – which include notable criminal elements – they are harvesting the fruit of the hatred they have sown. They have accepted defections from the party that was in power until recently, but it is impossible to get a clear picture of what they are about as public opinion has been gagged. From what I have been able to gather from my personal contacts, we are not dealing with isolated incidents. Under pressure from abroad, the regime had adopted milder methods and ordered that "not even a hair of a Jew's head be harmed." Their boycott – which denies individuals the possibility to engage in economic activities, denies them the dignity of citizens, and denies them their homeland – has led many to commit suicide. I myself know of five cases; and I am convinced that the phenomenon is widespread and will claim many more victims. One may claim that these unfortunates lacked the moral strength to endure their fate. But if the responsibility lies largely at the feet of those who pushed them to this act, it also falls to those who remain silent.

All that which has happened and which is happening daily is carried out by a government that describes itself as "Christian." Not only the Jews but also thousands of faithful Catholics in Germany and, I believe, the entire world have been waiting for weeks in the hope that the Church of Christ would make itself heard in condemning this abuse of the name of Jesus Christ. Is this idolatry of race and of the power of the state, with which the masses are bombarded daily over the radio, not open heresy? Is this war of extermination against Jewish blood not an outrage against the holiness and humanity of our Savior, against the blessed virgin, and the apostles? Is it not absolutely contrary to the behavior of our Lord and Redeemer who even on the cross prayed for His persecutors? And is it not a black mark on this Holy Year that should instead be a year of peace and reconciliation?

All of us who watch the current German situation as faithful children of the Church fear for the image of the Church should its silence continue any longer. We are also convinced that this silence will not in the long run pacify the current German government. The war against Catholicism is carried out more quietly and in a less brutal way than that against the Jews, but it is not for that less systematic. It will not be long until no Catholic will be able to engage in any professional activity without first submitting to the new way of things.

> Begging apostolic blessing at the feet of Your Holiness,
> Edith Stein, PhD
> lecturer at the Institute for Pedagogy
> at the Collegium Marianum of Münster

Pius XI's nocturnal meditation, transcribed by Pacelli during his audience of 6 November 1937[2]

With regard to the *main tendue*: we take that hand and offer ours in return with the prayer that it be accepted. For we do not want the one nor offer the other except insofar as we make our own, as we have both the right and the duty, the words of our Lord Jesus Christ: *venite a me, omnes qui laboratis et onerati estis, et ego reficiam vos*. We take your hands and offer ours in order to do good for you. This act represents no ideological commingling or confusion, as some are wont to say; it is not a betrayal of those principles that all the world recognizes as belonging to the Catholic Church. It is to do good for you. As this situation emerged in France, it might be best for the French episcopacy to make a gesture of this sort. If they should do so, it would not be one episcopacy praising another, but the Holy Father himself would respond: good, you have well interpreted the thought of the Holy Father, as you have done nothing other than interpret the thought of Jesus Christ Himself. Jesus Christ came to this world to offer salvation and benefit to all. *Venite a me, omnes* . . .

To His Eminence the most Reverend Cardinal Eugenio Pacelli, secretary of state to His Holiness[3]

Nunciature apostolique de France
n. 3267
subject: communist Catholics

Paris, 10 November 1937

Most reverend Eminence,

Returning from his "*ad limina*" visit to Rome, the Most Excellent Mons. Serrand, bishop of Saint-Brieuc, came to see me the day before yesterday in the nunciature.

He spoke to me of the paternal greeting that he and many of his colleagues received in the audience of 6 November; the prelate related to me that the Holy Father referred, among other things, to the question of collaboration proposed several times now by the French Communist Party. Mons. Serrand added that he and some of his colleagues noted with interest and surprise that, with regard to the "*main tendue*," the august Pope let it be understood that it might be inopportune wholly to ignore this oft-repeated invitation. It might instead be better to take up that invitation, "not of course so that we might be drawn toward the communists, but rather so that we can draw the communist proffered hand toward us."

The Holy Father then added that he had in mind to assign one of the most excellent bishops the task of exploring the possibility of a public declaration on the part of the French episcopacy in this regard.

I thought it opportune to reply to Mons. Serrand that it was perhaps better not to take the ideas expressed by the Holy Father too literally, as He likely put them forward as a simple and distant hypothesis meriting study, in the light, moreover, of His marvelous encyclicals, especially the *Divini Redemptoris*.

It is indeed pointless for me to mention to Your Eminence that, should the French episcopacy ever make a pronouncement on the "*main tendue*," it would be necessary in my humble opinion that we think long and hard on that possibility and be alert to the serious consequences that could follow from a declaration that is not sufficiently clear and precise.

For the rest, the repeated and formal declarations of perfect loyalty to laicism that have appeared in the communist paper and in other papers of similar stripe, following the discourse of Deputy Thorez, seem to me to render useless any intervention on the part of the episcopacy.

I bow to kiss the Sacred Purple with a sense of profound obsequiousness and have the honor to affirm that I am to Your Most Reverend Eminence

your most devout and devoted servant
V. Valeri

To His Excellency the Most Reverend Monsignor Valerio Valeri, papal nuncio, Paris[4]

Secretariat of State to His Holiness
n. 4828/37

From the Vatican, 26 November 1937

Most Reverend Excellency,

I received from Your Most Reverend Excellency your accurate report N. 3267 on the subject "Catholics and Communists," and hastened to submit it for the venerable consideration of the Holy Father.

The event related to Your Excellency by Mons. Verrand, bishop of Saint-Brieuc, has some foundation in truth in that during an audience granted to several French bishops the Holy Father opened his soul on the question of whether or not any consideration should be given to the offer – one cannot know how sincere it may be – of the "*main tendue.*" It was not a case of a definite proposal – the Holy Father is very far from that – but rather a simple thought inspired by the desire to open the way to the wellbeing which the Church offers to souls who have been deceived by communist error.

The Holy Father knows well that this is a delicate matter and must be studied with the greatest calm and without taking rash measures, thinking only of the glory of God, the honor of the Church, and the salvation of human souls.

As pastor to all the faithful He hopes that the day will not come when He can be reproached for not having seized a favorable opportunity by rejecting a hand offered to Him.

Indeed, the Holy Father maintains that one does not have the right to deny the possibility of good faith behind an offer of this sort, and so He is obliged to keep alive the possibility of one day taking advantage of such an offer for the good of souls. Moreover, who having a soul free of preconceptions could ever criticize the Church for taking into consideration in the appropriate way and with the appropriate precautions the needs of these souls and this their impulse – one cannot know how sincere – to come toward us?

Nonetheless, the Holy Father thinks that it would be necessary to proceed in such a way that the maternal gesture of the Church, inspired purely by charity, should not result in any harm to souls due to false interpretations that might arise or any confusion of ideas, for example that the Church was somehow revoking the condemnation of atheist communism.

So to protect the honor of the Church it would not be enough for the communists to give ample guarantees to respect the religious credo of the Catholics; but it must also be clear that Catholics, in accepting the proffered hand, are not renouncing the principles of order and social justice proclaimed by the Catholic Church, especially in recent times, and that they are reclaiming as their own doctrine any good that can be derived from the so-called conquests of socialism.

His Holiness spoke at greater length on this topic with the Most Excellent Cardinal Liénart and authorized him to speak with the Most Excellent Cardinal Verdier, as may have already occurred.

Your Excellency therefore is requested to make the necessary contacts with the most excellent cardinal archbishop in order to study what might be done in the sense described above and with the necessary caution.

The Holy Father thinks, for example, that, should favorable conditions prevail for an initiative of this sort, the French bishops might ask those who are proffering their hand to tell us clearly in what manner we might take that hand that they offer us and offer ours in return in order to do good for them and with them on behalf of society, but on the condition that nothing is sacrificed to that first supreme good which is the truth, even if only with regard to possible confusion of words and ideas. An opportunity might present itself, for example, with regard to some work of charity that might relieve a social ill and to which the Church could not remain indifferent, as for example a case of crushing poverty or an illness for which no succor has yet been offered. In such a circumstance, we must demonstrate even more clearly and forcefully than in the past that the

Catholic Church has always been the first to address social ills, even when civil society has remained indifferent, and it has done so not out of vain ostentation but to carry out the teachings of its Divine Founder to Whom the communists themselves often appeal. So if the communists offer the Church an opportunity to reduce a social ill without destroying among the masses the principles of morality and faith, then Catholics will be happy to find a way to carry out the evangelical teachings of their Divine Master. Yet no true and lasting moral and material gain can be achieved without accepting the norms of Christian justice and morality, norms that temper the exaggerated desire for earthly goods and condemn all excess, even in the demand for legitimate rights.

Obviously the question of the proffered hand can only be studied in this regard and with due caution; meanwhile it will be well for this study to be undertaken so that the bishops can offer an adequate response should the occasion arise.

The Holy Father thinks it probable that nothing will come of this; but the Church must not be reproached for not having at least made an effort on its part, as the honor of God and the need to save souls demands. Finally, regarding those works of charity and assistance that the bishops may propose, the Holy Father makes available to the French bishopric the sum of one million francs.

I happily take advantage of this occasion to confirm my sense of distinct and sincere esteem

servant of your most reverend Excellency
Card. Pacelli

To His Eminence the Most Reverend Cardinal Eugenio Pacelli, secretary of state to His Holiness – audience with Minister Ciano[5]

Rome, 2 August 1938

Most Reverend Eminence,

Last Saturday I was invited by the cabinet council of the His Excellency the Minister of Foreign Affairs to meet with him that afternoon at 17:30.

Count Ciano greeted me with his usual courtesy and, after having told me that he was worried about the health of one of his daughters, who suffers from an ear infection and may have to undergo an operation, came to the point.

He said to me: "Monsignor, where are we headed? This morning *il Duce* called me [it must have been a telephone call, as Mussolini was in Forlì], very upset by the pope's discourse to the students of Propaganda Fide [*L'Osservatore Romano*, 30 July 1938, n. 175], so upset that he has replied publicly." And so saying he showed me the *Giornale d'Italia* (31 July 1938, n. 181) and read me the brief response.

He added: "The government must regulate the relationship between whites and blacks in the empire, where had we pursued a healthy racist policy from the start, namely had there not been encounters between white men and black women, we would have avoided the revolt of Asmara. Above all we must prevent the birth of half-castes, for we do not choose to repeat the horrors of Portugal, England, and France. The Anglo-Saxon races now pursue a strict racist policy, and Italy must do the same.

Along with the question of the blacks, we must also deal with that of the Jews, for two reasons: 1. because they are being expelled everywhere and we don't want those expellees to think that Italy is some sort of promised land; 2. because it is in their doctrine, consecrated in the Talmud, that the Jew must mix with other races like oil with water, namely staying on top, in a position of power. And we seek to prevent the Jews from taking control in Italy.

Finally the minister told me that Mussolini was also upset by the Holy Father's reference to the five days of Milan, a reference which bears on the Rome–Berlin axis.

Count Ciano spoke to me calmly, though with emphasis, and at the end he did raise his voice a bit.

I believe that I succeeded in keeping calm and replied that the discourse of the Holy Father was strictly religious, as racism unmitigated by the necessary qualifications and limitations is a heresy. One need only consider what has taken place in Germany, where the Minister of Culture, Mister Rust, has said that Jesus Christ was a bastard and has carried out a careful program of de-Christianization in defense of the race. I added that in Germany Catholicism is combated as a religion of the Jews because Our Lord was Jewish, and myths of the race are substituted for Christian dogmas. Given the alliance between Germany and Italy and the affirmations of racism that proliferate in all our newspapers, the Holy Father felt it a pastoral necessity to say what he said, adding even that his comments were not inspired by dislike for the Germans, as one could imagine given that he is Milanese.

I also spoke of the care that the Church has always taken to prevent not only sexual relations between blacks and whites, but also marriages in order to avoid the creation of half-castes, which combine, as is well known, the worst of both races.

In this regard I referred to the declaration of the Holy See made last year on my behalf to Minister Lessona (see my respectful reports of 5 August and 1 October 1937, nn. 5526 and 5577).

With regard to the Jews, I explained to him my concern that Germany continued to persecute as Jews even those who were baptized and converted and so had left their people. In Italy, instead, thanks to the concordat, one could not block the marriage of a converted Jew and a Catholic.

Minister Ciano reassured me that Italian racism, as proclaimed by *il Duce*, was much different from German racism and sought simply to regulate with appropriate laws the relations between whites and blacks in the new empire and also to regulate the Jewish question. Though he did not add further clarifications on the issues I had raised. He told me that Italy is a Catholic country and that, if anyone here were to say that Jesus Christ was a bastard, he would be punished as a blasphemer.

I asked in the end if I needed to do anything, and he replied, "No, you needn't do anything."

I did believe, however, that it was my duty to inform the Holy Father during the audience of last Sunday and Your Eminence verbally on Saturday evening and now in writing with this respectful report.

Bowing over to kiss the Sacred Purple, I take this opportunity to confirm my sense of profound veneration

for Your Most Reverend Eminence
Apostolic nuncio in Italy
Francesco Borgongini Duca

Notes by Monsignor Domenico Tardini[6]

Montini called me. Cardinal Pacelli had called him to issue the following orders:

1. that Monsignor Confalonieri hand over all the material he has regarding the discourse of his Holiness Father Pius XI that he had prepared for the assembly of 11 February;

2. that the printer destroy all he possesses relative to that same discourse (drafts, set type);
3. that Cardinal Pizzardo is authorized to read that discourse for his own knowledge.

13:00. I went to Confalonieri, who gave me everything he had. Another typescript and His Holiness's manuscript. He assured me he would give the appropriate instructions to the printer.

18:15. Confalonieri called to tell me that the vice-director of the print shop was himself taking care to destroy all the material that had been prepared so that there did not survive "even a line."

The last discourse of Pius XI, written on the nights of 31 January and 1 February 1939[7]

Venerable Brothers,

Ten years of Conciliation – seventeen and now eighteen years of this papacy – twenty years as a bishop – sixty years as a priest: here are the great occasions that, in the bright and miraculous splendor of Lourdes, together invite you to offer consolation and cheer with your always beloved presence to an aging pope.

Your revered presence says much, or will soon say much, to the Church and the faithful throughout the world. It says much especially to Us and inspires Us to say many things in turn to you! . . .

The short time available forces Us to choose Our arguments carefully and treat them with great care, with God's help and your good will and patience We will try to do that.

Certainly the conciliation is the most important topic and the one that must be treated with the greatest care. For We can well say that it is a topic of collective and universal importance, and not only for Italy. In this regard We can, indeed We must, invoke the apostle: *et grati estote* (Colossians 3.15).

We shall speak of that great topic tomorrow, after having praised and thanked our Lord in the majesty of the great Basilica that cheers us so close at hand.

For now We want to engage in brief – have no doubt about that – but important reflections with such a great number of priests and bishops. Indeed it is not so much Our paltry numbers that impel Us but still more your numerous presence.

How many are you? How many are the years of sacerdotal and episcopal vocation that you represent before Us? How great and magnificent an accumulation, a truly inestimable treasure of divine grace – grace received and grace bestowed on so many souls – a treasure of correspondence, of beatification, of gospel, of merits in the face of God and of men?

But of these and many other obvious reflections We prefer to offer one that seems to Us – in light of this final lesson that life has allowed Us among the Congregation whose guidance has been entrusted to Us – the most practical, with the promise of bearing the greatest and most valuable fruit.

What is the source of the priesthood and the bishopric?

It is the Seminaries.

Of course the hand and grace of God works above all of this: the grace of election and vocation, the grace of beatification and consecration. But all of these graces are spread, cultivated, perfected, and completed in the Seminaries. It is from these, and (by rule) only from these, that We have the hope and, dare We say, the possibility to develop a sound priesthood, and from that priesthood the bishopric. What is more primordial and substantial for the Church?

For whoever bears a responsibility regarding the organization of the Seminaries, these observations are at once consoling and tremendous; especially for Us whom divine Providence prepared for many years of responsibility as priest, bishop, and pope, with a number years of seminary that, as We see, is granted to few: twelve years in Milan and then three here in Rome.

In order to respond to the needs of this great theme, and benefiting from that final lesson to which We referred above, We cannot overlook the fact there are Seminaries and Seminaries: *diocesan* Seminaries and *interdiocesan* Seminaries, and a scale of great and still greater importance.

Do not imagine that We wish to enter into the many details that might occur to one, especially to vigilant, experienced, and illuminated spirits like yourselves. Piety and study, spiritual direction and external control, discipline and cleanliness, economy and administration, library and kitchen, the teaching and administrative corps and the domestic personnel, and every great and small thing. And yes, these last as well, for daily life is made up of small things, and great things are rare. Such is the teaching of our Lord in heaven, who rules the world and knows the small bird who dies in the forest and the hair that falls from our head. (Matthew 6.26; Luke 21.18)

Yet these few and poor words must suffice for many important things, for Our intention in calling your attention to both diocesan and interdiocesan Seminaries is to beseech you with all Our heart to aid Us always in insuring their greater welfare; aid Us by seconding the directives and the care of Our, indeed of your, Congregation, fully consecrated to those Seminaries that belong to you; aid Us by considering your own not only the diocesan Seminaries but also the interdiocesan Seminaries that in fact exist and labor for all Seminaries within their ambit; aid Us by making once again *corde magno et animo volenti* the sacrifice of some thing that is particularly useful to the diocese, understanding that it is for a still greater and broader good, as well as representing a true charity to the pope; aid Us seconding the rigor of the Rectors regarding admission and promotion, understanding that they bear a special and formidable responsibility, assisted by special thanks and help . . .

Here We would like to conclude, among so many other things that are pressing and should be considered. We would like to conclude with two personal recollections from our youth, because they seem to Us particularly instructive. The first recalls Our revered Archbishop who, in the children's seminary, granted our first Communion. He was a man of great experience and a fine orator; the Rector of his Seminary was a remarkable and exemplary man, though a hard and authoritarian one, and he was Our Rector too. The Archbishop said to a holy priest, Our paternal uncle and in some ways a second father: "I always end up accepting his judgments regarding admissions and promotions; only once did I think that I was right; and even that time in the end I had to agree that actually he had been right."

The other memory regards the great and luminous figure of Cardinal Agostino Riboldi, who was Our physics professor and then the zealous Bishop of Pavia and finally the well-remembered Cardinal Archbishop of Ravenna. It was said to him one day: "with this generosity in granting exemptions and rigor in recruiting, we will soon have parishes without priests." To which he responded: "If the holy Mass is not said, then the faithful will be excused for not hearing it." Few dioceses have had a bishop more zealous and more productive of pastoral fruit.

And so for the Seminaries We hope to have finished; though We must add a few things urged on and indeed obliged by your presence.

The Acts of the Apostles (4.4) state that the ministry of the word – *ministerium verbi* – is the greatest responsibility of the apostles and so of you who are their successors.

And it is to the topic of episcopal words that We would like briefly to draw your attention, just as an aging father does to his children. Public words and private words, private words directed to a private person or to a person holding a public office; public words spoken, written, or printed; words spoken over the telephone . . .

I said draw your attention because the Pope too is Bishop, Bishop of Rome and of the Catholic Church, as Pope Eugene underlined at the Council of Florence, if only to associate that great event with our celebrations in these days.

That which I intend to say to you and of you, we must first of all say to Ourselves and of Ourselves. You know, dear and venerable brothers, how the words of the Pope are often construed. There are some, and not only in Italy, who take Our allocutions and Our audiences, and alter them in a false sense, and so, starting even from a sound statement, have Us speak incredibly foolish and absurd things. There is a press capable of saying most anything that is opposed to Us and to Our concerns, often twisting in a perverse way the recent and more distant history of the Church, arriving even at the persistent denial of any persecution in Germany and adding to that the false accusation of Our engagement in politics; just as the persecution of Nero carried with it the accusation of having burnt Rome. They arrive at true irreverence; and these things are said while our press is forbidden to contradict or correct them.

You cannot expect that your words will be treated any differently, even when they are the words of a sacred pastor divinely inspired, words spoken in prayer or written or printed to illuminate, protect, or save souls.

Be careful, dearest Brothers in Christ, and do not forget that often there are observers and informers (you would do well to call them spies) who, of their own initiative or because charged to do so, listen to you in order to condemn you, after, it is understood, having understood nothing at all and if necessary just the opposite. In their favor they have the great excuse and advantage of ignorance; we must remember that just as Our Lord did for those who crucified Him. It is far worse when rather than this excuse we encounter those who in their foolish presumption believe and claim to know all when in fact they do not understand the Church or the Pope or a Bishop or the link of faith and charity that binds us all in the love and service of Our Lord, Jesus the King. Alas there are these pseudo-Catholics who seem happy when they believe they have identified a disagreement or discrepancy between one Bishop and another, or even better between a Bishop and the Pope.

Dear Brothers, you must take care not only about the abuse of what you say in public but also about what you say in private, especially if you should have occasion, with paternal goodness and faith, to speak with individuals holding a government or party office, the so-called hierarchs. Combined with the necessary caution, you must have for them a certain indulgent understanding, as for them it is a question of their career, in simple terms of their livelihood.

We know that there are many good and consoling exceptions: distinguished individuals who are able in a virile and noble fashion to combine their state occupations with their Catholic faith and who thereby bring great benefit to religion, to the conscience and souls of many, especially the young of our country. We should like to know each of them personally, just as many of you have singled them out to thank and bless them all one by one.

There are other words to which I draw your attention, words that some may imagine protected by a natural secrecy, but they are not; indeed they are perhaps still more carefully controlled, namely words spoken on the telephone . . . Here is something about which Saint Peter, the first Pope, did not have to worry.

For the sake of brevity and completeness, We will come immediately to Our recommendations: do not ever speak on the telephone words that you do not want to be known. You may believe that your words are travelling to your distant correspondent, and yet at a certain point they may be noticed and intercepted.

The Behm brothers have given Us a magnificent network with a splendid telephone apparatus, and We welcome this happy occasion to thank them; and yet We have never once in all these years used the telephone. We have always been happy to welcome each of you, in person and not over the telephone, *in osculo et amplexu Christi*, and, also in person, to ask that you obey, on such a solemn occasion and for the greater benefit of divine Goodness, the Apostle's solemn summons: *et grati estote* (Colossians 3.15), as, God willing, we shall do tomorrow in the great Basilica of the Apostles, who certainly exult in the glorious appeal – as the Psalm says, *exultabunt ossa humiliata*. We can and must say *exultabunt ossa glorificata*, and We say it with all our heart, as in prayer. Exult in the glorious bones of the great among the friends and apostles of Christ who have honored and blessed Italy with their presence, with their works, with their glorious martyrdom, with the purple of their noble blood; exult in this memorable day, which recalls when God was given back to Italy and Italy to God, fine omen of a happy future.

And in the presence of that omen, you too, sacred and glorious bones, prophesy like those of the aged Joseph . . . Prophesy the perseverance of Italy in the faith preached by you and sealed by your blood; sacred bones, prophesy a complete and firm perseverance

214

against all the blows and threats that from near and far threaten it and fight against it; prophesy, sacred bones, peace and prosperity, honor, above all, the honor of a people aware of its dignity and human and Christian responsibility; prophesy, dear and revered bones, prophesy the arrival or the return of the true Faith to all the peoples, all the nations, all the races, all joined together and all of the same blood in the common link of the great human family; prophesy, apostolic bones, order, tranquility, peace, peace, peace for all the world that instead seems seized by a homicidal and suicidal folly of weapons; peace demands that we implore the God of peace and hope to attain it. So be it!

NOTES

1 Ernst von Weizsäcker, *Erinnerungen* (Munich, Leipzig, and Freiburg: P. List, 1950), p. 253.

2 Numerous diplomatic reports describe this climate. Among others, see Sir D'Arcy Osborne's reports to Lord Halifax. For expressions of admiration and consensus made by French and British diplomats, see Owen Chadwick, *Britain and the Vatican during the Second World War* (Cambridge: Cambridge University Press, 1986), pp. 13–29, and the memoir of F. Charles-Roux, *Huit ans au Vatican, 1932–1940* (Paris: Flammarion, 1947), pp. 244ff., 255, 272. Monsignor Bernardini, nuncio to Bern, reported to the Italian minister in July 1939 that "during his last visit to Rome he had noted great satisfaction among the cardinals and the environment completely changed." Archive of the Italian Ministry of Foreign Affairs, dispatch from Tamaro, the Italian minister to Switzerland, Bern, 21 July 1939, MIAE, scatola 43, fasc. 2.

3 This interpretation can be found in several works by Giovanni Miccoli. See his *I dilemmi e i silenzi di Pio XII: Vaticano, Seconda guerra mondiale e Shoah* (Milan: Rizzoli, 2000), and in particular the chapters "La posizione di Pio XI: una prospettiva sempre piú esplicita di rottura" (pp. 125, 150) and "Pio XI e il problema di antisemitismo: una prospettiva di revisione" (pp. 295–308). This work has been further enriched by sources made available in Germany in 2003 and included in the French edition *Les dilemmes e les silences de Pie XII* (Paris: Complexe, 2005).

4 Although not explicit, this line is broadly implied in the excellent reconstruction of Giacomo Martina, "L'ecclesiologia prevalente nel pontificato di Pio XI," in Alberto Monticone, ed., *Cattolici e fascisti in Umbria (1922–1945)* (Bologna: Il Mulino, 1978), pp. 221–35.

5   To my mind, this thesis is overstated in Fabrice Bouthillon, *La naissance de la Mardité: une théologie politique à l'âge totalitaire: Pie XI (1922– 1939)* (Strasbourg: Presses universitaires de Strasbourg, 2001), p. 334.

6   Daniele Menozzi, *Sacro Cuore: un culto tra devozione interiore e restaurazione cristiana della società* (Rome: Viella, 2001).

7   On the spiritual and interior aspects of the cults of Benedict XV and Pius XI, see Giorgio Rumi, "Il cuore del re," in *Achille Ratti, Pape Pie XI*, proceedings of the conference organized by the École française de Rome, 15–18 March 1989 (Rome: École française de Rome, 1996), pp. 285–6.

8   ASV, Arch. Nunz., b. 204, copy of the letter of Benedict XV.

9   The best-known anecdote, and one that provides a notable contrast with his successor, is Bottai's description from 19 May 1939 of a papal audience Pius XI had granted him. Entering into the papal rooms, he was reminded of that previous encounter with Ratti: "Pius XI made a display of divine inspiration in his intuitive, illuminating discourse, full of insights and subtleties. Out of his humanity and work with men and with things of this world, Pius XI conveyed, as though inspired from above, immediately a sense of mysticism, but a mysticism that works, that speaks carefully, that knows what it wants and where and when." Giuseppe Bottai, *Diario 1935–1944* (Milan: Rizzoli, 1996), p. 148; see also Renzo De Felice and Renato Moro, eds., *Carteggio Giuseppe Bottai–don Giuseppe De Luca 1940–1957* (Rome: Edizioni di Storia e Letteratura, 1989), p. xxiii.

10   Unpublished diary of Tardini, in Carlo Felice Casula, *Domenico Tardini (1888–1961)* (Rome: Studium, 1988), pp. 384–5.

11   Gaetano Salvemini, "Il Vaticano e la guerra d'Etiopia," *Giustizia e libertà*, 9 October 1936, now also available in Salvemini, *Opere*, III/3: *Preludio alla seconda guerra mondiale*, ed. A. Torre (Milan: Feltrinelli, 1967), pp. 741–63.

12   On the well-known discourse delivered by Pius XI on 27 August 1935, we can now consult the work of Lucia Ceci, *Il papa non deve parlare: Chiesa, fascismo e guerra d'Etiopia* (Rome and Bari: Laterza, 2010), p. 33; Sergio Pagano, Marcel Chappin, and Giovanni Coco, eds., *I "Fogli di udienza" del Cardinale Eugenio Pacelli, Segretario di Stato, I (1930)* (Vatican City, 2010), p. xx; Agostino Giovagnoli, "Il Vaticano di fronte al colonialismo fascista," in Angelo Del Boca, ed., *Le guerre coloniali del fascismo* (Rome and Bari: Laterza, 1991), pp. 11–32.

13   For a reconstruction of the cultural debate among European intellectuals in the interwar period, see Renato Moro, *La formazione della classe dirigente cattolica (1929–1937)* (Bologna: Il Mulino, 1979), pp. 413–525.

14   This according to Germano Lustrissimi, prior of Finalpia; see Maria Paiano, *Liturgia e società nel novecento: percorsi del movimento liturgico di fronte ai processi di secolarizzazione* (Rome: Edizioni di storia e letteratura, 2000), p. 98.

15 AES, Stati Ecclesiastici, pos. 430a, fasc. 354, audience of 16 November 1937.

16 In addition to the French edition of Miccoli's book (see n.3 above), I will refer here to a study that makes rigorous use of the new documentation: Alessandro Duce, *La Santa Sede e la questione ebraica (1933–1945)* (Rome: Studium, 2006).

17 Sigmund Freud, *Moses and Monotheism: Three Essays*, in *The Standard Edition of the Complete Psychological Works of Sigmund Freud* (London: Hogarth Press, 1953–74), pp. 54–7.

18 Discourse to pilgrims on Belgian Catholic Radio in *La Documentation Catholique*, 39 (1938), c. 1459; see Miccoli, *I dilemmi e i silenzi*, p. 309.

19 AES, Stati Ecclesiastici, pos. 566, fasc. 599–601.

20 AES, Germania, 1933–45, pos. 643, fasc. 158, ff. 16–17.

21 Angela Ales Bello, "Edith Stein, la Germania e lo stato totalitario," in Bello and Philippe Chenaux, eds., *Edith Stein e il nazismo* (Rome: Città Nuova, 2005), pp. 61–81.

22 "E. Stein: filosofa e Carmelitana," in Waltraud Herbstrith, OCD, *Edith Stein: vita e testimonianze* (Rome: Città Nuova, 1987). Romano Guardini had seen already in the early 1930s the possibility of a new messianic politics according to which National Socialism might respond to the general need for salvation by means of a neo-pagan recasting of the myth of the Savior. Romano Guardini, *Der Heilbringer in Mythos, Offenbarung und Politik: eine theologisch-politische Besinnung* appeared in 1946 (Stuttgart: Deutsche Verlags-Anstalt), but its first part had already been published in 1935: "Der Heiland," *Die Schildgenossen*, 14 (1935), pp. 97–116.

23 Edith Stein, *Vie d'une famille juive, 1891–1942* (Paris: Cerf, 2001), p. 493.

24 In this regard, D. Menozzi and R. Moro do well to recall points made by the young Augusto Del Noce, who asked what fascism's claim to be a "totalitarian solution" meant in relation to the Church and replied that, in this way, fascism "laid claim on the individual in his entirety and so failed to recognize the duality between the external man, the subject of politics, and the internal man, the subject of religion." Daniele Menozzi and Renato Moro, eds., *Cattolicesimo e totalitarismo* (Brescia: Morcelliana, 2004), p. 381.

25 One exception is the classic sourcebook put together by Pietro Scoppola, *La Chiesa e il fascismo: documenti e interpretazioni* (Rome and Bari: Laterza, 1973).

26 The limited inclination in Italy to publish large collections of sources relative to the relationship with fascism owes much to the fact that, while in Germany it was strongly felt "that these were issues that needed explanation and justification; that there was more here than attacks, debates, and manipulations, but in some sense the historical memory of the Church. Such was not the case with regard to fascism

the Holy See and the Church felt that there was really nothing to clarify or justify in this regard." Giovanni Miccoli, "Chiesa cattolica e totalitarismi," in Vincenzo Ferrone, ed., *La Chiesa cattolica e il totalitarismo*, conference proceedings (Turin, 25–6 October 2001) (Florence: Olschki 2004), p. 5.

27 On the ambiguous nature of German political Catholicism – torn between its national identity and its identity in the Church – and its role in having aided the rise of Nazism, it may be worthwhile returning to the thesis of Ernst-Wolfgang Böckenförde, "Der deutsche Katholizismus im Jahre 1933: eine kritische Betrachtung," *Hochland*, 53 (1960–1), pp. 21–39.

28 In particular, the studies of the sacralization of politics undertaken by Emilio Gentile and Renato Moro have opened a path where both lay and Catholic research can enrich one another on common ground. Renato Moro, "Religione e politica nell'età della secolarizzazione: riflessioni su di un recente volume di Emilio Gentile," *Storia Contemporanea*, 26/2 (1995), pp. 255–325.

29 Luigi Salvatorelli, *Pio XI e la sua eredità pontificale* (Turin: Einaudi, 1939). This is a text of extraordinary lucidity, written immediately after the death of the pope, one that expresses the sense of anticipation but moves beyond that and also contains an acute analysis of his entire papacy.

30 Chadwick, *Britain and the Vatican during the Second World War*, p. 27.

31 Giuseppe Dossetti, "Introduzione," in Luciano Gherardi, *Le querce di Monte Sole* (Bologna: Il Mulino, 1994), p. xxxv.

32 Trans. note: Sturzo was the founder of Italy's first Catholic political party, the Italian Popular Party, in 1919 and an exile from fascism between 1924 and 1945.

33 On 8 May 1977, from the pulpit he cited the pope he loved the most – "if from time to time politics touches the altar, the Church must defend its altar" – and added: "The Church must not trouble itself with the laws of the state, for that is not its domain, but when the laws of the state tread upon divine law, then the Church must condemn those laws and forbid Catholics from following them." Oscar Romero, typescript of his *Ideología de la Iglesia en la Independencia* of 1962, cited in Roberto Morozzo della Rocca, *Primero Dios: vita di Oscar Romero* (Milan: Mondadori, 2005), p. 68. Romero's was not a common integralist vocation, then, but one that entailed great "pride" in his faith and insistence that the centrality of Christ (*Primero Dios* was a saying of his) must never take second place to earthly powers, whatever their political and cultural connotations.

34 Andrea Riccardi, "Pio XI e i vescovi italiani," in *Achille Ratti, Pape Pie XI*, pp. 529–48.

35 Oral testimony given to Andrea Riccardi, in Riccardi, *Le politiche della Chiesa* (Milan: Cinisello Balsamo, 1997), p. 114.

CHAPTER 1   A POPE'S ILLUSIONS AND THE REBIRTH OF CHRISTIAN SOCIETY

1   C. Puricelli, "Le radici brianzole di Pio XI," in *Achille Ratti, Pape Pie XI*, proceedings of the conference organized by the École française de Rome, 15–18 March 1989 (Rome: Ecole française de Rome, 1996), pp. 24–52.

2   Domenico Tardini, "Diario inedito (1933–1936)," in Carlo Felice Casula, *Domenico Tardini (1888—1961)* (Rome: Studium, 1988), p. 292; Domenico Tardini, *Pio XII* (Vatican City: Tipografia Poliglotta Vaticana, 1960), p. 147. Ratti would always pay careful attention to money matters, just as he would personally follow building projects. The latter even absorbed him during his daily walks of about an hour in the Vatican gardens. "Even when seated under the ancient Holm oaks, near to the round chapel and breathing in the air that blew across the Roman countryside, he would often trace out on the ground the outlines of building projects." Carlo Confalonieri, *Pio XI visto da vicino* (Cinisello Balsamo: Edizioni Paoline, 1993), p. 216; John F. Pollard, *Money and the Rise of the Modern Papacy: Financing the Vatican, 1850–1950* (Cambridge: Cambridge University Press, 2005), pp. 127–49.

3   Ibid., pp. 169–70.

4   Marina D'Amelia, *La mamma* (Bologna: Il Mulino, 2005), pp. 155–68.

5   He wrote this passage as part of a booklet he prepared: "Due piante iconografiche di Milano, da codici manoscritti del secolo XII," in Angelo Novelli, *Il cardinale Ratti* (Milan: Pro Familia, 1921), p. 102.

6   From Pius XI's audience with Monsignor Picaud, bishop of Bayeux, in *Annales de Sainte Thérèse*, 1932, n. 5.

7   "Ai dirigenti della Gioventù femminile dell'Azione Cattolica," in Domenico Bertetto, *I discorsi di Pio XI*, 3 vols (Vatican City: Libreria editrice vaticana, 1985), vol. 3, pp. 853–4.

8   Confalonieri, *Pio XI visto da vicino*, p. 190.

9   AES, Stati Ecclesiastici, pos. 430, fasc. 355, udienze Pacelli.

10   In the first years of his ministry, Achille Ratti worked in poor relief for the Istituto di Nostra Signora del Retiro del Cenacolo, a religious order founded in 1826 by Father Terme and Marie-Victoire Couderc, the "Mère Thérèse" who would be canonized by Paul VI in 1970.

11   Sermon to the Cenacle of Rome, 1921, in "Pie XI et notre société," f. 3, unpublished typescript kept in the Archive of the Cenacle of Rome. This archive includes an unpublished 48-page declaration, hand-written in French, that gathers together the memories of the religious there who had known Achille Ratti. It constitutes an excellent source for evaluating the relationship between the priest and women.

12   Ibid.

13   His close relationship with Antonio Ceriani lasted for twenty years; when it began Ratti was thirty and Ceriani seventy. Achille Ratti would

write about his friend: "his paternal affection, his trust, his openness knew no limits and so I am heir, executor, and final judge of all that is his." This text is cited in Nello Vian, "L'epistolario di Achille Ratti: una fonte ancora inesplorata," in *Achille Ratti, Pape Pie XI*, p. 91.

14 *Israel*, 30–31 (26 April–2 May 1935).

15 AES, Stati Ecclesiastici, pos. 576, fasc. 607.

16 During his tenures as prefect of the Ambrosiana and the Vatican Library, Achille Ratti carried on an intense correspondence with important figures of scholarship, art, and science; that correspondence is still not available for consultation. Various factors, not least of which being his character and temperament, suggest that Ratti would be an excellent correspondent, and he was a fine writer of letters. Giovanni Galbiati, his successor at the Ambrosiana, referred to "a mountain of correspondence all written in his hand." This enormous correspondence terminated completely, save for a few short notes to the Belgian Cardinal Mercier, when Ratti became pope. In contrast to Pius X, who wrote perhaps thousands of letters, Pius XI stopped all personal hand-written correspondence. Vian, *L'epistolario di Achille Ratti*, p. 91.

17 Tardini, *Pio XII*, p. 148.

18 E. Cattaneo, "Achille Ratti prete e arcivescovo di Milano," in *Pio XI nel trentesimo della morte (1939–1969)* (Milan: Opera Diocesana per la Preservazione e Diffusione della Fede, 1969), p. 114.

19 The modernist group responded to the condemnation of modernist positions contained in the decree *Lamentabili sane exitu* by holding a meeting in Molveno (Trentino). Ratti was unaware of this secret meeting. Nicola Raponi, "I veri promotori del convegno di Molveno," *Fonti e Documenti*, 16–17 (1987–8), pp. 348–9.

20 Luigi Salvatorelli, *Pio XI e la sua eredità pontificale* (Turin: Einaudi, 1939), p. 48.

21 Marco Cuaz, *Le Alpi* (Bologna: Il Mulino, 2005), p. 122.

22 AES, Stati Ecclesiastici, pos. 430, fasc. 340, audience of 16 August 1930.

23 Alessandro Pastore, *Alpinismo e storia d'Italia: dall'Unitá alla Resistenza* (Bologna: Il Mulino, 2003). Much of the information discussed in this section comes from this interesting work.

24 Annibale Ancona, "Cinquant'anni di alpinismo: ideali ed entusiasmi: uomini, fatti, cose," in Club Alpino Italiano, *Cinquant'anni della sezione di Milano, 1873–1923* (Milan, 1923), p. 25. Gaetano Negri, who held important administrative offices in Milan, was also secretly involved in the repression of 1898.

25 One example was a group tour of Etna in April 1924 that numbered 600 participants and included a stop in Rome for an audience with the Alpinist pope and a visit to the Tomb of the Unknown Soldier. The organizer of this successful trip was the important Popular Party deputy Francesco Mauro, a Catholic fascist who in 1923, on the fiftieth anniversary of the Milanese club, published together with Giovanni Bobba

a collection of mountaineering articles by the pope: Francesco Mauro and Giovanni Bobba, *Scritti alpinistici del sacerdote dottor Achille Ratti* (Milan: Bertieri e Vanzetti, 1923).

26 *Le Alpi al popolo* (Milan, 1945).

27 Roberto Morozzo della Rocca, "Achille Ratti e la Polonia (1918–1921)," in *Achille Ratti, Pape Pie XI*, p. 97.

28 Ibid.

29 Ibid., p. 110.

30 Ibid., p. 108.

31 Here is Pacelli's description of the shocking scene that confronted the auditor sent by the Munich nunciature to negotiate with the revolutionaries: "an unseemly task for me a crowd of suspicious looking women; they were Jews like the others and filled the offices there, provocative and slyly smiling. The head of that group of women was Levien's lover, a young divorced Russian Jew who ruled with authority Levien is a young man, also a Russian Jew, pale and dirty with dull eyes and a hoarse, vulgar voice; a truly revolting individual, and yet with a clever and intelligent face." AES, Pacelli to Gasparri, "Sulla situazione politica," 28 March 1919, Germany 442.

32 AES, Bavaria 129, Pacelli to Gasparri, "Sulla rivoluzione in Baviera," Munich, 15 November 1918, n. 10,856.

33 AES, Bavaria 129, Pacelli to Gasparri, 19 April 1919.

34 AES, Germany 494, "Sulla questione dell'Alta Slesia," Pacelli to Gasparri, 6 March 1921.

35 AES, Germany 494, "Conferma e dichiarazione di cifrato," n. 127, Warsaw, Ratti to Gasparri, 30 November 1920.

36 On the plebiscite, see my chapter "Il nazionalismo polacco: il plebiscito in Alta Slesia," in Emma Fattorini, *Germania e S. Sede* (Bologna: Il Mulino, 1992), pp. 231–65.

37 J. Schmidlin, *Papstgeschichte der neuesten Zeit: Pius XI* (Munich: Kösel & Pustet, 1939), pp. 156–67.

38 Fattorini, *Germania e S. Sede*, p. 251.

39 ASV, copy of the letter from Benedict XV, Arch. Nunz., Warsaw, b. 204.

40 Salvatorelli, *Pio XI e la sua eredità pontificale*, p. 54.

41 *L'Illustration*, 9 January 1937; citation taken from Yves Chiron, *Pio XI* (Cinisello Balsamo: Edizioni San Paolo, 2006), p. 131.

42 Allocution to representatives of Azione Cattolica on 21 July 1938; Bertetto, *Discorsi*, vol. 3, p. 775.

43 Salvatorelli, *Pio XI e la sua eredità pontificale,* p. 63.

44 Giorgio Rumi, "Il cuore del re," in *Achille Ratti, Pape Pie XI*, p. 287.

45 "Il trionfo del re pacifico del XXVI Congresso eucaristico di Roma, 24 May 1922," *Civiltà Cattolica*, 1922, n. 2, pp. 481ff.; Bertetto, *Discorsi*, p. 12.

46 As nuncio, Ratti was supposed to go abroad, but the authorities blocked his entrance, and Čičerin, foreign commissar, responded ironically to

Benedict XV's request. Andrea Riccardi, *Il Vaticano e Mosca* (Rome and Bari: Laterza, 1992), p. ix.

47 Addressing the Turin Congress of April 1923, Luigi Sturzo asked: "Might the obstacle of nationalism dissolve tomorrow and give way instead to internationalism? The small states created by the war will feel the need to form a hegemonic coalition encompassing both intellectual agreements and political defenses." Giuseppe Donati, director of *Il Popolo*, held that it was the position on nationalism/imperialism that distinguished democratic Catholics from conservative ones, while Francesco Luigi Ferrari expressed similar ideas in *Il domani d'Italia*; see Danilo Veneruso, *Il seme della pace: la cultura cattolica e il nazionalimperialismo fra le due guerre* (Rome: Studium, 1987), pp. 62ff.

48 Luigi Sturzo, "Nazionalismo e fascismo," in Sturzo, *Il partito popolare italiano* (Bologna: Zanichelli, 1956), pp. 203–17.

49 Giacomo Martina, *La Chiesa nell'età dell'assolutismo del liberalismo del totalitarismo*, vol. 4 (Brescia: Morcelliana, 1983), p. 103. Jacques Prévotat, *Les catholiques et l'Action Française: histoire d'une condamnation 1899–1939* (Paris: Fayard, 2001).

50 Louis Picard, *Projections de la doctrine évangélique* (Louvain: Édition du secrétariat général de la Jeunesse étudiante catholique, 1937). On the liturgical movements in the various European countries, see Maria Paiano, *Liturgia e società nel novecento* (Rome: Edizioni di storia e letteratura, 2000).

51 Philippe Chenaux, "De Mercier à Maritain: une seconde génération tomiste belge (1920–1930)," *Revue d'histoire ecclésiastique*, 92 (1997), n.2, pp. 475–98.

52 Prévotat, "La condamnation de l'Action Française," pp. 360–95.

53 "Al Pellegrinaggio internazionale della gioventú cattolica, 20 settembre 1925," in Bertetto, *Discorsi*, vol. 1, p. 452.

54 Jacques Maritain, *Primauté du spirituel* (Paris: Plon, 1927).

55 Cardinal Gasparri to Monsignor Julien, 2 June 1925, in G. Bellart, *Monseigneur Julien, 1856–1930, évêque d'Arras: inventaire de ses papiers personnels* (Lille: Université de Lille, 1980), vol. 3, p. 191.

56 Consistorial allocution "Misericordia Domini," in Bertetto, *Discorsi*, vol. 1, p. 648.

57 Ibid.

58 Fabrice Bouthillon, *La naissance de la Mardité: une théologie politique à l'âge totalitaire: Pie XI (1922–1939)* (Strasbourg: Presses universitaires de Strasbourg, 2001), pp. 269–89.

59 Philippe Boutry, "Hagiographie, histoire et Révolution française: Pie XI et la béatification des martyrs de septembre 1792 (17 décembre 1926)," in *Achille Ratti, Pape Pie XI*, pp. 305–55.

60 Pietro Scoppola, "La storiografia italiana sul pontificato di Pio XI," in *Achille Ratti, Pape Pie XI*, pp. 181–93.

61 AES, Italy, pos. 617, fasc. 50, 4; Giovanni Sale, *Il fascismo e il Vaticano prima della Conciliazione*, preface by Pietro Scoppola (Milan: Jaca Book, 2007), p. 80.

62 According to Veneruso, Ratti's early concern that the Church might become a political party remained with him always. His hostility to nationalism was fundamental and prior to the Lateran Treaties (*Il seme della pace*, p. 40). The studies of Martina, Miccoli, and Bouthillon carefully differentiate his papacy in the 1920s from that of the 1930s and in particular the condemnation of totalitarianism that characterized the last two years of his life.

63 Mussolini's speech to the Chamber of Deputies, 13 May 1929, cited in Pietro Scoppola, *La Chiesa e il fascismo: documenti e interpretazioni* (Rome and Bari: Laterza, 1973), pp. 207–8.

64 *Acta Apostolicae Sedis, Commentarium officiale*, vol. 21, 11 June 1929, n. 7, pp. 297–306.

65 Luigi Sturzo, *Chiesa e stato: studio sociologico-storico* (Bologna: Zanichelli, 1959), vol. 2, pp. 174–8.

CHAPTER 2   THE SPIRITUAL TURN

1 "All'Assemblea generale della Gioventù cattolica italiana," in Domenico Bertetto, *I discorsi di Pio XI*, 3 vols. (Vatican City: Libreria editrice vaticana, 1985), vol. 1, p. 39.

2 There is a vast literature on the Sacred Heart; see, e.g., Daniele Menozzi, *Sacro Cuore: un culto tra devozione interiore e restaurazione cristiana della società* (Rome: Viella, 2001); Fulvio De Giorgi, *La scienza del cuore* (Bologna: Il Mulino, 1995). Also useful are the observations of Annibale Zambarbieri, "Per la storia del Sacro Cuore in Italia tra '800 e '900," *RSCI*, 41 (1987), pp. 361–432.

3 Daniele Menozzi, "Devozione al Sacro Cuore e instaurazione del regno sociale di Cristo: la politicizzazione del culto nella chiesa ottocentesca," in Emma Fattorini, ed., *Santi, culti, simboli nell'età della secolarizzazione (1815–1915)* (Turin: Rosenberg & Sellier, 1997), pp. 161–94; Fulvio De Giorgi, "Il culto del sacro cuore di Gesù: forme spirituali, forme simboliche, forme politiche nei processi di modernizzazione," ibid., pp. 195–211.

4 Agostino Gemelli, *Idee e battaglie per la cultura cattolica* (Milan: Vita e pensiero, 1933), p. 33; see also his editorial "Medievalismo" in the first issue (December 1914) of *Vita e Pensiero*.

5 *Quas primas*, paragraphs 17–19, at www.newadvent.org/library/docs_pi11qp.htm.

6 Giorgio Rumi, "Il cuore del re," in *Achille Ratti, Pape Pie XI*, proceedings of the conference organized by the École française de Rome, 15–18 March 1989 (Rome: Ecole française de Rome, 1996), pp. 285–6.

7 Menozzi, *Sacro Cuore*, p. 300.

8 Pius XI rejected the proposal to combine the two holidays and so render complete the political linkage between the devotion, daily conduct, and interior faith of the believer. He held that the current dramatic situation required that even liturgical language be used to impose the supreme spiritual authority of the Church and brought the discussion to a conclusion in that manner. Menozzi, *Sacro Cuore*, pp. 296ff.

9 "La regalità di Cristo: relazione, atti e voti del primo congresso nazionalc della regalità di G. Cristo: 20–21–22 maggio 1926," *Vita e Pensiero* (1926).

10 Germano Lustrissimi, "Anno liturgico fonte di redenzione sociale: avvento-natale-attesa e principio," *Rivista liturgica*, 24 (1937), pp. 269–72. On all of these aspects, see the interesting work of Maria Paiano, *Liturgia e società nel Novecento: pecorsi del movimento liturgico di fronte ai processi di secolarizzazione* (Rome: Edizioni di storia e letteratura, 2000), in particular the chapter on "La politicizzazione del culto," pp. 75–147.

11 All of these citations are taken from Thérèse de Lisieux, *Oeuvres complètes* (Paris: Cerf, 1992), Lett. 197, p. 553.

12 Ibid., Lett. 144, p. 469.

13 Ibid., p. 997.

14 "13 febbraio 1923, In occasione della lettura del decreto di riconoscimento dei miracoli praticati da santa Teresa del Bambin Gesú," in *Inviti all'eroismo: discorsi di SS. Pio XI nell'occasione della lettura dei brevi per le canonizzazioni, le beatificazioni, le proclamazioni del eroicità delle virtú dei santi, heati, servi di Dio, 3 volo.* (Rome. La Civiltà Cattolica, 1942), vol. 1, p. 93.

15 "4 maggio 1934, In occasione della beatificazione della venerabile Elisabetta Bicchier des Âges," ibid., vol. 2, p. 181.

16 "7 gennaio 1928, In occasione della lettura del decreto sull'erocità delle virtú praticate dal fratel Benilde delle scuole cristiane," ibid., vol. 1, pp. 155–6.

17 Nadine-Josette Chaline, "La spiritualité de Pio XI," in *Achille Ratti, Pape Pie XI*, p. 165.

18 Carlo Confalonieri, *Pio XI visto da vicino* (Cinisello Balsamo: Edizioni Paoline, 1993), p. 219.

19 "A gruppi di Azione Cattolica e a novelli sposi," in Bertetto, *Discorsi*, vol. 3, p. 688.

20 Diego Venini, *D. Venini, collaboratore di Pio il Grande: diari 1923–1939*, ed. F. Cajani (Milan, 2004), p. 185.

21 Giacomo Martina, "L'ecclesiologia prevalente nel potificato di Pio XI," in Alberto Monticone, ed., *Cattolici e fascisti in Umbria (1922–1945)* (Bologna: Il Mulino, 1978), pp. 221–35.

22 Confalonieri, *Pio XI visto da vicino*, p. 209.

23 *L'Osservatore Romano*, 4 January 1937.

24 Monsignor Arthur Hinsley was the archbishop of Westminster and consultant for the Sacred Congregation for the Propaganda of the Faith; Pacelli wrote to him asking about the varicose vein treatments of Professor Eidinow. AES, Stati Ecclesiastici, pos. 430, fasc. 354, audience of 11 January 1937.

25 Confalonieri, *Pio XI visto da vicino*, pp. 209–10.

26 Ibid.

27 Ibid.

28 Venini, *D. Venini, collaboratore di Pio il Grande*, p. 199.

29 The Gregorian reform emphasized this iconographic sensibility, in particular with the metaphors of nudity and illness. Clement IV's sepulcher is located in the Church of the Franciscans in Viterbo, and his image is one of suffering marked by a visage of sadness, fatigue, and age. In contrast, the funereal statue of Boniface VIII, by Arnolfo di Cambio, exudes serenity. Gerhart B. Ladner wrote: "His classic calm is that serenity that defeats death." *Die Papstbildnisse des Altertums und des Mittelalters,* 3 vols. (Vatican City: Pontificio istituto di archeologia cristiana, 1941–84), vol. 2, p. 308.

30 Agostino Paravicini Bagliani, *Le chiavi e la tiara* (Rome: Viella, 1998), p. 88. See also Bagliani, *Il corpo del papa* (Turin: Einaudi, 1994).

31 Confalonieri, *Pio XI visto da vicino*, p. 222.

32 Luigi Salvatorelli, *Pio XI e la sua eredità pontificale* (Turin: Einaudi, 1939), pp. 191–2.

33 Federico Alessandrini, "Memoriale II," *Studium*, fasc. 3, 1988, p. 420.

34 Venini, *D. Venini, collaboratore di Pio il Grande.*

35 Alessandrini, "Memoriale II," p. 421.

36 Giuseppe Dalla Torre, *Memorie* (Verona: Mondadori, 1965).

37 AES, Stati Ecclesiastici, pos. 560, fasc. 592, 1935–8.

38 It was with this same attitude of reluctance that he wrote to Tardini from Gardone Riviera on 7 November 1939: "I am enjoying splendid days of repose and meditation, though you may have a different opinion if, however, my absence causes difficulty for anyone or is harmful to the offices, please let me know, as it would create no difficulty for me to return immediately." Ibid.

39 Oral testimony from Cardinal Achille Silvestrini.

40 Confalonieri, *Pio XI visto da vicino*, p. 217.

41 See the critical edition from the Archivio Segreto Vaticano: Sergio Pagano, Marcel Chappin, and Giovanni Coco, *I "Fogli di udienza" del Cardinale Eugenio Pacelli, Segretario di Stato, I (1930)* (Vatican City, 2010), p. xx.

42 Tardini's audiences ran from 27 September to 29 October 1938.

43 Pacelli hoped to stay in Switzerland till 2 November. "Charged by him to speak with the Holy Father, who was still at Castelgandolfo, I observed that after such an intense year of work he would have been happy to prolong his stay by even a few days. Pius XI listened to me benevolently and replied: 'The most excellent secretary of state should

do as he pleases. But let him know that we will return to Rome for the feast of Christ the King (the last Sunday of October) and it would be a good thing if he returned also. In fact' – he added – 'let him know that if he comes we will receive him at 10 a.m.' I phoned Cardinal Pacelli in Switzerland and conveyed the pope's wishes. He arrived in Rome on Sunday the 30th at 7 a.m. and by 10 was already with the pope." Domenico Tardini, *Pio XII* (Vatican City: Tipografia Poliglotta Vaticana, 1960), pp. 151–2.

44 Ibid., p. 147.

45 Carlo Felice Casula, *Domenico Tardini (1888–1961)* (Rome: Studium, 1988), pp. 292–3.

CHAPTER 3 FRANCE AND COMMUNISM AS CHRISTIAN HERESY

1 "His holiness would like the Holy See to be kept informed of communist activity in France of various sorts and in particular of attempts to establish cells of communist infection among Catholics." Letter cited in Paul Christophe, *1936, les catholiques et le Front Populaire* (Paris: Editions ouvrières, 1986), p. 43.

2 Giorgio Caredda, *Il fronte popolare in Francia 1934–1938* (Turin: Einaudi, 1977), pp. 64–155.

3 Emmanuel Mounier, "Rassemblement populaire," *Esprit*, 1 June 1936.

4 "Per l'inaugurazione dell'esposizione mondiale della stampa cattolica," 12 May 1936, in Domenico Bertetto, *I discorsi di Pio XI*, 3 vols. (Vatican City: Libreria editrice vaticana, 1985), vol. 3, pp. 487–8; "Ad un pellegrinaggio ungherese: il nuovo pericolo per la civiltà umana e cristiana," 13 May 1936, ibid., p. 492.

5 *L'aube*, 15 May 1936.

6 *L'aube*, 9 June 1936. On 31 May 1936 the pope had said: "There is a newspaper that assumes the honor of calling itself Catholic and has referred to our ideas in such a way as to make it seem that we had not already warned against, or had forgotten, or had judged less serious the threat that communism poses to religion." Bertetto, *Discorsi*, vol. 3, pp. 501–4. On this whole affair, see René Remond's preface in Françoise Mayeur, *"L'aube": étude d'un journal d'opinion* (Paris: Colin, 1966), pp. 100–1.

7 On Gay, see the excellent biography by Jean-Michel Cadiot, *Francisque Gay (1885–1936) et les démocrates d'inspiration chrétienne* (Paris: Salvator, 2006).

8 It would be interesting to explore further the figure of Guido Manacorda. His book on Bolshevism was a great success, and he criticized Croce for having a poor knowledge of German.

9 Giuseppe Bottai, *Diario 1935–1944* (Milan: Rizzoli, 1996), p. 223.

10 AES, Francia, pos. 805, fasc. 367–70, "Intesa cattolici–radicali–comunisti."

11 AES, Francia, pos. 804, fasc. 367, p. 41.
12 AES, Francia, pos. 805, fasc. 368, "Il settimanale 'Sept' e la politica della main tendue." Nuncio Valeri asked Pacelli for a deferment of the suppression of *Sept*: "This deferment will make it seem less an imposition from the supreme authority, following the well-known controversy, and would prevent the spread of tendentious comments among public opinion and so would avoid having the suppression of the periodical fall at a moment when the memory of the triumphal visit of Your Eminence in France is still vivid." AES, Francia, pos. 805, fasc. 367, Valeri to Pacelli, 31 July 1937.
13 AES, Stati Ecclesiastici, pos. 548, fasc. 577, *Enciclica Divini Redemptoris*.
14 Giorgio Petracchi, "I gesuiti e il comunismo tra le due guerre," in Vincenzo Ferrone, ed., *La Chiesa cattolica e il totalitarismo*, conference proceedings,Turin, 25–6 October 2001 (Florence: Olschki, 2004), p. 123.
15 Friedrich Muckermann, *Im Kampf zwischen zwei Epochen: Lebenserinnerungen* (Mainz: Matthias Grünewald, 1973), pp. 624–6.
16 See, e.g., circular no. 561 of 1936, containing directives from the Secretariat of State regarding the battle against communism, or circular no. 967, which warned representatives of the Holy See about the spread of communism. There are also numerous files coming from all over the world and including a variety of arguments relative to communist propaganda. AES, Stati Ecclesiastici, pos. 474, fasc. 475–90, "Propaganda comunista nel mondo."
17 See Petracchi, "I gesuiti e il comunismo tra le due guerre," p. 144.
18 Ibid., p. 150; Paul Droulers, *Politique sociale et christianisme: le père Desbuquois et l'Action Populaire, 1919–1946* (Paris: Éditions ouvrières, 1981), p. 196.
19 AES, Stati Ecclesiastici, pos. 548, fasc. 574. All the following citations come from this *posizione*, which combines various files on the same topic (fasc. 575–7).
20 AES, Francia, pos. 800, fasc. 357, "Corrispondenza del nunzio Valerio Valeri con Tardini."
21 AES, Stati Ecclesiastici, pos. 548, fasc. 576.
22 Ibid., Cicognani report of 4 May 1937.
23 Luigi Salvatorelli, *Pio XI e la sua eredità pontificale* (Turin: Einaudi, 1939), p. 221. On the Oxford Group, see AES, Stati Ecclesiastici, pos. 554, fasc. 587.
24 AES, Francia, pos. 824, fasc. 391, "Missione pontificia a Lisieux," 1937.
25 Ibid.
26 Philippe Chenaux, *Pio XII: diplomatico e pastore* (Rome: San Paolo, 2004), p. 185.
27 This text appeared for the first time in *Études Carmélitaines*, in April 1932. It is now included in the interesting volume on Delbrel: Maurillo Guasco, ed., *Madeleine Delbrel: chiesa, ateismo, evangelizzazione* (Fossano: Esperienze, 2005), p. 47.

28 AES, Francia, pos. 824, fasc. 392.
29 Ibid.
30 "Pius XII's style is marked by a certain abundance of phases and asides, as if he wanted to explore even the most hidden subtleties of his thought, like a jeweler who seeks to display all the facets and plays of light of a precious jewel. The jewel is there, but finding it requires careful study of those texts. What I mean is that, among those broad and elegant turns of phrase, there are some that could not be any clearer, more incisive, or forceful. And there lies the essence of Pius XII's thought." Domenico Tardini, *Pio XII* (Vatican City: Tipografia Poliglotta Vaticana, 1960), p. 82.
31 Philippe Chenaux, "Il cardinale Pacelli e la questione del nazismo dopo la enciclica 'Mit brennender Sorge' (1937)," in *Annali dell'Istituto storico italo-germanico in Trento* (Bologna: Il Mulino, 2006), p. 265.
32 AES, Francia, pos. 824, fasc. 392.
33 AES, Francia, pos. 824, fasc. 393.
34 Ibid.
35 Ibid.
36 *DDF*, 1932–9, 2nd series (1926–39), vol. 1, "Delbos aux réprésentants diplomatiques de France," Paris, 16 July 1937, pp. 413–14.
37 Ibid., vol. 6, "M. de Saint-Jouan, ministre de France à Lima, à Delbos, ministre des affaires etrangères," Lima, 30 August 1937.
38 Ibid.
39 AES, Stati Ecclesiastici, pos. 430a, fasc. 354, audience of 6 November 1937.
40 *Avvenire d'Italia,* 7 November 1937.
41 Ibid.
42 AES, Stati Ecclesiastici, pos. 430a, fasc. 354.
43 AES, Francia, pos. 805, fasc. 368.
44 AES, Francia, pos. 805, fasc. 367–70: "Intese cattolici–radicali–comunisti."
45 Ibid.
46 AES, Francia, pos. 805, fasc. 368: "Intese cattolici–radicali–comunisti."
47 Ibid.
48 Ibid.
49 AES, Stati Ecclesiastici, pos. 430a, fasc. 354.
50 AES, Francia, pos. 805, fasc. 368, minuta n. 4828/37.
51 AES, Francia, pos. 805, fasc. 367.
52 Ibid.
53 AES, Francia, pos. 805, fasc. 368, pp. 40–1.
54 Salvatorelli, *Pio XI*, p. 218.
55 AES Francia, pos. 805, fasc. 369, Christmas message of Cardinal Verdier (1937).
56 Ibid.

57 *L'aube* of 23 December 1937 includes large excerpts of Verdier's discourse. On 28 December the Catholic paper published a piece by Gaston Tessier, explaining that "for some time now the Catholic union has pursued a policy of cooperation with the communists."

58 AES, Francia, pos. 805, fasc. 369.

59 AES, Francia, pos. 800, fasc. 357–59, "Corrispondenza personale fra il nunzio in Francia mons. Valerio Valeri e mons. Tardini (1936–1944)." The following quotations are also taken from this source.

60 Ibid., Report of 29 December 1937, p. 73.

CHAPTER 4   SPAIN AND THE CRUSADE

1 Georges Bernanos, *I grandi cimiteri sotto la luna* (Milan: Il Saggiatore, 1996), p. 127.

2 Arturo Carlo Jemolo, *Chiesa e stato in Italia dalla unificazione ai giorni nostri* (Turin: Einaudi, 1981), p. 261.

3 Fulvio De Giorgi, "La Spagna franchista vista dalla Chiesa italiana," in Giuliana Di Febo and Renato Moro, eds., *Fascismo e franchismo: relazioni, immagini, rappresentazioni* (Soveria Mannelli: Rubbettino, 2005), pp. 422ff.

4 Hilari Raguer, "El Vaticano y la guerra civil española (1936–1939)," *Cristianesimo nella Storia*, 3 (1982), pp. 137–209.

5 AES, Stati Ecclesiastici, pos. 430a, fasc. 353, audience of 11 August 1936.

6 Ibid., audience of 25 August 1936.

7 *DBFP*, 2nd series, vol. 17, p. 219, F. D'A. G. Osborne (the Vatican) to Mr. Eden, The Vatican, 3 September 1936.

8 "Ai terziari francescani," in Domenico Bertetto, *I discorsi di Pio XI*, 3 vols. (Vatican City: Libreria editrice vaticana, 1985), vol. 3, p. 550.

9 "Ai figli perseguitati della Spagna: eroismi di fede e di martirio," 14 September 1936, ibid., p. 556.

10 One of the listeners had this to say about Pacelli: "His Eminence is a careful man, unable to allow temporary uncertainty cloud the most urgent facts of this terrestrial world; it was as if we ourselves were gazing into the tear-filled eyes of the young nuns and saw there reflected the pools of blood flooding the sacred altars of Barcelona." Cited in Hilari Raguer, "Spagna franchista e Vaticano (1939–45)," in Di Febo and Moro, eds., *Fascismo e franchismo*, p. 149.

11 Gabriella Mezzanotte, "Cronologia," in Georges Bernanos and Paola Messori, eds., *Romanzi e "Dialoghi delle Carmelitane"* (Milan: Mondadori, 1998), p. lxxxvi.

12 *Esprit*, 1 November 1936.

13 Anastasio Granados, *El cardenal Gomá* (Madrid: Espasa-Calpe, 1969), pp. 96–7, 170–1. On this whole affair, see Guy Hermet, *Les Catholiques dans l'Espagne franquiste* (Paris: Presses de la Fondation nationale des sciences politiques, 1981), p. 58.

14   "Carta colectiva del Episcopado Español," in Isidro Gomá y Tomás, *Por Dios y por España* (Barcelona: R. Casulleras, 1940), pp. 560–90 (at p. 576).

15   Citation taken from Josep Maria Lloréns, *La Iglesia contra la República Española* (Vieux: Grupo de Amigos del Padre Llorens, 1968), p. 232.

16   AES, Stati Ecclesiastici, pos. 430a, fasc. 353, 20 February 1936.

17   AES, Stati Ecclesiastici, pos. 430a, fasc. 354, 22 December 1936.

18   On 15 May, *L'aube* and *Vie Catholique* published an appeal by a number of personalities – Mauriac, Maritain, Madaule, Gabriel Marcel, and also Claude Bourdet, future resistance fighter, founder of *France Observateur* and journalist for *Témoignage Chrétien* – "that the world be spared the merciless massacre of Christian populations." Jean-Michel Cadiot, *Francisque Gay (1885–1936) et les démocrates d'inspiration chrétienne* (Paris: Salvator, 2006), pp. 284ff.

19   On this affair, see the excellent synthesis of Guy Hermet, "Pie XI, la République espagnole et la guerre d'Espagne," in *Achille Ratti, Pape Pie XI*, proceedings of the conference organized by the École française de Rome, 15–18 March 1989 (Rome: Ecole française de Rome, 1996), pp. 500–27.

20   ASV, Arch. Nunz. Madrid, b. 968, fasc. 3, Monsignor Antoniutti, chargé d'affaires. On these months, see also his *Memorie autobiografiche* (Udine: Arti grafiche friulane, 1975), pp. 29–40. Following this posting, Antoniutti served as nuncio in Canada and, starting in 1953, returned to Spain for ten years.

21   ASV, Arch. Nunz. Madrid, b. 968, fasc. 6, Roma Rapporti Politici.

22   Ibid.

23   Ibid. The following citations also come from this source.

24   Consistorial allocution "Quod iterum: la preghiera del papa per l'umanità," in Bertetto, *Discorsi*, vol. 3, p. 671.

25   *FRUS*, 1938, vol. 1, p. 132. The ambassador in France (William Bullitt) to the secretary of state, Paris, 25 January 1938.

26   Arch. Nunz. Madrid, b. 968, fasc. 4, notes to the government.

27   Ibid.

28   AES, Francia, pos. 800, fasc. 359.

29   *FRUS*, 1938, vol. 1, p. 209, The ambassador in Italy (William Phillips) to the secretary of state, Rome, 6 June 1938.

30   Cited in Raguer, "Spagna franchista e Vaticano," p. 155.

31   We do, however, have a good reconstruction in Vincente Cárcel Ortí, "Nunzio in Spagna (1938–1953)," in Franco Gualdrini, *Il cardinale Gaetano Cicognani (1881–1962)*, preface by Mons. A. Silvestrini (Rome: Studium, 1983), pp. 174–82.

32   *Acta Apostolicae Sedis*, 31 (1939), pp. 151–4.

33   "Pius XI never felt any sympathy for Franco's regime. Franco's ties to Nazi Germany meant that the encyclical *Mit brennender Sorge* applied to him as well . . . disapproval of the July 1937 collective letter

of the Spanish bishops in favor of the 'crusade' suggest that [Ratti's] sentiments did not coincide precisely with those of his secretary of state. Whether or not he actually said 'No, cardinal, not that,' that phrase probably well sums up his thought." Hermet, *Pie XI, la République espagnole et la guerre d'Espagne*, p. 527.

34 Jean Meyer, *Apocalypse et révolution au Mexique: la guerre des Cristeros (1926–1929)* (Paris: Julliard, 1974); Meyer, *La Christiade: l'Église, l'état et le peuple dans la Révolution mexicaine (1926–1929)* (Paris: Payot, 1975).

35 Consistorial allocution "Jam Annus: i fulgori dell'Anno Santo," in Bertetto, *Discorsi*, vol. 1, p. 501.

36 "Paterna sane sollicitudo," 2 February 1926, in *Achille Ratti, Pape Pie XI*, pp. 131–8.

CHAPTER 5   NAZISM AS PUBLIC ENEMY NUMBER ONE

1 AES, Germania, pos. 643, fasc. 158, ff. 16–17.

2 Teresia Renata de Spiritu Sancto, *Edith Stein* (London: Sheed & Ward, 1952), pp. 118–19.

3 AES, Germania, pos. 643, fasc. 158, f. 15.

4 ASV, Segr. Stato, anno 1933, rubr. 256, protocollo 127 230.

5 AES, Germania, pos. 621, fasc. 138; Göring met with Monsignor Pizzardo.

6 AES, Germania, pos. 643, fasc. 157, "Il governo e la Chiesa cattolica," Orsenigo to Pacelli, 8 May 1933.

7 AES, Germania, pos. 643, fasc. 159, Orsenigo to Pacelli, 6 April 1933.

8 Monsignor Berning, bishop of Osnabrück, was in Berlin during those days and summarized Hitler's words as follows: "Hitler spoke with both passion and calm, not a word against the Church and expressing great esteem for the bishops: 'I have been attacked for the way I deal with the Jewish question. For 1500 years the Church has considered the Jews a source of evil and restricted them to the ghettos . . . I am doing a great service to Christianity.'" Hans Müller, *Katholische Kirche und Nazionalsozialismus: Dokumente 1930–1935* (Munich: Deutscher Taschenbuch, 1963), n. 48, p. 118.

9 AES, Germania, pos. 643, fasc. 157, "Il governo e la Chiesa cattolica," Orsenigo to Pacelli, 8 May 1933.

10 Ibid.

11 The youth situation had been noted with particular concern by the nuncio since 1930: AES, Germania, pos. 604, fasc. 113, 4 August 1930, "Descrizioni sulla propaganda bolscevica presso i giovani contro il Natale."

12 AES, Germania, pos. 641–3, fasc. 157, "Il governo e la Chiesa cattolica," 8 May 1933.

13 Kardinal Faulhaber, *Judentum, Christentum, Germanentum: Adventspredigten gehalten in St Michael zu München 1933* (Munich: Huber, 1934), p. 9.

14 Letter from Faulhaber to Wurm, 8 April 1933, in Ludwig Volk, *Akten Kardinal Michael von Faulhabers 1917–1945*, 1, VKZG, Reihe A, p. 705.

15 Giovanni Miccoli, "Santa Sede, guerra e Shoah: una proposta di discussione," in *Annali dell'Istituto storico italo-germanico in Trento* (Bologna: Il Mulino, 2006), p. 232.

16 AES, Germania, pos. 643, fasc. 158, f. 5.

17 AES, Stati Ecclesiastici, pos. 430, fasc. 353, audience of 28 February 1936.

18 Pius XI knew and esteemed Orsenigo when prefect at the Ambrosiana, and he appointed him, beginning in June 1922, as internuncio to the kingdom of the Netherlands; in 1925 he became nuncio in Budapest and in 1930 succeeded Pacelli as head of the prestigious nunciature in Berlin. He was always attentive and faithful to the directives of the secretary of state, who managed first hand the relations with Germany from Rome. Monica M. Biffi, *Mons. Cesare Orsenigo, nunzio apostolico in Germania (1930–1946)* (Milan: Nuove Edizioni Duomo, 1998).

19 Alessandro Duce, *La Santa Sede e la questione ebraica (1935–1945)* (Rome: Studium, 2006), p. 37.

20 See Emma Fattorini, *Germania e Santa Sede: le nunziature di Pacelli tra la Grande Guerra e la Repubblica di Weimar* (Bologna: Il Mulino, 1992).

21 With regard to Von Papen, for example, he noted that, when acting as godfather for the great-grandchild of Marshal Hindenburg, "he obtained no authorization from the ecclesiastic authorities." AES, Germania, Pacelli–Orsenigo correspondence, 6–8 April 1933, fasc. 159. Meanwhile, regarding Gœbbels's visit to the Vatican on 25 April 1933, he wrote: "Last year he married a protestant without making any effort to accord with the norms of the Code of Canonical Law that regulates mixed marriages. In fact he celebrated the rite in the presence of a protestant minister in Berlin, causing great sadness among Catholics. Given these precedents, I doubt he plans to visit the Vatican" – as if these were the important details about a figure such as Gœbbels. His concern about mixed marriages with protestants was a constant one. Even given the need to protect a Catholic minority, his insistence on these concerns strikes one as pathetic in the face of events of a much more serious nature. Even his comment on *Kristallnacht* was entirely taken up with the scandal of the Nazi leaders, who in that period were frequently divorcing in order to acquire wives in keeping with their new elevated political and social status.

22 In this regard, see dispatch N.46 48 of 3 December 1938 sent to Monsignor Orsenigo: Sergio Pagano, Marcel Chappin, and Giovanni

Coco, eds., *I "Fogli di udienza" del Cardinale Eugenio Pacelli Segretario di Stato, I (1930)* (Vatican City, 2010), pp. xix–xx.

23 The nunciature repeatedly sent documents on "the moral pressure that the government exercises on German youth to enroll in the organizations of the state." This documentation was kept in the so-called white boxes of the private archive that Pacelli kept in his bedroom, proof of the importance of the issue. AES, Germania, pos. 160, scatola 2, Archivio Pio XII, Associazioni giovanili cattoliche, 4 March 1934.

24 See Jean Dujardin, *L'Église catholique et le peuple juif: un autre regard* (Paris: Calmann-Lévy, 2003); Renato Moro, *La Chiesa e lo sterminio degli ebrei* (Bologna: Il Mulino, 2002), pp. 35–77.

25 Hubert Wolf, " 'Pro perfidis Judaeis', die 'Amici Israel' und ihr Antrag auf eine Reform der Karfreitagsfürbitte für die Juden (1928), oder Bemerkerungen zum Thema katolische Kirche und Antisemitismus," *Historische Zeitschrift*, 279 (2004), pp. 612–58.

26 The dossier on the condemnation can be found in the Archives of the Holy Office, ACDF, "Rerum Varium," 1928, n.e., vol. 1.

27 Ibid.

28 "Der Heilige Vater hatte einen 'schmerzlichen Eindruck' von dessen Votum," Wolf, " 'Pro perfidis Judaeis,' " p. 640.

29 Suppression of the "Amici Israel," 25 March 1928, in *Acta Apostolicae Sedis*, 20 (1928), p. 103.

30 Giovanni Miccoli, "L'enciclica mancata di Pio XI sul razzismo e sull'antisemitismo," *Passato e Presente*, 15 (1997), n. 40, p. 39.

31 Enrico Rosa, "Il pericolo giudaico e gli 'Amici d'Israele,' " *Civiltà Cattolica*, 79 (1928), n. 2, p. 338; see the always insightful observations of Renato Moro, "Le premesse dell'atteggiamento cattolico di fronte alla legislazione razziale fascista: Cattolici ed ebrei nell'Italia degli anni venti (1919–1932)," *Storia Contemporanea*, 19 (1988), pp. 1071ff.

32 Miccoli, "Santa Sede, guerra e Shoah," p. 237.

33 AES, Scatole Archivio privato Pio XII, fasc. I, October 1933 – January–February 1934.

34 AES, Germania, pos. 641–3, fasc. 157, "Inaugurazione del Reichstag," 22 March 1933.

35 Thomas Martin Schneider, "Reichsbischof Ludwig Müller: Untersuchung zu Leben, Werk und Persönlichkeit," *Arbeiten zur kirchlichen Zeitgeschichte*, 19 (Göttingen, 1933), pp. 66ff.

36 AES, Germania, pos. 738, scatola 4.

37 Ibid.

38 "Deutsche-Evangelische Korrespondenz," n. 49, 10 December 1934, attached to a report of Orsenigo from 11 December 1934, AES, Germania, pos. 738, scatola 4, "Crisi della chiesa evangelica."

39 Federico Alessandrini, "Memoriale II," *Studium*, fasc. 3 (1988), p. 746; Maurillo Guasco, "L'ufficio giornali," in *La figura e l'opera di Federico*

Alessandrini: recanati, 29–30 October 1988 (Rome: Istituto Luigi Sturzo, 1989), pp. 14–28.

40 Renano, "La vittoria del 'vescovo Müller,' " *Avvenire d'Italia*, 1 February 1934.

41 Renano, "Confusione babelica nel protestantesimo tedesco, le aberrazioni sacrileghe del 'movimento tedesco di fede,' " *Avvenire d'Italia*, 4 January 1934.

42 Eberhard Bethge, "Dietrich Bonhöffer: Person und Werk," in *Die mündige Welt*, 1 (Munich, 1955), p. 23.

43 Angelo Martini, "Il cardinale Faulhaber e l'enciclica 'Mit brennender sorge,' " *Archivium Historiae Pontificiae*, 2 (1964), p. 305.

44 A complete analysis of this documentation, conducted with the usual precision and clarity, can be found in the French edition of Giovanni Miccoli, *Les dilemmes et les silences* (Paris: Complexe, 2005), pp. 129–220.

45 AES, Germania, pos. 604, fasc. 115.

46 AES, Germania, pos. "Scatole," 1936, pp. 11–15.

47 The documents have been published in Peter Godman, *Hitler and the Vatican: Inside the Secret Archives that Reveal the New Story of the Nazis and the Church* (New York: Free Press, 2004). On Hudal, see Philippe Chenaux, "Pacelli, Hudal et la question du Nazisme (1933–1938)," *RSCI*, 57/1 (2003), pp. 133–54.

48 "The lack of a direct link between those first preparatory works, which remained internal documents, and the drafting of the final document is indeed singular; on the basis of the available sources it is impossible to proceed beyond hypotheses. One cannot, however, rule out the possibility that priorities changed over time. At first the need for a doctrinal declaration on racism may have prevailed, while subsequently the need to address the emergency in the German Church became more important (a question of life or death)." Duce, *La Santa Sede e la questione ebraica*, p. 57. And though the documentary sources are available, the question remains unanswered. The full dossier on the encyclical can be found at pos. 719, fasc. 312–22.

49 AES, Stati Ecclesiastici, pos. 430, fasc. 354.

50 AES, Germania, 1938–9, pos. 719 P.O., fasc. 313.

51 Martini, "Il cardinale Faulhaber."

52 AES, Germania, pos. 719, fasc. 312, *Mit brennender Sorge*, the Italian translation reviewed and corrected by Pacelli.

53 AES, Germania, pos. 719, fasc. 315, contains the manuscript version of the encyclical drafted by Faulhaber.

54 Alfred Baudrillart and Paul Christophe, *Les carnets du cardinal Alfred Baudrillart, 20 novembre 1935–11 avril 1939* (Paris: Cerf, 1996), p. 437.

55 AES, Germania, pos. 719, fasc. 312, includes the various drafts and reworkings.

56 AES, Germania, pos. 719, fasc. 316, "Nota di protesta dell'ambasciatore tedesco presso la Santa Sede," von Bergen to Pacelli, 12 April 1937.

57 AES, Germania, pos. 719, fasc. 317, Pacelli's response to Ambassador von Bergen, 30 April 1937.

58 AES, Germania, pos. 720, scatole 323–37; these files hold all the information on the conflict that followed delivery of the encyclical.

59 Note from 23 March 1937, cited in Maria Bocci, *Agostino Gemelli, Rettore e francescano: Chiesa, regime, democrazia* (Brescia: Morcelliana, 2003), p. 481.

60 AES, Germania, 1937–8, pos. 720, fasc. 328.

61 In the note on the response, Pacelli defends Kaas, "who contrary to the assumption of Hitler was not the author of the encyclical" (AES, Germania, pos. 720, fasc. 329). Regarding this conversation, in another report from 4 May, the nuncio related the comment of Kurt von Schuschnigg, "who knows Hitler well. According to him, the anger and hatred of the German chancellor have become especially intense following publication of the learned encyclical. As for Kaas, Hitler thinks him a traitor not because he believes him to be the author of the encyclical but because in his raving he imagines him working against Germany. In any case, all have understood how to judge the value of Chancellor Hitler's words." AES, Germania, pos. 720, fasc. 329.

62 The apostolic delegate to Japan, Paolo Marella, wrote on 15 October 1937: "The faithful here, eminence, are very few and largely ignorant. They have little conception and still less concern about the Church in foreign countries . . . the non-Christians are happy to raise objections to the Church itself, labeling it a foreign presence and so a threat to the integrity of the nation . . . Until Christianity has taken firmer hold among the Japanese, we must proceed with extreme caution with regard to the press when it comes to referencing religious questions among other peoples." He added that, "with regard to the unfortunate ideological positions of right-wing extremists, 100% Japanese and threatening to seize power, they could open the way to any sort of political or ideological intolerance." AES, Germania, pos. 720, fasc. 324.

63 AES, Germania, pos. 720, fasc. 328.

64 Ibid.

65 AES, Germania, pos. 720, fasc. 328. On 16 June Pacelli wrote: "The Holy Father approves of the actions of the bishop of Berlin and wishes that other bishops burn without question all that which might cause problems." Ibid.

66 AES, Germania, fasc. 335.

67 Ibid.

68 There are extensive dossiers on this persecution: AES, Germania, pos. 720, fasc. 334.

69 AES, Germania, pos. 720, fasc. 327.

70 On 1 June Austrian Catholic newspapers criticized Goebbels's speech. On 17 June they wrote that "it would be useful for the religious to

know that violation of the German law on uniforms has led to persecution in the convents and the uncovering of secret archives; such is the basis of Goebbels's claims. Moreover, it is important that reference to Goebbels's speech not damage the religious themselves." AES, Germania, pos. 720, fasc. 327.

71 For a reconstruction of the positions of the German bishopric, including during the war years, see Giovanni Miccoli, *I dilemmi e i silenzi di Pio XII: Vaticano, Seconda guerra mondiale e Shoah* (Milan: Rizzoli, 2000), pp. 169–200.

72 "In these months, von Preysing himself and the bishop of Münster, von Galen, had fruitlessly proposed a more consistent and systematic use of *Mit brennender Sorge* in daily services, in order to break the wall of silence that the regime sought to build around it." Miccoli, *I dilemmi e i silenzi*, pp. 171ff.

73 AES, Germania, pos. 311, Bertram to Pacelli, 28 December 1936.

74 Ludwig Volk, *Akten Kardinal Michael von Faulhaber 1917–1945*, vol. 2: *1935–45* (Mainz: Matthias Grünewald, 1978), n. 607, p. 281.

75 Miccoli, *I dilemmi e i silenzi*, p. 173.

76 See the correspondence between Monsignor Gröber, archbishop of Freiburg, and Otto Wacker, Baden's minister for education, culture, and justice, who writes that he will maintain his loyalty to the homeland, in this time of trial, specifically insofar as he is Catholic.

77 AES, Germania, pos. 643, fasc. 158, ff. 16–17.

78 Edith Stein, *Life in a Jewish Family: Her Unfinished Autobiographical Account (Collected Works of Edith Stein*, vol. 1), trans. Josephine Koeppel (Washington, DC: ICS), 1986, p. 35.

79 Angela Ales Bello and Philippe Chenaux, eds., *Edith Stein e il Nazismo* (Rome: Città Nuova, 2005).

80 "Edith Stein: filosofa e Carmelitana," in Waltraud Herbstrith, ed., *Edith Stein: vita e testimonianza* (Rome: Città Nuova, 1987).

81 Angela Ales Bello, "Edith Stein, la Germania e lo stato totalitario," in Ales Bello and Chenaux, eds., *Edith Stein e il Nazismo*, pp. 62–82.

82 This is carefully explored by Philippe Chenaux, who places the letter in the context of the other documentation that has become available since the opening of the archives. Chenaux, "La Santa Sede e la questione dell'antisemitismo sotto il pontificato di Pio XI," ibid., pp. 5–37.

CHAPTER 6 "ANOTHER CROSS THAT IS NOT THE CROSS OF CHRIST"

1 AES, Germania, pos. 721–4, fasc. 339.

2 Ibid.

3 "At my daily audience with the Holy Father I read in its entirety my proposed article for *Osservatore Romano*; he approved of it fully – jokingly telling me he gave it a 'ten *cum laude*' – and ordered

that it be printed today on the front page in large font." AES, pos. 720, fasc. 332, 14 September 1937.

4 Protests from ecclesiastical authorities failed to prevent "official propaganda and the imposition of Rosenberg's ideology from assuming ever greater proportions, so that it has become the foundation of all the courses for training teachers at state and party institutions, teachers who then take positions in state schools. *Der Mythus des 20. Jahrhunderts* has been laid as the first stone in the foundation of the Nuremberg edifice and with such brazen gestures the declarations and assurances made by the government of the Reich become hollow." AES, Germania, pos. 720, fasc. 323.

5 AES, Germania, pos. 604, fasc. 115.

6 AES, Germania, pos. 719, fasc. 316.

7 AES, Stati Ecclesiastici, pos. 430a, fasc. 341, audience of 3 April 1937.

8 Ibid.

9 On 5 June 1937, regarding "the rash order, contrary to the concordat, that the bishop of Münster not publish anything regarding school grades in the diocesan newsletter," Orsenigo wrote: "I went to the Foreign Ministry and they told me that it was not their responsibility. I pointed out that application of the concordat was indeed their responsibility. So far they have not responded, and I am not sure how to proceed." AES, Germania, fasc. 223, ff. 13–14. On the side of Orsenigo's document, there is a penciled comment (perhaps by Tardini; certainly not by Pacelli) asking: "How to respond?"; and then "Monsignor Pizzardi says to put it in the archive." AES, Germania, pos. 720, fasc. 335, 19 June 1937.

10 AES, Germania, pos. 720, fasc. 326.

11 Ibid.

12 These events and the relative documentation were already reconstructed in 1965 in Angelo Martini, "Pio XI e Hitler," *Civiltà Cattolica*, 1 (1965), p. 345, and Giovanni Miccoli, *I dilemmi e i silenzi di Pio XII: Vaticano, Seconda guerra mondiale e Shoah* (Milan: Rizzoli, 2000) – see the exhaustive note 125 on p. 450. There is an ample dossier in the Vatican on the archbishop from Chicago and his attacks on Hitler: AES, Germania, pos. 720, fasc. 326.

13 Ibid.

14 Ibid.

15 Ibid.

16 John Evans, "Cardinal Urges Church to Fight Isms with Votes," *Chicago Tribune*, 3 January 1938, p. 14.

17 AES, Germania, pos. 720, fasc. 326.

18 *DDF*, 1932–9, 2nd series (1936–9), vol. 8, pp. 777–8, Charles-Roux to Paul-Boncour, foreign minister, Rome, 14 March 1938; this includes the meeting with Tardini.

19 *FRUS*, 1938, vol. 1, p. 458, the chargé in Austria (John C. Wiley) to the secretary of state, Vienna, 19 March 1938.

20 AES, Stati Ecclesiastici, pos. 430, fasc. 355.

21 Ibid.

22 Ibid.

23 *DDF*, 1932–9, 2nd series (1936–9), vol. 9, p. 302, Rivière to Paul-Boncour, Rome, 8 April 1938.

24 *FRUS*, 1938, vol. 1, p. 474, "Memorandum by the Vatican secretary of state (Cardinal Pacelli) to the American ambassador in the United Kingdom (Joseph Kennedy) [copy transmitted to the department by the ambassador as an enclosure to his despatch no. 206, 19 April; received 26 April].

25 *DDF*, 1932–9, 2nd series (1936–9), vol. 10, Rivière to Bonnet, foreign minister, Rome, 18 June 1938.

26 AES, Austria-Ungheria 1938–46, pos. 918, fasc. 76.

27 AES, Stati Ecclesiastici, pos. 430, fasc. 355.

28 AES, Austria-Ungheria 1938–46, pos. 918, fasc. 76.

29 *The Times*, Monday, 10 October 1938, p. 14.

30 AES, Austria-Ungheria 1938–46, pos. 918, fasc. 76.

31 Ibid.

32 AES, Stati Ecclesiastici, pos. 560, fasc. 592, Udienze Tardini, 27 September – 29 October 1938.

33 AES, Germania, pos. 336, fasc. 72–3, L. Kaas, 12 November 1938.

34 The paper *Avvenire d'Italia* on 22 October 1936 commented on an article written by the Austrian agency entitled "No separate paths": "While Bolshevism is essentially anti-religious, indeed incarnates brutality against religion . . . National Socialism plans to stay on religious terrain even if it does not understand religion in a traditional sense, but views spiritual and religious values instead in a political sense." Speaking in Saarbrücken on 17 October, Alfred Rosenberg expressed his satisfaction over Monsignor Hudal's article, because in his view the rector of Santa Maria dell'Anima had conceded that in order to combat Bolshevism a new spiritual ideology was needed. *Avvenire d'Italia* sought valiantly to justify the article, but recognized that, for Hitler's press, it would have supported an unconditional linking of Catholicism and racism in the face of a simple choice between Bolshevism and Nazism: "The psychological consequences of this transformation will not fade quickly. The lesson to be learned from this episode is that in their debates Catholics must never lose sight of the absolute supremacy of religious values that must never be clouded by worries about contingencies." The article was signed "Danubiano," and so was written by Alessandrini, surely approved if not suggested by the secretary of state.

35 For the complete reconstruction, see Philippe Chenaux, "Pacelli, Hudal et la question du Nazisme (1933–1938)," *RSCI*, 57/1 (2003).

36 Renzo De Felice, *Mussolini il duce* (Turin: Einaudi, 1981), p. 466; see the section "Dall'asse al 'patto d'acciaio,' un cammino di timori e incertezze."

37 Ibid., p. 478. De Felice identified three reasons for Italian reluctance: first, the unpopularity of the Axis following the Anschluß, then the opposition of military leaders and the king to a military alliance, and finally, and most importantly, concern about the Alto Adige.

38 AES, Germania, pos. 800, fasc. 359, 10 May 1938.

39 On Hitler's visit I would like to mention Maddalena Vianello's graduate thesis, which reconstructs its various steps by means of an original study of the material available from the Istituto Luce (academic year 2003, degree in contemporary history from the Faculty of Letters and Philosophy at the University of Rome "La Sapienza").

40 ASDMEI, Affari politici (1931–45), Germania, b. 49 (1938), fasc. 2, "Viaggio di Hitler in Italia."

41 M. Casella, "La crisi del 1938 tra stato e Chiesa nella documentazione dell'Archivio storico del ministero degli affari esteri," *RSCI*, 54 (2000), pp. 91–186.

42 Carlo Confalonieri, *Pio XI visto da vicino* (Cinisello Balsamo: Edizioni Paoline, 1993), p. 225.

43 AES, Germania, pos. 720, fasc. 329.

44 Ibid.

45 AES, Germania, pos. 720, fasc. 329. See the audience of 10 April 1938. When Pacelli was elected, "Mussolini was pleased and promised to forward some advice on how to govern the Church profitably. He did not, however, plan to use Tacchi-Venturi, whom he considered "used up." Galeazzo Ciano, *Diario, 1937–43* (Milan: Rizzoli, 1980), p. 48.

46 AES, Stati Ecclesiastici, pos. 430, fasc. 355.

47 AES, Germania, pos. 720, fasc. 329.

48 Pacelli's corrections are shown here in brackets: "I have the pleasure of informing your reverence that the Holy Father was most pleased by the many fine and good things learned from you in yesterday's audience [even though mailed on the 10th, the letter is dated the 8th, the day after the audience] and communicated in the name of the head of the government in the audience granted to you yesterday. Nonetheless, His Holiness was especially [added] pained today by articles on the visit to Rome by Hitler [substituted with] the chancellor of the German Reich that appeared in papers, like *Il Messaggero* of this morning [added], that are well known to [deleted] call themselves fascist. He does not understand how the fulsome statements of Mussolini [substituted for *il Duce*] can be reconciled with the positions taken by a press that is well known [here he has deleted "that can well be taken"] to take orders from above . . ." And so Pacelli's version continues with its thousand subtleties. Ibid.

49 There is no copy of this letter of 8 January 1938 in the Vatican Secret Archives; it can be found instead in ACS, Segr. Part. Duce, Carteggio riservato, b. 64. On Tacchi-Venturi's activities in these months of 1938, see Andrea Riccardi, *Roma, "città sacra"? Dalla*

conciliazione all'operazione Sturzo (Milan: Vita e Pensiero, 1979), pp. 177–86.

50 AES, Germania, pos. 720, fasc. 329.
51 Ibid., audience of 10 April 1938.
52 On 10 July 1938, Bottai wrote: "When I told Mussolini of my recent visit to Germany, I noted his intolerance for any criticism of things German. He was amused by descriptions of the Germans' lack of punctuality or the disorder of their ceremonies . . . but responded with passionate defense . . . to comments of disapproval regarding their mysticism of land and blood." Giuseppe Bottai, *Diario 1935–1944* (Milan: Rizzoli, 1996), p. 123.
53 AES, Stati Ecclesiastici, pos. 430, fasc. 355.
54 AES, Italia, pos. 720, fasc. 329.
55 Ibid.
56 Ibid.
57 AES, Germania, pos. 720, fasc. 330.

CHAPTER 7 "SPIRITUALLY WE ARE ALL SEMITES"

1 John LaFarge, *The Manner is Ordinary* (New York: Harcourt, Brace, 1954), pp. 272–3.
2 Georges Passelecq and Bernard Suchecky, *The Hidden Encyclical of Pius XI* (New York: Harcourt, Brace, 1997), p. 36.
3 Ibid., pp. 36–7.
4 Giovanni Miccoli, "L'enciclica mancata di Pio XI sul razzismo e sull'antisemitismo," *Passato e Presente*, 15 (1997), n. 40, p. 40.
5 Passelecq and Suchecky, *The Hidden Encyclical*, p. 69. Six letters from Gundlach and five from other American Jesuits sent to LaFarge are published in their entirety in Passelecq and Suchecky's text. It is especially clear in Gundlach's letters that he believes the superior general responsible for delaying delivery of the text to the ailing pope; see also the letters of 18 November 1938 and 28 January, 15 March, and 10 May 1939.
6 AES, Stati Ecclesiastici, pos. 541, fasc. 563.
7 DDF, 1932–9, 2nd series (1936–9), vol. 8, pp. 134–6, Rivière to Delbos, Rome, 29 January 1938.
8 AES, Stati Ecclesiastici, pos. 574–5, fasc. 606.
9 AES, Stati Ecclesiastici, pos. 566, fasc. 599–601.
10 ADSS, vol. 6, pp. 211–12, doc. 125, note 2, 29 December 1938. For a reconstruction of the initiatives in support of the emigration of Jewish refugees, see Susan Zuccotti, *Under his Very Windows: The Vatican and the Holocaust in Italy* (New Haven, CT: Yale University Press, 2000), pp. 70–81.
11 Passelecq and Suchecky, *The Hidden Encyclical*, p. 80.

12 "Alle suore di Nostra Signora del Cenacolo," in Domenico Bertetto, *I discorsi di Pio XI*, 3 vols. (Vatican City: Libreria editrice vaticana, 1985), vol. 3, p. 770.

13 Ibid.

14 A. Brucculeri, "Razzismo italiano," *Avvenire d'Italia*, 17 July 1938, cited in Renzo De Felice, *Storia degli ebrei sotto il fascismo* (Turin: Einaudi, 1988), p. 293.

15 Zuccotti, *Under his Very Windows*, p. 29.

16 These passages come from his discourse to the students of Propaganda Fide and also appeared in *L'Osservatore Romano* on 30 July 1938. Another piece, entitled "A Berlin Citation," from *L'Osservatore Romano* on 12 August, denied that the pope had ever spoken of the Italian racial measures as copies of the German ones.

17 ASV, Arch. Nunz. Italia, 3, fasc. 5–6, protocol Borgongini Duca, audience with Minister Ciano, 2 August 1938.

18 Ibid.

19 AES, Stati Ecclesiastici, pos. 560, fasc. 592, summary of the audience with Tardini, 28 October 1938.

20 AES, Stati Ecclesiastici, pos. 430, fasc. 355.

21 Published in *La Documentation Catholique*, 39 (January–December 1938), c. 1459; see Giovanni Miccoli, *I dilemmi e i silenzi di Pio XII: Vaticano, Seconda guerra mondiale e Shoah* (Milan: Rizzoli, 2000), p. 309.

22 "Il paterno elogio di Sua Santità ai pellegrini della Gioventù Cattolica del Belgio," *L'Osservatore Romano*, 9 September 1938. On the few Catholic papers that reproduced the text, such as *La Croix* of 17 September, see Zuccotti, *Under his Very Windows*, pp. 45–6.

23 On these affirmations, see the recollections of Dossetti: "I learned about it only indirectly via France, nearly at the same time as Maritain's piece on 'L'impossible antisémitisme.' The forceful theological intuition of Pius XI and Maritain's piece has decisively directed my thought in this regard up to the present day." Giuseppe Dossetti, "Introduzione," in Luciano Gherardi, *Le querce di Monte Sole* (Bologna: Il Mulino, 1994), p. xxxviii.

24 AES, Stati Ecclesiastici, pos. 560, fasc. 592, audience of 20 October 1938.

25 Ibid., 21 October 1938.

26 Ibid., 22 October 1938.

27 "Un tremendo atto di accusa," *Il regime fascista*, 30 August 1938.

28 AES, Stati Ecclesiastici, pos. 460, fasc. 592, 24 October 1938; the summary of the audience continues: "After the storm had passed, Father Tacchi-Venturi took out a photo of His Holiness, asking for an autograph. It was for Mussolini's son, who will be married on the 29th. The Holy Father looked carefully at it and then said: 'I take little pleasure in signing my name below the name of Mussolini.' He also recalled that Mussolini's son wrote an objectionable article a few

years back. Father Tacchi-Venturi observed: 'Yes, Holy Father, but that was not Bruno but rather Vittorio, the brother. Indeed, that article upset his father a good deal.' The Holy Father interrupted: 'He should have given him four good slaps! He deserved them.' And then His Holiness signed."

29 ASV, Arch. Nunz. Italia, 9, fasc. 5–6, audience with the Holy Father, 8 November 1938.

30 AES, Stati Ecclesiastici, pos. 576, fasc. 607. This position includes the dossier entitled "Decennale della Conciliazione" and put together by Tardini in 1941; it contains, among other things, copies of the official letters on mixed marriages, the signed letters of 4–5 November, and the exchange of letters between Pacelli and the Italian ambassador to the Holy See. Tardini compiled another thematic dossier dedicated entirely to the racial laws and entitled "Matrimoni misti e leggi razziste (violazione dell'art. 34 del Concordato)"; it can be found in the *posizione* Italia 1063.

31 "A proposito di un nuovo decreto legge," *L'Osservatore Romano*, 14–15 November 1938.

32 "Agli assistenti ecclesiastici della gioventù di Azione Cattolica," in Bertetto, *Discorsi*, vol. 3, p. 775.

33 "Agli alunni del collegio di 'Propaganda Fide,'" ibid., p. 781.

34 "Now that the Church is reconciled with the state, thanks to the generosity of the pope, the wisdom of the government, and the applause of the people, Italy is taking great steps toward becoming once again, as it was in the past, a center and fulcrum of spiritual life and activity." Report from the representative of *Rivista Liturgica* at the International Liturgical Conference, Antwerp, 22–7 July 1930, "Il movimento liturgico in Italia," *Rivista Liturgica*, 17 (1930).

35 Maria Paiano, *Liturgia e società nel novecento: percorsi del movimento liturgico di fronte ai processi di secolarizzazione* (Rome: Edizioni di storia e letteratura, 2000), p. 96.

36 AES, Stati Ecclesiastici, pos. 560, fasc. 592, 10 October. The pope approved changes in the diocesan board in exchange for removal of the *Federale* and desired that the changes take place immediately, not delaying a single day.

37 Ibid., audiences with Tardini on 11 and 15 October.

38 www.vatican.va/holy_father/pius_xi/encyclicals/documents/hf_p-xi_enc_29061931_non-abbiamo-bisogno_en.html, paragraphs 52 and 62.

39 Maria Cristina Giuntella, "I fatti del 1931 e la formazione della 'seconda generazione,'" in Pietro Scoppola and Francesco Traniello, eds., *I cattolici tra fascismo e democrazia* (Bologna: Il Mulino, 1975), pp. 183–235. According to Scoppola, it was not just "a simple conflict between Church and fascism but a conflict between Catholic base and leadership on the one side and fascist base and leadership on the other. Nor was the conflict between base and leadership any less profound, if

less noted, than that much more studied between the leadership on both sides." Ibid., p. 15. See also Renato Moro, *La formazione della classe dirigente cattolica (1929–1937)* (Bologna: Il Mulino, 1979).

40　"Alla Federazione francese dei sindacati cristiani," in Bertetto, *Discorsi*, vol. 3, p. 811.

41　AES, Stati Ecclesiastici, pos. 560, fasc. 592, audience with Tardini, 14 October 1938.

42　ASV, Arch. Nunz. Italia, 9, fasc. 6.

43　"29 settembre 1938: un'offerta sublime," *L'Osservatore Romano*, 28 September 1942.

44　Angelo Martini, "Pio XI, la pace e gli accordi di Monaco," *Civiltà Cattolica*, 20 September 1975.

45　AES, Stati Ecclesiastici, pos. 547, fasc. 571–2, European situation in March 1937.

46　Ibid., fasc. 572, hand-written note by Tardini, 14 March 1938.

47　*DDF*, 1932–9, 2nd series (1936–9), vol. 10, p. 99, Rivière to Bonnet, foreign minister, Rome, 18 June 1938.

48　Martini, "Pio XI, la pace e gli accordi di Monaco"; see also François Charles-Roux, *Huit ans au Vatican, 1932–1940* (Paris: Flammarion, 1947), pp. 124–7.

49　*DBFP*, 3rd series, vol. 2, p. 136, Torr (Vatican) to Viscount Halifax, Rome, 23 August 1938.

50　*DDF*, 1932–9, vol. 10, p. 100, Rivière to Bonnet.

51　"Pio XI agli alunni del Collegio di Propaganda Fide, 21 agosto 1938," *L'Osservatore Romano*, 22–3 August 1938, cited in Bertetto, *Discorsi*, vol. 3, pp. 777–84.

52　Martini, "Pio XI, la pace e gli accordi di Monaco," p. 464.

53　Ibid., p. 469. In the positions of the Secretariat of State I have found no trace of the "12 pages of notes written hurriedly in pencil and with a few corrections" that Martini cites and uses at length. There are instead many brief notes by Tardini that we will cite here and there.

54　For the pope's reaction to the Munich Agreement, see Ludwig Volk, "Päpestliche Kritik an der Appeasement-Politik von 1938: ein unveröffentlicher Bericht des britischen Vatikangesandten," *Stimmen der Zeit*, 197 (1979), p. 532.

55　Martini, "Pio XI, la pace e gli accordi di Monaco," p. 472.

56　AES, Stati Ecclesiastici, pos. 560, fasc. 592.

57　Martini, "Pio XI, la pace e gli accordi di Monaco," p. 470.

58　AES, Stati Ecclesiastici, pos. 560, fasc. 592.

59　Andrea Riccardi, *Roma, "città sacra"? Dalla Conciliazione all'operazione Sturzo* (Milan: Vita e pensiero, 1979), pp. 192–3.

60　Andrea Riccardi, *Le politiche della chiesa* (Cinisello Balsamo: San Paolo, 1997), p. 18.

61　ASV, Arch. Nunz. Italia, 9, fasc. 6.

62　Georges Bidault, "Faire du durable," *L'aube*, 3 September 1938.

63 Martini, "Pio XI, la pace e gli accordi di Monaco," p. 471. The comment the pope made to Tardini regarding Munich is famous: "This is not a capitulation but a headlong fall [*capitombolo*]," Domenico Tardini, *Pio XII* (Vatican City: Tipografia Poliglotta Vaticana, 1960), a judgment repeated in the introduction to ADSS, vol. 1, p. 8.

CHAPTER 8 THE END OF A PAPACY

1 Letter from 18 November 1938 to LaFarge, cited in Georges Passelecq and Bernard Suchecky, *The Hidden Encyclical of Pius XI* (New York: Harcourt, Brace, 1997), p. 73.
2 Maria Bocci, *Agostino Gemelli, rettore e francescano: Chiesa, regime, democrazia* (Brescia: Morcelliana, 2003); see in particular chapter 4: "Un rettore antisemita: Gemelli e gli ebrei," pp. 475–554.
3 Ibid., p. 484.
4 AES, Stati Ecclesiastici, pos. 430a, fasc. 355.
5 Cited in Bocci, *Agostino Gemelli*, p. 505. With many caveats, including the fact that statements of this sort must be contextualized and it does not "ooze anti-Semitic hatred," Bocci adds: "Certainly, speaking at that moment, following the introduction of the anti-Jewish laws and the condemnation of those laws by the pope, his comments may have another meaning." Ibid. Miccoli notes in this regard that these are phrases "laden with multiple signals," as Gemelli's invocation of the deicide portrays Mussolini's racial laws in the context of the ancient condemnation of the Jews and the curse of a fatal destiny against which opposition is pointless, so that he ends up adopting the "confusedly racist criterion that had inspired those laws." Giovanni Miccoli, "Agostino Gemelli, Università cattolica e regime fascista," *Studi Storici*, 45/2 (2004), p. 617.
6 Owen Chadwick, *Britain and the Vatican during the Second World War* (Cambridge: Cambridge University Press, 1986), pp. 26–7.
7 Bocci, *Agostino Gemelli*, p. 502.
8 Ibid., p. 504.
9 Carlo Confalonieri, *Pio XI visto da vicino* (Cinisello Balsamo: Edizioni Paoline, 1993), p. 190.
10 AES, Stati Ecclesiastici, pos. 576, fasc. 607. Where there are no specific citations, the unpublished material referred to in this section comes from this position. The title of the dossier is "Decennale della conciliazione."
11 Ibid., Tardini's note from 8 February.
12 Giacomo Martina, *Storia della Chiesa da Lutero ai nostri giorni* (Brescia: Morcelliana, 1993), p. 113.
13 Angelo Martini, "L'ultima battaglia e gli ultimi giorni di Pio XI," *Civiltà Cattolica* (1959), no. 2, pp. 574–91; no. 3, pp. 572–90; no. 4, pp. 236–50, 237.

14 Giovanni XXIII, "Lettera all'Episcopato d'Italia nel ventesimo anniversario della morte di Pio XI e nel trentesimo della Conciliazione," 6 February 1959, *Civiltà Cattolica* (1959), no. 1, pp. 337–43.

15 Ibid.

16 So, for example, the controversy raised by Cardinal Tisserant, the ardent and extroverted friend of Ratti from 1911, when the latter was prefect of the Ambrosiana, who presumably wrote a memoir about the last days of Pius XI. According to the presumed memoir of Tisserant, the text published by John XXIII was not authentic: "First of all because it was an innocuous, antiseptic text that could certainly have been published earlier. Secondly, any literary critic familiar with the style of Pope Ratti could tell that this was not the writing of Pius XI." These declarations were made by Paule Hennequin, Cardinal Tisserant's niece, and Monsignor Georges Roche, with whom Tisserant intended to spend the last years of his life in Montferrer (France). According to the statements made by these two to the Italian and international press on 12 June 1972, Tisserant was of the opinion that the pope had been poisoned on orders from Mussolini. A long piece ran in *Panorama*, 29 June 1972, p. 55.

17 Martini, "L'ultima battaglia," p. 28.

18 Tommaso Gallarati Scotti, *Interpretazioni e memorie* (Milan: Mondadori, 1960), p. 30.

19 Nicola Raponi, "La denuncia dei totalitarismi," in *Pio XI e il suo tempo*, conference proceedings, February 2000 (Milan, 2000), pp. 115–23.

20 Ernesto Buonaiuti, *Pellegrino di Roma: la generazione dell'esodo* (Bari: Laterza, 1964), pp. 238–40.

21 Angelo Crespi died in 1949; his book *Dall'io a Dio* was published posthumously with an introduction by Gallarati Scotti: "He felt ever more to be a citizen and combatant for Western Christian civilization, understood in its highest form: not a closed citadel in defense of capitalist interests, but a sort of new Thebes with one hundred doors opened to all the peoples of the earth for the future of the world." Angelo Crespi, *Dall'io a Dio* (Modena: Guanda, 1950), "Introduction" by Tommaso Gallarati Scotti, p. 13.

22 "From his conversations with Sturzo he had acquired a sort of neo-Guelphian historical vision; in that vision he also included possible 'future paths' for the history of Europe and the possibility of a reconciliation between democracy and Christianity." Raponi, "La denuncia dei totalitarismi," p. 121.

23 Ibid.

24 Gallarati Scotti, "Ultimo colloquio," in *Interpretazioni e memorie* (Milan: Mondadori, 1960), p. 31.

25 Galeazzo Ciano, *Diario, 1937–43* (Milan: Rizzoli, 1980), 9 February, p. 37.

26 Ibid.

27 The file includes a number of nice photographs of the funeral, the book of the liturgy, translated by Giuseppe De Luca, and the declaration of the director of the Istituto LUCE, read by Bacci, who spoke of the documentary *Laudatio funebris* by Monsignor Angelo Perugini.

28 ASV, Arch. Nunz. Italia, 1, fasc. 7, 20 February 1939.

29 "Incredible but true. They are trying to pass off Pius XI, hated supporter of the wars in Ethiopia and Spain, as a pacifist and an anti-fascist . . . Enough. The Vatican will remain that foundry of lies that it has always been, an agent of international reaction and opposition to human rights, a function of its claim to divine rights." "Un papa morto," *Risveglio Anarchico*, 21 February 1939.

30 "La morte di Pio XI," *L'Unità*, 11 February 1939.

31 "We are aware that over the past three years the pope has found the human courage to condemn the abomination of racist persecution . . . Nor has it escaped anyone's notice that this condemnation was motivated by other more serious worries: the opposition of the Vatican to the rash politics of the Rome–Berlin axis But we are not persuaded by this sermonizing pacifism. There have been two wars (and they continue to this day): one against Ethiopia – against which the pope remained silent – and one against Spain – and the pope sided with the invaders and assassins of the Spanish people." "Il destino di Pio XI: da cappellano del fascismo ad avversario del razzismo," *Nuovo Avanti!*, 18 February 1939. Citations from this article are included in Marcello Elli, "Pio XI e l'azione della Santa Sede nella stampa degli antifascisti italiani in esilio! 1935 1939," *Sociologia*, 40/2 (2006), pp. 3–26.

32 "The Filipelli memorandum referred to the crisis in late 1924 following the assassination of Giacomo Matteotti. Mussolini placed everything on the same plane, as, egocentric to the point of madness, he saw himself as the center of the universe. The possibility of a moral testament from this great pope inspired in him nothing more than recollection of the bother of the Filipelli memorandum." Ciano, *Diario*, p. 39.

33 ASV, Arch. Nunz., 1, fasc. 7. Borgongini to Monsignor Vincenzo Santoro, Rome, 13 February 1939.

34 According to the claims of, again, Roche and Hennequin, on Easter Monday 1970 Cardinal Tisserant declared: " 'They eliminated him,' 'they assassinated him'; no one at the time dared to ask if they had any proof. Professor Francesco Petacci had access to the private chamber of the pope immediately after his death. Petacci was responsible for preserving the corpse. According to the cardinal, his intervention may have served to erase any traces of poisoning." Memoir published in *Panorama*, 29 June 1972, p. 55. These claims are unverified and unverifiable, but we report them here for the sake of completeness and once again to evoke the climate of suspicion and conspiracy that arose.

35 Seven days after the publication of *Summi Pontificatus*, Pius XII's first encyclical, the *New York Times* wrote that, "according to authoritative Vatican sources, the theme of the encyclical, especially as regards the totalitarian states, was inspired by an unpublished piece that Pius XI, his predecessor, wrote before he died."

36 Cited in Giovanni Miccoli, "Santa Sede, guerra e Shoah: una proposta di discussione," in *Annali dell'Istituto storico italo-germanico in Trento* (Bologna: Il Mulino, 2006), p. 243.

37 "To my mind, it was a moment when the Church could and should have made a statement, at considerable risk but also with some likelihood of having an effect. This was the moment between Pius XI and his successor, during the months between February 1939 and the following autumn, before the war made everything more complicated, both for the Holy See, obliged as it was not to take sides in the conflict, and for the German Church and bishopric, which must have felt the need to remain loyal to the fatherland." Giuseppe Dossetti, "Introduzione," in Luciano Gherardi, *Le querce di Monte Sole* (Bologna: Il Mulino, 1994), p. xxxiv.

38 On von Galen, see the recent collection of proceedings from the 2006 conference in Münster: Hubert Wolf, Thomas Flammer, Barbara Schüler, eds., *Clemens August von Galen: ein Kirchenfürst im Nationalsozialismus* (Darmstadt: WBG, 2007).

39 Text cited in Giovanni Miccoli, *I dilemmi e i silenzi di Pio XII: Vaticano, Seconda guerra mondiale e Shoah* (Milan: Rizzoli, 2000), p. 184; see the chapter "Lacerazioni e dilemmi, l'episcopato tedesco e la guerra," pp. 169–201.

40 "Sermon by the bishop of Münster, Clemens August Count von Galen, on Sunday 13 July 1941 in St Lambert's, Munster," www.churchinhistory.org/pages/booklets/vongalen%28n%29.htm.

41 The correspondence between von Galen and Pius XII consists of twelve letters written between 1940 and 1946; three of them remained unpublished until recently and are kept in the archive of the postulation for the beatification and canonization of Pius XII. Those three letters, discussed here, can now be found in Stefania Falasca, *Un vescovo contro Hitler* (Cinisello Balsamo: San Paolo, 2006); it includes the von Galen–Pius XII correspondence in an appendix.

42 ADSS, vol. 2, pp. 229–32, letter from Pius XII to Konrad von Preysing, 30 September 1941.

DOCUMENTARY APPENDIX

1 AES, Germania 1933–45, pos. 643, fasc. 158, ff. 16–17. The letter was sent on 12 April 1933.

2 AES, Stati Ecclesiastici, pos. 430a, fasc. 354, audience of 6 November 1937.

3 Sacra Congregazione degli Affari ecclesiastici straordinari, Francia, 1936–9, pos. 805, fasc. 368.
4 Ibid.
5 ASV, Arch. Nunz. Italia, b. 24, fasc. 5.
6 AES, Stati Ecclesiastici, pos. 576, fasc. 607.
7 Ibid.

INDEX